CHANGE AGENT

A Life Dedicated to Creating Wealth for Minorities

Praise for James H. Lowry's CHANGE AGENT:
A Life Dedicated to Creating Wealth for Minorities

"Jim Lowry has lived one of the most interesting lives of any person I know. He's traveled the world. He's consulted with heads of state and heads of the largest companies in the world. He's been a pioneer and a catalyst for major changes in massive organizations. He has been a friend and mentor to me and many others. His story is inspiring. His insights have been developed through years of illuminating study and work. I've known him for 20 years, but what I knew about him only scratched the surface of the life full of amazing stories contained in this book. I'm excited for the world to know more about this dynamic man I love and respect."

—John Legend, Founder FREEAMERICA Singer, songwriter, producer and activist

"If there is a book that should be on your 2020 reading list, it must be *Change Agent: A Life Dedicated to Creating Wealth for Minorities,* written by one of the most profound and knowledgeable black business experts and advisors on black wealth that I know, James Lowry. I am proud to say that long before he wrote this information-filled and intellectually-grounded book, James has been a friend and advisor to me throughout my business career. I credit him with a lot that my companies, over the years, have accomplished and I invite anyone—whether you are an entrepreneur, CEO or just a person seeking smart business ideas, to read *Change Agent."*

—Bob Johnson, Founder of Black Entertainment TV (BET) and The RLJ Companies

"A must read for African American success in the 21st century and beyond. With an analytical, historical lens and his years of training as a management consultant, James Lowry adeptly outlines what is needed and what has not worked and why. As the late Ossie Davis said, "It is the plan, not the man." Strategically coming together as a community with a business mindset is what will take the African American community forward."

—Julieanna L. Richardson, Founder & President, The History Makers

Jim generously shares his life lessons honed as not only a trailblazing corporate pioneer and leader but as an African-American on the bleeding edge of change. His nearly 50-year track record is a blueprint for those looking to become change agents that transform business as usual.

—Jerri DeVard, EVP, Chief Customer Officer at Office Depot

"Change Agent — A Life Dedicated to Creating Wealth for Minorities is indeed the 21st Century's North Star for Black America. His chronicle of his personal and professional life experiences allows his words to clearly amplify what needs to be done to ensure Black economic success in the fourth industrial revolution of the Gig Economy. *Truly, a Must Read!"*

—Ronald C. Parker, Former President/CEO, The Executive Leadership Council & SVP, Human Resources, PepsiCo

"Too often in our lives, we become burdened by limitations imposed by ourselves. This book shows you how to take control of your own financial destiny and prosper with confidence. Jim Lowry has been a champion for wealth creation within the minority community for years. I am so happy that he is sharing his passion for all of us to benefit from."

—Michael Hyter, Managing Partner, Korn Ferry International

Change Agent – A Life Dedicated to Creating Wealth for Minorities is destined to become an iconic business book because Jim Lowry is a business icon. The book acknowledges the laudable progress we have made in the minority business community and is also a call to action for the important work that remains to be done. Thank you, Jim, for sparking much-needed dialogue and much-needed action at a much-needed time!"

—Dr. Randal Pinkett, Chairman and CEO of BCT
Partners, Winner of The Apprentice

"I was blown away by the extraordinary story of how a young man from Chicago with a passion for economic development became a civic leader, an entrepreneur, a trusted advisor to corporate titans and political leaders and a business legend who mentored hundreds of business leaders and helped to design, and develop programs that drove well over $5 Billion of revenue to black and minority business enterprises."

—Shawn D Rochester, author of The Black Tax: The Cost of Being Black in
America
CEO of Good Steward LLC, Founder of PHD Enterprises & The IDEA Institute

"Jim Lowry is a pioneer and visionary. In this timely book he chronicles how the gains made in the Civil Rights Movement need equivalent progress in economic inclusion so that America can achieve its full potential as a nation."

—Leonard Greenhalgh, PhD, Professor Emeritus, Tuck Diversity
Programs Tuck School of Business at Dartmouth

"With his lifelong efforts to promote and increase investment in minority communities, Jim Lowry has been a pioneer and trailblazer for African Americans. Thanks to Jim, today many corporations across a wide range of industries are more accountable and engaged in efforts to promote diversity and inclusion."

—John W. Rogers, Jr., Chairman, Co-CEO & Chief
Investment Officer Ariel Investments

"I was so pleased to learn more about the man I have known and admired for my entire life. As a Chicagoan, his insights and reflections on our city resonate for all of us, shed light on our city and its history and provide lessons on where we are today."

—Gigi Pritzker, CEO Madison Wells Media

CHANGE AGENT

A Life Dedicated to Creating Wealth for Minorities

JAMES H. LOWRY

ARCHWAY
PUBLISHING

Archway Publishing books may be ordered
through booksellers or by contacting:

Archway Publishing
1663 Liberty Drive
Bloomington, IN 47403
www.archwaypublishing.com
1 (888) 242-5904

Cover image - Victor Powell
Cover design - Michele Lomax & PMM Agency

ISBN: 978-1-4808-8724-4 (sc)
ISBN: 978-1-4808-8723-7 (hc)
ISBN: 978-1-4808-8725-1 (e)

Library of Congress Control Number: 2020901478

Printed in the United States of America.

Archway Publishing rev. date: 04/02/2020

Nettie Camille, Camille Aisha, and Camille Lowry.

I'd like to dedicate this book to the three Camilles in my life. My mother, Camille Lowry, who inspired me to be the man I am today. My former wife Nettie Camille Anthony who supported me in my early career and in raising our beautiful daughter. And finally, my daughter, Camille Aisha Lowry, who since the day she was born has brought me joy and the motivation to be a change agent.

CONTENTS

ACKNOWLEDGMENTS

I offer special acknowledgment to my James H. Lowry & Associates team—my assistant, Julia Rastelli, for the many drafts she typed; my former associate, Jerome Simmons, for his hours of research in the initial drafts; and my lawyer, Michele Lomax, who turned out to be an exceptional editor, encouraging me to dig deep and speak my truth, while she endeavored to make the green pea greener. Without their help, dedication, and friendship, the words on these pages would still just be memories.

I also want to thank those individuals who, over the years, assisted my core team in reviewing multiple drafts of this book, providing insights, feedback, and encouragement: Jacque Edmonds Cofer, Michele Rogers, Anthony Licata, Larry Kirshbaum, Marilyn Booker, Maurice Cox, Al Smith, Toni Fay, Faith Childs, William A. Lowry, Larry Shulman, Tom Woodard, William Matassoni, and my special friend and ex-wife Sharon Collins.

Throughout the book, I acknowledge the many individuals who played significant roles in my life and on whose shoulders I was lifted. I wish to further acknowledge my family; my BCG partners and Black/LatinX cadre; all the former members of James H. Lowry & Associates; my Francis W. Parker and Grinnell College classmates; the clients I served over forty-five years; my fellow board members at Grinnell College, Kellogg School of Management, Toyota Diversity Advisory Board, and Howard School of Business; the alumni of the Kellogg National Minority Supplier Development Council Advanced Management

Education Program; my many fellow members of the Executive Leadership Council and its former presidents Carl Brooks and Ron Parker, along with my good friends Camilla McGhee and Jennifer Vasquez; Linda Johnson Rice, John Rogers, Mellody Hobson, and all my friends at Ariel Capital; the Richard Holland family; Harriet Michel; William Pickard; Tony Miller; Joan Robinson-Berry; Susana Robledo; Beatrice Louissaint; Senator Carol Moseley Braun; Virginia Clarke; Tahnee Lacey; Randal Pinkett; Dorothy Davis; Jim Simmons; John Rice; Cindy, Gigi, and Margo and Tom Pritzker; John Legend and his family, Chrissy, Luna, and Miles, and his brother Bumper Stephens and cousin Dawn Bell, and their extended family Hassan and Kiki Smith, and David Levin; the many Peace Corps volunteers who crossed my path; Joe, Dan, Ricky, and Eddy Arriola; and the Hashemipour family.

Lastly, I offer a special remembrance with gratitude to those corporate business leaders we recently lost. Barry Rand, Price Cobb, and Bernard Tyson helped diversify corporate America, were strong advocates of social change, and were my personal friends. These titans of business broke barriers and were change agents in their own right. They hold a special place in my heart for the efforts they made in leveling the playing field for blacks in corporate America and beyond. Their legacies live on in the hearts of the many they touched and who, as a result of their tireless efforts, were able to gain entry into C-suites in Fortune 500 companies.

PREFACE

"Jim, what is happening in Chicago? Why are so many young blacks killing other young blacks?" These were not new questions. But when posed to me last year by a dear friend I was visiting in Washington, DC, I recalled an article I read by Phillip Jackson, founder of the Black Star Project. In the article, Phil highlighted the following:

- 89% of 16 to 19-year-old young black men in Chicago are not working;
- 43% of 20 to 24-year-old young black men in Chicago are not working;
- Only 7% of 8th grade black boys in Chicago read at a proficient level;
- black people have a harder time finding jobs in Illinois than in any other state in the country;
- Chicago had 762 murders and 4,331 shootings in 2016, mostly young black men killing other young black men, mainly because of the economics and violence associated with the drug trade.

He ends by saying: "Few people or organizations or foundations or government agencies are working on solutions to these issues."

Facing these negative statistics, statistics that only appear to be getting worse in Chicago, citizens are demanding the mayor, the police superintendent, and Chicago civic leadership take *immediate action* to address these serious problems that are threatening lives and the economic stability of Chicago. While immediate action should be taken, I feel it's unfair to put the entire blame on the mayor and others who were holding leadership positions in 2017. Looking at the awful situation in Chicago today forces me to reflect on a 1968 *Life* magazine issue devoted entirely to poverty in America. The magazine cover read: *The Negro and The Cities: The Cry That Will Be Heard.*[1]

The issue presented a detailed description of the causes, symptoms, and key factors of deep poverty in the inner cities in the United States. At the end of the issue, there was an article about the Bedford-Stuyvesant Restoration Corporation and Bed-Stuy D&S Board created by Senator Robert Kennedy. In the issue, Senator Kennedy was praised for putting two bills before the Senate that would "offer private industry tax credits, incentives and accelerated depreciation to get them into the ghettos. I think we can at least do as much for the ghettos as for the oil industry." The article ended with a statement from a young community organizer:

> "The task is so great that no single program, no single project can touch the lives of more than a fragment of Bedford-Stuyvesant. But if the work does not go on, if the money stops pouring in, then there is no question that the ghetto will explode."

That community organizer was me.

Close to fifty years later, I strongly feel that statement is just as valid today in Chicago as it was in Brooklyn in 1968. The inner cities are not on fire with flames, but drugs and gun violence are destroying them just as effectively. I still believe

---

[1] *Life* 64, no. 10 (March 8, 1968).

in a comprehensive economic plan to attack poverty in areas such as Bedford-Stuyvesant, but the plan must be developed by people truly committed to change who possess the skills necessary to implement such change, not just by folks wanting photo opportunities. What we need are seasoned problem solvers willing to spend months, if not years, analyzing the major elements of the problems. Too often, when we get people who truly want to solve the problems of the poor, they don't understand or appreciate the US economic system or how to produce and transfer wealth. Often, attempts to address these highly complex problems grounded in historic realities have failed.

Looking back over the years, I clearly see there has been:

- no comprehensive, well-thought-out and implemented US strategy to prevent drug trafficking in our communities;
- no comprehensive US economic and business strategy to create growth-oriented companies in the inner city;
- no comprehensive US training programs to prepare our youths for jobs in a rapidly changing global industry; and,
- no comprehensive US plan to better educate our children in the public school system to ensure they get jobs in growth industries.

What I have observed over the past fifty years are institutions, government agencies, and individuals working in their own silos. As a result, there have been many, many projects and hurriedly developed, reactive plans operating with limited vision. As a result, the impact on the problems have been minimal.

The other thing I have observed over the past fifty years is that too often these major initiatives, programs, and projects were designed and developed by academics. Many of these highly educated and well-intentioned authors carried a strong desire to effect change, but they were unable or unwilling to accept the historic complexity of poverty. Even our noted great civil rights leaders, such as Martin Luther King Jr., Whitney Young, and Reverend Ben Hooks, were emotional activists and tactical geniuses, but they were not analytical and did not have a deep understanding of business, economic, or management strategies. One of the highest compliments I ever received was from Reverend Jesse Jackson, when he said, "Jim, if we had you with us in the civil rights movement with your managerial and business knowledge, our movement would have been so much stronger." I thanked him for the compliment, but I wonder if young Jesse would have welcomed me as an equal partner at the table.

Black people will always need bold, charismatic, inspirational leaders like the Rev. Jacksons of the world, but as an ethnic group, we must expand the number of seats at the table to include geniuses from all walks of life who are not driven by the desire to have their photos taken for *Jet, Ebony, Black Enterprise, Savoy, Time,* the *Washington Post, New York Times,* or the *Chicago Defender,* or be seen on the six o'clock news.

In spring of this year, I went to an outstanding gala sponsored by the nonprofit group The History Makers, an institution created by visionary Julieanna Richardson. Over the past eighteen years, the organization has captured and told the stories and historic contributions of African American leaders from all walks of life. I came away from that dinner thinking about the wealth of knowledge, history, and potential power that Julieanna Richardson and her team had accumulated. The sad truth is that the average person probably does not even know the institution exists. Upon returning to my office after the event, I said it was time we should accept the advice of our beloved actor and civil rights leader Ossie Davis that he gave after the assassination of Martin Luther King Jr. He said, "If we want to move forward, we must accept it is the plan, not the man." For me, that plan must be comprehensive and in partnership with other ethnic and religious groups appealing to all generations and with a strong economic focus. I do not know who the driver of the plan would be today, but for the good of America, we must start the discussions. This book is my attempt to do just that.

INTRODUCTION

BECOMING A CHANGE AGENT

I have been incredibly blessed. In many ways, I am a product of the times. As a beneficiary of the civil rights movement, I will always be grateful to the young blacks and whites who gave their lives to challenge past social injustices and racism in the South—injustice and inequality for blacks and other minorities that lasted more than four hundred years. Because of those brave and selfless efforts, affirmative action laws and policies were enacted, opening the door to institutions and companies that only a few years earlier denied entry to people of color.

Throughout my life, my parents, teachers, and later even my professors would remind me of my unique status as an affirmative action baby. I was also made keenly aware that many of my educational and career opportunities might not have been possible had historical standards and metrics been used to evaluate me. As a result, at each critical juncture in my career, I was motivated to excel. I made it my personal goal to prove that such standards of entry were unfair in evaluating my talents, my unique contributions, and the size of my heart. I never wanted to be a token black. My success was made possible because those high-level doors had been opened for me by others who came before me. I hope that in sharing my story, it will serve as a reminder of our history and how important it is to continue to open doors for those who follow.

This book reflects the journey of an old warrior who early in his life had simple professional and personal goals. My goals were to have a family, be a good father and husband, excel in my field of choice, become financially secure, and be a community leader. Whether it was six years in the Peace Corps, a liberal education, societal changes of the times, or the many injustices I witnessed, or perhaps a combination of all these factors, I decided to become a change agent instead—a change agent motivated to help not only my family but the millions of people of need in the United States and emerging countries. It became clear to me that people both in America and developing nations desperately wanted to escape poverty. They did not want to be uneducated, unhealthy, or jobless. I concluded early in my career that these people had the same hopes and goals for their families as I did, but they lacked the wealth or connections to lift themselves out of their predicament. They had to face life with the cards they were dealt. A select few of those disadvantaged individuals were able to rise from the depth of poverty, but in most cases, the odds were stacked against them.

My career taught me that although a good education and key relationships were critical to achieving success, without wealth, the road traveled was more challenging. I learned then, and believe even more strongly today, that if more minority communities had accepted the need to create wealth, many of the problems confronting blacks would not exist.

Despite the progress we have made over the past fifty years, economic growth has still not been achieved for so many people on the lower end of the societal ladder. This failure of progress is particularly true for African Americans. When Martin Luther King Jr., Senator Robert Kennedy, and other leaders gave their lives for social and economic advancement, their goal was not to create wealth for those only at the top. Their goal was to create jobs for the jobless, to uplift poor communities in the North and South, and to rectify past injustices for all citizens, securing a stronger and more competitive America.

I have dedicated my life to the field of minority business enterprise development to address the wealth gap and change the mind-set of blacks to one of wealth creation as a means to level out the playing field and create capital for those less fortunate. In this book, I share how I achieved financial wealth and advanced throughout my career. I attempt to address the issue of economic disparity and the social, political, and economic reasons that caused it. I also outline a strategy for change. I write this book as a person of color who is a firm believer in the US free enterprise system, with all its strengths and weaknesses. I also write this book as a proud black American man who worked and aspired to assist less fortunate people in my community as well as in the villages and towns of South America, Africa, and the Caribbean that I spent time in and still hold dear in my heart. It was those global experiences that opened my eyes to cultural differences. They also made me realize that the same factors that prevented economic growth for the lower classes in Peru, Tanzania, and Brazil are the same factors that slowed progress in Inglewood, California, the West Side of Chicago, and the Bronx, New York.

In hindsight, I am forced to accept we are products of the families who raised us, the education we received, the training provided, and the times in which we lived. Concerning the latter, the civil rights struggle, federal policies, and the opportunities offered to me altered my formative years. Thus, at the beginning of each chapter, I briefly outline the historical events that were occurring, the principal government laws and policies that were impacting our communities, and, as a result, what opportunities were presented to me—a black man from the South Side of Chicago—during that period.

Throughout the book, I share how each experience equipped me to be and do better in the next phase of my life. I share the key players of different ethnic, religious, and other groups who supported, motivated, or mentored me, because any success I have achieved over the last fifty-plus years, I achieved on the shoulders of others.

I dedicate this book to the younger generations of all colors, races, and genders. It is my belief that today's youth controls the destiny of the United States and the world. When I saw thousands of young people of all colors, religions, and sexual orientations at the Parkland rally in Washington, DC, I gained a renewed faith in the goodwill of people and emerging leadership of youth in America. I share my wisdom to embolden the millions of millennials and younger to become the next wave of change agents. I want to arm them with my lessons learned and empower them to navigate the tricky and often depressing complexities of the world in which they live. It is my hope that by sharing my historical account and those of other trailblazers from the past, I will motivate this younger generation to be agents of change for the future. As a nation, we can no longer be mere observers of challenges. We must be active participants in the struggle. I end the book with two open letters, one to black leaders and the other to young future leaders. I firmly believe we must have a new plan of action to strengthen the many black communities in need of capital investment—new strategies and possibly an entirely new direction.

Each year, people ask me if I will finally retire. In the final chapter, I outline the reasons I cannot withdraw from the fight. There is still too much to do, too many lessons to share, and too many people who need help. So as long as my services are needed and people, especially young people, continue to ask for my advice, I will continue to work. I feel it is my duty and an honor. In my limited way, I will continue to be a change agent and join others to make this great nation more inclusive and prosperous for all its citizens.

Historical Background 1939–1952

In 1919, there had been a major race riot in Chicago. Fifteen whites and twenty-three blacks were killed, leaving five hundred injured (60 percent of them black). From this point on, the tension was high and growing as millions of blacks were pouring into the city to escape the South and take advantage of the higher-paying jobs in auto plants and steel mills. These jobs were published in black newspapers such as the *Chicago Defender* and *Pittsburgh Courier*, the same newspapers that reported the stories of our heroes in politics, athletics, and our communities, while also publishing the news of weekly lynchings in the South. Willard Francis Motley, whose well-known pen name was Bud Billiken, kept all *Chicago Defender* readers abreast of the times. It was a very segregated time in Chicago.

The Democratic Party led the United States under the leadership of President Franklin Delano Roosevelt (and many would say by his wife, Eleanor). Eleanor Roosevelt was a progressive thinker and champion of black, labor, and women's rights. The Democrats controlled Congress, relying on a coalition of blacks, women, and Southern Dixiecrats.[2]

- 1941: On June 25, 1941, President Franklin Delano Roosevelt issued Executive Order 8802,[3] desegregating war production plants and creating the Fair Employment Practice Committee (FEPC), which banned discriminatory

---

[2] Southern Dixiecrats were a short-lived segregationist political party in the United States. Its members were referred to as Dixiecrats, a portmanteau of Dixie, referring to the Southern United States, and Democrat. This political party was committed to the maintenance of segregation and opposed to federal intervention into race and, to a lesser degree, labor relations.

[3] https://www.britannica.com/event/Executive-Order-8802.

employment practices by federal agencies and all unions and companies engaged in war-related work—including the defense industry.

- 1944: President Truman is elected president.
- 1946: On April 18, 1946, Jackie Robinson integrated baseball when he joined the Montreal Royals, the Dodgers' best farm team. After huge success that year, he joined the Dodgers the following spring. He often faced death threats, teammate boycotts, and constant racial epithets from white fans.
- 1948: President Truman signed Executive Order 9981[4] desegregating the United States Armed Forces.
- 1948: On January 30, 1948, Mahatma Gandhi was assassinated, leaving the world shocked and saddened by the news that India's great beacon of peace was gone. Gandhi's teachings and strong beliefs were a significant influence on future leaders, such as Martin Luther King Jr. in the United States and Nelson Mandela in South Africa.
- 1948: In the case of *Shelley v. Kraemer*,[5] the US Supreme Court ruled that a court "may not constitutionally enforce a restrictive covenant which prevents people of a certain race from owning or occupying property."
- 1950: In the case of *McLaurin v. Oklahoma State Regents*,[6] the US Supreme Court ruled to prohibit racial discrimination in places of public institution of high learning such as colleges or universities.

---

[4] Executive Order 9981, July 26, 1948; General Records of the United States Government; Record Group 11; National Archives.

[5] *Shelley v. Kraemer,* 334 U.S. 1 (1948).

[6] *McLaurin v. Oklahoma State Regents,* 339 U.S. 637 (1950).

CHAPTER 1

MY EARLY YEARS — WHEN WOODLAWN WAS A VILLAGE

I grew up in the village of Woodlawn, and it truly was a village back then—a stable, working-class, black community where everyone knew one another and families worked, played, partied, and worshipped together. I was one of two sons of postal worker parents, William E. and Camille Lowry, and I grew up realizing that, compared to quite a few others in our neighborhood, we were pretty well off, comfortable. Our parents' combined salaries meant that we lived in a nice house, never went hungry, and were treated with respect by the neighbors. My parents were part of the Great Migration, and while Chicago was racially segregated, they knew that living in Chicago in the thirties was far superior to the lives they might have lived in Tennessee or Mississippi, where they had been born.

The year my father was born, thirty-seven African American men were lynched in Tennessee. While my dad refused to speak much about his childhood in Memphis, my relationship with my mother was much more open. Through many conversations over the years, I learned a detailed account of my mother, Camille Caldwell's, life in Hollandale, Mississippi, where she grew up. According to my mother, her family lived a very comfortable existence because my grandfather was an accomplished carpenter, a trade he passed on to his two sons. My grandmother, Emma Jane, was a real leader and a powerful influence in her community. She was deeply religious, providing daily spiritual uplifting for the many people she met. She often toured the farmlands with her horse-drawn buggy, selling or trading her homemade medicines and preaching the Gospel to whoever would listen. The Caldwells owned land and had enough money to send their eldest daughter to a historically black college, and my mother and her sister to Mary Holmes Seminary Boarding School. However, the lifestyle as they knew it came to an abrupt end one night when a Jewish storekeeper, who was a close friend of the family, contacted my grandfather to warn them that the KKK was coming to lynch him. Although he denied it until the day he died, it was alleged my grandfather had flirted with a white woman who had hired him for carpentry work.

I never met my grandfather before he died. When I saw photos of him, he had a light complexion with straight hair and was very handsome. Considering this and hearing how he was forced to leave Mississippi, I had to wonder who really did the flirting. Was it my grandfather or the white woman accusing him, whose attentions he might have spurned?

With that ominous news, my grandparents made a fast decision and purchased three tickets for my grandfather and his two sons to escape via the Illinois Central Railroad to Chicago. According to my uncle William, my grandfather and his two sons stayed hidden in the restroom until the train crossed the Mason-Dixon line into perceived safety. My grandfather told my grandmother that once they arrived in Chicago and got established, they would send word to have the rest of the family join them. Alone in Mississippi, my grandmother remained with her three daughters for another two years until they reunited with my grandfather. The Caldwell family never returned to Mississippi. One of my uncles found employment with the US Postal System, and the other as a carpenter for the railroad.

My parents were good providers, and as children, we were well fed, with a refrigerator full of healthy, if not gourmet, foods. My father used to do all the shopping and buy all our staples from a store called Hillmans in downtown Chicago. Since we did not own a car, every Friday, my brother, William E. Lowry, Jr. (Bill), and I would meet my father at the L train at the Sixty-First Street Station to help him carry those shopping bags home, often heavily laden with canned goods. That heavy lifting was my early-childhood experience in bodybuilding. It never occurred to me then, but looking back, I always wondered how my father carried all those heavy bags alone from the store to the downtown train station.

For the first twenty years of my life, the only steak I ever ate was round steak tenderized by my mother and smothered in gravy. At every dinner, my mother would serve some kind of greens— collard, mustard, or turnip. My mother not only worked a forty-hour week at the post office, but she was also an outstanding housewife and a superb cook. When it came to fried chicken, no one could fry a chicken like my mother. Every Sunday, my mother would fry five chickens for the family, extended family, and neighbors.

Sunday was a happy day, playing sports in the park and coming home to my mother's chicken, family card games, and ending it by watching the *Ed Sullivan Show*. We watched that show with pride as he hosted guests the likes of Nat King Cole, the Nicholas Brothers, Lena Horne, and Sammy Davis Jr. These stars were the first blacks who were exposed to white audiences on TV. Originally, Sammy Davis Jr. did not receive star billing. Sullivan would introduce the Will Mastin Trio starring Sammy Davis Jr. The family would laugh in unison because after Sammy's father and uncle would dance for about three minutes, they would fade into the background, and Sammy would go on to perform for twenty minutes and steal the show.

My brother and I loved sitting by our parents as they played cards with neighbors and friends. There was always much laughter along with copious amounts of gin and tonics. One night, being the bad boy I was even in my early years, I started drinking the remnants of those gin and tonics. Later, my brother found me passed out on the floor and very sick to my stomach. Needless to say, as a result of my first official hangover, I had no desire to drink hard liquor until my freshman year in college.

I had an extraordinary bond with my mother—a relationship that grew stronger every year until she died at ninety-seven and a half. She was always my strongest supporter and my greatest inspiration. She came home every night to prepare dinner and kept our apartment spotless. My mother always had a smile on her face and never showed a hint of anger, despite growing discord between her and my father.

My brother and I attended Austin O. Sexton Grammar School, where we received an excellent education from a cadre of outstanding and highly motivated teachers. Many of our teachers at A.O. Sexton had graduate degrees, but the color of their skin blocked them from other career paths. For the vast majority of blacks of this time, the top careers were teachers, social workers, waiters, and Pullman porters on the railroad. At the top of the ladder were doctors and dentists. Many black professionals also worked in the post office, as it gave them financial stability. In fact, my first two dentists worked full-time in the post office. In our extended family, we always looked up to my uncle Sam Cooksey. Uncle Sam Cooksey always had the most money because he was a head waiter at the Palmer House Hotel. Even in the fifties, he made thousands of dollars in tips.

My favorite teacher at A.O. Sexton was the unforgettable Ms. Madalen Stratton. She was a very tall and impressive woman who maintained total control of her classroom. She always pushed us to be the best students we could be. She also made us take pride in our black history, years before there was a Black History Month. On every wall in her classroom were banners and photos of famous African and African American heroes. Under her guidance, I wrote a well-researched essay on Paul Robeson, for which I received an A. It pains me today that I never kept that essay. I was Mrs. Stratton's favorite in the classroom, and we had a special bond. She not only sent me a nice note when I graduated, saying how proud of me she was, but she continued this practice for many years without fail every time she saw me acknowledged in the press. Mrs. Stratton never knew the positive impact her notes had on me or how she inspired me throughout my career. Like many young blacks in Chicago, we led an isolated and protected life. We were fearful of racists, especially white youths and white policemen. But one policeman we feared the most was a black policeman named Two Gun Pete. Two Gun Pete was an officer in Woodlawn and feared by everyone in the community—a big black policeman who had unlimited and unlawful latitude to be the enforcer on black youths and criminals in the neighborhood. I am sure every police department in urban America had their version of Two Gun Pete.

As kids, we were aware of the dangers of racism in Chicago, so we knew what to do or not to do when confronted by whites. An incident involving my father left an indelible mark on me. One day he took us to a Cubs game. At the game, a foul ball landed two feet from my brother, who eagerly picked it up. To our dismay, a large white man confronted my brother and took the ball out of his hand. We both looked at our father, who we thought would take the ball back, but instead he sheepishly looked away and returned to watching the game. Both my brother and I cried.

I was only ten years old, but on that day, I vowed no one

would ever take the ball from me or my family again. I told myself that looking away was something that might be normal for black men from Memphis, Tennessee, growing up in the 1920s trying to survive, but this was not to be the case for Jim Lowry growing up in Chicago in the 1950s. My teachers and my mother had instilled in me the pride that would prevent me from looking the other way when confrontation was needed. I would later discover looking away and swallowing my pride was indeed going to be a part of my journey.

Chicago was an extremely segregated city in the fifties. Within our designated boundaries, we functioned as a separate community or a small town. In our neighborhood, Sixty-First Street operated as the main business street for us, with many retail stores, mostly owned by nonblacks, including one supermarket, one library, four liquor stores, one movie theater, one drugstore, and a barbershop. On our block were trade unionists, a doctor, and a highly acclaimed artist. We had friends in the adjacent neighborhoods of Englewood and Hyde Park, and we would often compete against our friends in athletics in Washington Park, our home away from home. The joke I heard as a youngster was that they named Washington Park after our first president, but once blacks became the majority population in the neighborhood, the park was renamed Booker T. Washington Park. I don't know if this was true, but it is a story we heard often. My uncle Sam Cooksey once posed the question, "Jim, what is the name of our first president?" I quickly answered, "George Washington." He replied, "Correct." He then asked, "Jim, how many white people you know with the last name Washington?" Think about that, people.

It was so much fun roaming and playing in Washington Park. Washington Park was bordered by Sixtieth Street on the south, Martin Luther King Drive on the west, and Cottage Grove on the east—a park covering over 372 acres of green space and much diversity. I watched the African Americans participate in baseball or sixteen-inch softball games throughout the park. On the east side of the park, which bordered the prestigious University of Chicago, I would often see Italians playing bocce ball and West Indians practicing cricket.

Leaving my house at Sixtieth Street on the southern boundary of the park at age eleven, I would eagerly walk through the park to meet my friends without a care in the world, which likely is not the case for today's eleven-year-olds. I would often make new friends, watch old men fish in the lagoon, and eat wild mulberries off the trees. Our house was near the famous 1922 Fountain of Time monument, created by sculptor Loredo Taft and influenced by the 1893 World's Columbian Exposition, to which he had earlier contributed. Later this fountain and the surrounding area were designated a historic site by the city of Chicago. It was named after the first black tenured professor at the University of Chicago, Dr. William Allison Davis.

I had many pleasant memories of Washington Park, but the ones that have stayed with me for more than fifty years are the images of hundreds of black families having picnics and loving one another while listening to the latest Motown hits. There was much laughter, friends giving high fives, all while eating from picnic baskets filled with fried chicken, deviled eggs, and potato salad. The families were not rich, but most were happy.

Washington Park was a place we escaped to play baseball, basketball, and football. One year, my brother, Bill, represented the Washington Park Bears in the city's park district Biddy football league, which was well organized and had great coaches. The teams represented parks around the city. Occasionally, the teams were asked to play as entertainment during halftime at Chicago Bears football games. My brother was one of the stars of the team, and I was the eight-year-old mascot. Although I was not officially on the team, I remember one time, one of the coaches, Coach Earl Davis, gave me a jersey with the number four on it so I could be with the team on the sidelines at Wrigley Field. The first game I attended, my parents were in the stands, and to their and my surprise, the Bears fans behind the bench started screaming "Put number four in the game!" Suddenly, the entire section started chanting, "Put number four in!" Coach Davis thought it would be funny so he quickly gave me a helmet, and there was little Jimmy Lowry, running onto the field to the cheers of forty-five thousand fans, as the announcer made endless jokes about "little number four" lost in the line of scrimmage. The next two times we played at the Bears games, I was able to get a uniform and a helmet to fit, and I would run on the field as the comic relief, bringing a smile to my mother's face and laughter to all the fans.

Back in those days, we were free to wander anywhere over acres of land to find a game. Afterward, we would retreat to Jimmy Wooley's house. Jimmy had a great mother, Molly Wooley, one of the largest apartments in the neighborhood, and the first television in the community. It was a small twelve-inch TV, and five to seven of us would be leaning over one another, watching episodes of *Howdy Doody*, wrestling, the *Lone Ranger* and *Hopalong Cassidy*. Compared to us, Jimmy was rich. He was the only son of Johnny Wooley, a big-time "policy boss." Johnny Wooley was not only a policy boss, but he was an ardent supporter of community projects. He got the Third Ward Democrats to buy uniforms for our Little League baseball team, making us the only team in the neighborhood with uniforms, obviously the envy of our classmates. The support of the Third Ward Democrats and the financial donations of Mr. Wooley were questionable in terms of the legality of their source. I, like most of the players on the team, made no moral judgments.

In the fifties, "policy" might have been the largest black

industry in Chicago and other black communities across the nation. Every home in the neighborhood would warmly greet the "numbers" carrier as he stopped by almost monthly with his little notepad. It wasn't just men who played either. My grandmother, Emma Jane, played the numbers every day of her life.

Everyone knew the Jones brothers controlled policy on the South Side, that is until one of the Jones brothers, while in jail on a minor offense, happened to share with his cellmate how much money policy made. That cellmate was Sam Giancana, the infamous leader of the Chicago outfit. As soon as he got out of jail, he shared this information with Joey Esposito, Frank Nitti, and Tony Accardo and got approval to take over one of our only industries in the black community. Giancana told the brothers they could leave the country with their savings and their lives would be spared, so the story goes. Whether true or not, the Jones brothers left and retired to Mexico City. Ironically, thirty years later, a very smart young African American lady from Mexico City, who spoke fluent Spanish and was named Jones, applied for a job at my firm. She turned out to be the daughter of one of the Jones brothers. I would have gladly hired her, but we had no openings at the time. An interesting twist in black history, the father of one of my Francis W. Parker classmates wrote a book in 1946 titled *The Policy King,* which would become a model for change. Change came, and in 1974, the Illinois State Lottery began, and it basically destroyed the policy business industry.

Although it was never discussed openly, at an early age, I sensed my father favored my brother. I don't recall ever having discussions about anything with my father. Like many black men, he endured racial discrimination and suffered from it. He tried to be a strong head of the household, working long hours and suffering in silence. As a preteen, I discovered there was something else my father never discussed with me—and, it turns out, our entire family. One day in Washington Park, when I was watching my brother Bill play basketball on a court near our home, a young man about five years older than my brother approached us and, calling us by our names, introduced himself to us as our half-brother, Everett.

If you thought we were surprised, our reaction paled in comparison to the shock and pain of my mother when she heard the news. She immediately confronted my father, who, as it turns out, had been supporting Everett and his mother for more than fifteen years. Once it was out in the open, I admit that I was proud my father was so candid about having a son out of wedlock. It helped that it had taken place before he married my mother, and equally important, he supported them for thirteen years. Like other black families of my time, there was always one or two members of the family who seemed to have paid a price. In our family, it was my mother. My father was the leader of three households—our immediate family, his five-member family that he brought up from Memphis, and Everett Lowry's family. My mother always felt shortchanged financially and often taken for granted, which led her to make a bold move for the times. She decided to earn her own money, so she also got a job at the post office.

Deep down, I guess I also resented my father. It started with the way he treated my mother. My mother contributed to the family income, as my father did. However, my father expected my mother to still carry out all the household responsibilities with little or no help from him. My father and I pretty much kept our distance from each other as far back as I can remember. There was one thing that did bring us together—sports. Before TV, our family, like other families in the community, would gather around the massive radio and listen to the broadcasts of the Chicago Cubs, White Sox, Chicago Cardinals, and Bears football games. My favorite Cubs player was Peanuts Lowrey, for obvious reasons. We enjoyed those games, but the main attraction was Joe Louis fights. When Joe Louis won a match, you could hear the roar all over the black neighborhoods. In the forties and fifties, Joe Louis was the man. He was our hero.

Later, Jackie Robinson and Larry Doby in baseball, Marion Motley in football, and the Harlem Globetrotters in basketball would join our list of heroes. I will never forget a Harlem Globetrotters game my mother took me to. Often considered the clowns of basketball, they played it straight this game and beat the champion Minneapolis Lakers, led by George Mikan. With sports being ever present in our household, it was no surprise my brother and I aspired to be professional athletes. I probably wanted it even more than my brother. I yearned to please my father in the hopes that someday I would get his love and approval in return. The question I will always ask myself is, in his own way, did he love me? Did he appreciate me as his son? Did he take pride in my athletic and academic achievements?

It was by brother's skill and success as an athlete that inspired me to want to follow in his footsteps. My father made my brother my permanent babysitter, so I was regularly competing with youngsters four years older, forcing me to perform at a higher level in basketball, baseball, and football. My father was not a great athlete, but he had always aspired for my brother and me to be professional athletes. When my brother and I were not playing or hanging out at Washington Park, our weekly release was to go to the movies at our neighborhood theater. In many ways, that theatre was the neighborhood babysitter. We would all meet at the show and watch movies all day. We would eat too much candy and popcorn, and we probably made too much noise. For me, I looked forward to associating with my best buddies, while my brother, Bill, being a young "Mack Daddy," chased the girls.

The only blacks we saw in those movies were African warriors in *King Kong* movies; Bill Robinson dancing with Shirley Temple; Mantan Moreland in *Charlie Chan* movies; Willie Best in horror movies saying, "Feets, don't fail me now"; and Stephen Fletcher. When TV arrived, it did not get any better. *Amos and Andy* had been a very popular radio show created and starring white performers, Freeman Gosden and Charles Correll, between 1928 and 1953. When the show aired on TV in 1951, there was a black cast. Although the TV show was embarrassing, it was hilarious, and I laughed at jokes we knew we shouldn't laugh at—but they were very, very funny. Like the *Red Foxx* show many years later, *Amos and Andy* played to the black stereotype, making me feel embarrassed but at the same time entertained by their comical genius. This was our reality; we lived a closed life. But all this would soon change. A whole new world was about to open for my brother, Bill, and me.

When my brother graduated from A.O. Sexton, he was selected to be one of the first blacks to matriculate to the University of Chicago Laboratory School. The Lab School did not have a football team, but my brother started on the basketball and baseball team, and for two years, I went to every one of his games, cheering him on with uncontrollable enthusiasm.

In the 1950s, under the leadership of President Robert Hutchins, the University of Chicago developed a unique program that would allow Lab School students to enter the university after only two years. However, my brother opted not to take advantage of this opportunity and decided to transfer to another private school, Francis W. Parker, the only other private school in Chicago accepting blacks at the time, and it had a football team. My brother entered both the Lab School and Francis W. Parker with confidence, skills, and charm. As a result, he was highly successful at both schools academically and athletically. He set a high bar for me but one I eagerly wanted to reach and surpass.

There were a handful of local African Americans who were

leading the charge as true civil rights champions and would serve as early role models for me because of their lifelong leadership in business. Two leaders I remember from those days were Truman Gibson Sr. and Earl B. Dickerson, who together started and ran the Supreme Life Insurance Company of America for many years. They eventually sold it to another iconic black business leader, John Johnson, CEO of Johnson Publishing. Equally prominent was Robert Taylor. Robert Taylor was the son of the first African American to enroll in the Massachusetts Institute of Technology. Taylor studied architecture and finance at Howard University, the University of Illinois, and Northwestern University. He was a noted housing leader and, working with Sears and Roebuck Company's longtime board chairman, Julius Rosenwald, built low-income housing across the nation for blacks.

The Taylor family tradition of excellence and civic involvement continued over the generations. His granddaughter is Valerie Jarrett, who was a senior advisor to former president Barack Obama and one of that first family's closest friends. One of Taylor's other granddaughters, Antoinette Cook Bush, received a JD from Northwestern University Law School and a BA from Wellesley College. She has been the global head of government affairs and executive vice president at News Corporation since June 24, 2013. Formerly, she was a lawyer at Skadden, Arps, Meagher & Flom, LLP, where, over her nearly twenty-year tenure, she rose to become the partner in charge of the firm's Communications Group. I had the pleasure of hiring Antoinette one summer at my consulting firm, James H. Lowry & Associates, and wrote letters of recommendation for Antoinette's brother, Mercer, and sister, Janice, to Harvard Business School. Both were accepted, and they too have had outstanding professional careers.

The Cook offspring not only had an iconic leader on the Dibble side of the family in Robert Taylor, but their other grandfather Mercer Cook was an outstanding leader as well. Mercer Cook received a BA from Amherst College in 1925; a teaching diploma from the University of Paris in 1926; a master's degree in French from Brown University in 1931; and a doctorate from Brown University in 1936. In 1961, President John F. Kennedy appointed Cook the US ambassador to Niger. In 1963, he was designated as an alternative delegate to the General Assembly of the United Nations. In 1966, Ambassador Cook returned to Howard University and became the head of the Department of Romance Languages.

Unfortunately for me and others of my generation, model businessmen like Truman Gibson Sr., Earl B. Dickerson, and Robert Taylor were few. We lived on the southwest side of Chicago. Our view of the outside world was seen only through the papers of our community-based black newspapers like the *Chicago Defender* and later *Ebony* and *Jet* magazines. As a young teenager, I could not wait to read the latest *Jet* magazine to learn more about our iconic leaders. Of course, to be candid, I also liked to see the latest bikini centerfolds. John Johnson, owner of Johnson Publications, created the first centerfold much earlier than Hugh Hefner at Playboy. Through these publications, we soon discovered Adam Clayton Powell, Hazel Scott, Ambassador Mercer Cook, Thurgood Marshall, and others.

Historical Background 1952–1957

The fifties were the beginning of the civil rights movement in the South. In 1953, WWII hero Dwight D. Eisenhower was elected president of the United States. The following year, Rosa Parks refused to give up her seat on the bus to a white person, triggering a yearlong boycott of the buses in Montgomery, Alabama, led by Martin Luther King Jr. In 1956, the US Supreme Court ruled it unconstitutional to segregate buses.

Chicago's black population grows to four hundred thousand, but housing remains a problem. Because of segregation, several families would cram together and share the same bathrooms and kitchens in what was called the narrow Black Belt on the South Side.

We witnessed the election of two African Americans to the US House of Representatives, William Levy Dawson and Robert N.C. Nix Sr.

Ebony and *Jet* magazines replace the *Chicago Defender* as the principal translations of black affairs.

Blacks were integrating athletic teams at colleges.

Sammy Davis Jr. and Nat King Cole became crossover superstars, and Barry Gordy founded Motown Records.

Being black in America was still very difficult, but things were improving.

- 1953: President Eisenhower signed Executive Order 10479[7] that created the Government Contracts Committee, which is an antidiscrimination committee that ensured "all qualified candidates seeking employment on government

---

[7] Exec. Order No. 10479 (18 FR 4899).

contracts or subcontracts will not be discriminated against due to their race."

- 1954: In the milestone case *Brown v. Board of Education,*[8] the US Supreme Court ruled that separating children in public schools based on race was unconstitutional. It signaled the end of legalized racial segregation in the schools of the United States, overruling the "separate but equal" principle set forth in the *Plessy V. Ferguson*[9] case.
- 1955: President Eisenhower signed Executive Order 10590[10]—which excludes and prohibits discrimination against any employee or applicant for employment in the federal government because of race.
- 1955: Teenager Emmett Till was brutally murdered in Money, Mississippi, for allegedly whistling at a white woman. His mother insisted that his casket be opened at his funeral to show the damage to his face and his body at the hands of those who kidnapped and killed him. *Jet* magazine published a photo of Emmett Till in his casket, and the image was seen across the world. Like many young blacks, I felt what happened to Emmett Till could have easily happened to me. I was very upset seeing the photo of Emmett Till and learning that all of his murderers were found innocent at trial.

---

[8] 347 U.S. 483.

[9] 163 US 537 (*1896*).

[10] Exec. Order No. 10590, 20 FR 409 (1955).

CHAPTER 2

FRANCIS W. PARKER — A NEW WORLD

Surrounded by some of the wealthiest homes in the city, Francis W. Parker is set just off the shores of Lake Michigan on Chicago's North Side. When my brother arrived at Francis W. Parker, the school had more blacks enrolled from kindergarten to twelfth grade than the University of Chicago Lab School. You might wonder how this was possible considering Chicago was a very segregated and racially charged city in the fifties. The answer is simple. David Wallerstein and Truman Gibson Jr., two very powerful men, decided over dinner one night that it was time to integrate the school and bring diversity to the classrooms. So, just like that, it was done.

David Wallerstein was the pillar of the Jewish community, and Truman Gibson Jr. was the pillar of the black community. At the time, David Wallerstein was not only the chairman of the board of Parker, but he was also president of the Balaban-Katz movie chain, chairman of the local ABC TV Station, and later a vital member of the first board of directors of McDonald's. He and his wife, Caroline Wallerstein, were true liberals who practiced what they preached. When Jackie Robinson first started playing for the Brooklyn Dodgers, the Wallersteins welcomed him into their home when he was denied hotel accommodations. One day, the Wallersteins asked Jackie Robinson to visit the

Parker baseball practice. I was so in awe that Jackie Robinson was on our field that when he hit a ball to me, I was so nervous the ball went right through my legs.

The Wallersteins invited me to dinner often, but I will always remember the first dinner I had there with my classmate and good friend Jim Simmons. We were sitting at this long table when the black maid put before us a large plate of spaghetti. I looked at Jim, and Jim looked at me, and we just stared at each other, wondering how we were supposed to eat this spaghetti without looking like fools. You see, at this stage in my life, I did not know how to use a spoon to twirl the spaghetti to avoid having the long noodles hit me in the face. We both did what any young scared black from the South Side would do: we smashed the spaghetti to the point it was almost soup before eating. Sixty years later, Jim and I fondly remember that night.

I saw Truman Gibson Jr. as a type of crusader. He was also one of a very few blacks born into wealth. As I mentioned earlier, Truman's father, along with Earl B. Dickerson, founded Supreme Life Insurance Company of America, which at the time was one of the largest and most successful black companies in America. Truman Gibson Jr. graduated from the University of Chicago Law School and later served as a special assistant to President Truman. While serving in the White House, he persuaded President Truman to abolish many segregation laws in the US Army. After leaving employment in the Truman administration, Gibson Jr. became a highly successful entrepreneur, and with Willard Wirtz, he revolutionized the television industry. Wirtz and Gibson Jr. also founded the International Boxing Commission (IBC). Gibson Jr. was credited for bringing Joe Louis under management, and soon the nation watched major boxing matches every Wednesday and Friday nights. After helping Joe Louis with tax problems in 1949, Gibson Jr. took on the role of director and secretary of Joe Louis Enterprises, entering the world of professional boxing as a manager and promoter. He also played a unique and unheralded role in the civil rights movement, primarily as a member of the "black cabinet" of Presidents Franklin Delano Roosevelt and Harry S. Truman. As a second-generation wealthy lawyer, Gibson Jr. was fearless, bold, and ahead of his time.

The fifties were a period of transition for America. Having just defeated Hitler in the forties, we were abruptly faced with another world villain—Russia. In 1957, Russia launched *Sputnik 1*, hastening our entry into the space race. In 1959, Cuba was taken over by known Communist Fidel Castro, and whites were still lynching blacks in the South.

Chicago remained one of the most segregated cities in the United States. Young black men knew we could not venture into certain neighborhoods, or else we would have been beaten up or worse. We were also very aware that interracial dating was not accepted. Interracial marriage would not become legal in all states until the landmark Supreme Court case, *Loving v. Virginia*[11] in 1967. Hence, for Gibson Jr. and Wallerstein to be bold advocates for change said a lot about them and their character.

When my brother enrolled, both Truman Gibson Jr. and Earl B. Dickerson's daughters were students at Parker. Later, my brother dated Diane Dickerson, and I dated Karen Gibson. Dianne and Karen were both outstanding students and remained our friends for more than forty years. Looking back, I owe a lot to Truman Gibson Jr. and David Wallerstein and others for being the bold trailblazers ahead of their time.

My brother had a fabulous and joyous two years at Parker playing basketball, football, and baseball, acting in school plays, getting good grades, and becoming a student body leader. Being the envious and ambitious younger brother, I aspired to achieve the same, so I applied to Parker when I was in seventh grade.

---

[11] *Loving v. Virginia,* 388 U.S. 1 (1967).

I thought 1951 was going to be a great year, going to Parker with my brother. Unfortunately, I was not accepted because my standardized test scores were not high enough. It was a difficult pill to swallow because I was an A student at A.O. Sexton, and I desperately wanted to be at Parker with my brother during his final year. Throughout my school years, I never did well on standardized tests, which deeply affected me psychologically. I often thought I was not as smart as my classmates because of my poor performance on standardized tests. Upon reflection, I concluded maybe the problem might have been that standardized tests were not a fair judgment of my intellectual and problem-solving capabilities and the size of my heart.

The following year, I was encouraged to reapply by the Parker Admissions Department, which I did, and I even received a partial scholarship. Transferring to Francis W. Parker was one of the most significant events in my life. Traveling from the segregated South Side lower-income community of Woodlawn to the ultrarich Gold Coast school on the North Side opened my eyes in many ways. I was challenged culturally, academically, and emotionally.

Joining me in eighth grade was another student from A.O. Sexton, Jim Simmons. I knew Simmons but not well. For years, his mother had been the PE teacher at A.O. Sexton, noted for her tough classroom morning exercise and stern discipline. Mrs. Simmons must have known what she was doing because at one hundred years of age, she is living independently with her sharp mind intact.

Jimmy was a quiet, skinny kid at the time and not an outstanding athlete, but he had potential. When we started school together, he was four inches taller, but two years later, I grew four inches, and Jimmy and I both improved. Athletically, we put Parker on the map, winning football and basketball championships, beating public and private schools, and humiliating our close rival, Chicago Latin School, 77–12 in a basketball game our senior year.

With the help of another South Side sharpshooter recruit, George Gray, we lost only one game all season. Jim was All-Chicago basketball and All-Conference football. I was All-Conference for three years in football, basketball, and baseball and was awarded All-Chicago honors as well.

The transition from A.O. Sexton to Francis Parker was difficult in many ways. Although I was an A student in public school, private school was different. At A.O. Sexton, I received a solid education, but at Francis Parker, we were reading Shakespeare, Chaucer, and Hemingway. I remember a TV program entitled the *Whiz Kids* that had gifted students compete against one another. In my class, we had two students on the show. I had an inferiority complex because I felt overwhelmed academically. It did not help when one of my close friends, Don Richards, trying to praise me for my performance in a school play, stated, "Jim, you were great in the play, although I could not understand a word you said." You see, I brought from the South Side not only athletic skills but a thick African American accent. I had a problem "clearly articulating my vowels."

The same Don Richards also gave me some strong advice that I have often shared with others over the years. One day, I was totally frustrated with Don constantly raising his hand in the classroom, and I said: "Don, you ask too many questions!" He replied, "Jim, I ask a lot of questions, and I get As. You ask no questions and get Cs." This comment truly hurt, but I absorbed it and became a better student. I was never a whiz kid, but I became a B student, and I learned to clearly articulate my vowels. That brief exchange had a profound impact on me and my career. Because of Don Richards, I would ask questions without hesitating in any professional, political, or social situation. I learned to conduct research until I felt satisfied with the answers. Little did I know how valuable a trait this would be for me throughout the rest of my life. Too often, we accept what we perceive as fact because of the status of the author or presenter. I learned this was a mistake!

After a couple of years at Parker, when I returned to the South Side of Chicago, I was told I sounded like a white boy. Initially, I was embarrassed when confronted with this reality; I guess I did sound like a white boy. Many of us did in the fifties. I had two or three ways of talking, my Francis Parker way clearly articulating every vowel and my South Side way of talking. Although our friends on the South Side made fun of us for sounding white, we later found out they were also very proud of Jim Simmons and me because of our athletic achievements. They could report in great detail how many points we scored on the basketball court and how many touchdowns on the football fields.

Our same buddies would often ask us if we were dating any white girls. I lied and said no. I not only lied to my South Side male friends, but I also lied to the parents of my white girlfriend who I dated for two years. They never suspected I dated their daughter because I had my friend pick her up and take her home every weekend. They eventually found out the truth and took her out of school. Later they approached the school, asking if she could reapply on the condition that the school would get me to state I would not date their daughter. When the school asked me to do so, I immediately agreed, with every good intention, but I was weak. Fortunately for her parents, we broke up in my senior year, and soon after, I started dating a truly nice, beautiful, black, non–Francis W. Parker student by the name of Hope, and everyone was happy—her parents, the school, and, most importantly, me.

Early in my professional career, I was a chameleon, often not recognizing it until someone brought it to my attention. Even now, my close friends will say, "Lowry, you are using your Harvard voice." Initially, I felt I had to change my delivery to be accepted in each world. However, for me, I had three worlds: my inner-city world, my Francis W. Parker world, and my South Side black Jack and Jill world.

In the black community, there were Jack and Jill clubs established across the nation to facilitate the socialization of sons and daughters of prominent families, prominent light-skinned families. In the fifties, leaders of Jack and Jill chapters discriminated based on skin color and social status. My skin was light enough, but unfortunately, my father's occupation did not reach the threshold of prominence to be accepted, which hurt as a young teenager. I made up my mind then that any child I had was never going to be a member of any Jack and Jill club. I did not believe in social discrimination based on color, where the marker of acceptance was based on how light or dark one's skin.

While I was denied membership to the local Jack and Jill chapter, I was not denied access to the parties. Jimmy Simmons was a member because his mother was a schoolteacher and made sure I was invited to the club's functions. We were discouraged from dating Francis W. Parker students, who were mostly white. But we didn't care, because as a group, the Jack and Jill girls were gorgeous, so these parties were crucial to my dating life.

Francis Parker was not a perfect environment for Jim and me. Our student body would often meet as a group in the auditorium to listen to speakers and other entertainment or to view plays or movies. One day, the selected film was *Birth of a Nation*, by acclaimed director D.W. Griffith. Originally called *The Clansman*, it starred Hollywood's most prominent female silent movie star, Lillian Gish. Francis Parker felt it would be educational for the students because, produced in 1915, it was the nation's first feature film, the cinematography was ahead of its time, and it was Hollywood's first box office hit, grossing $50–100 million. The movie was proudly shown in the White House by then president Woodrow Wilson, who showed it again later when he was president of Princeton University.

But there was no pride felt by the two young black teenagers forced to watch in the all-white audience. The movie was disgustingly racist and glorified the Ku Klux Klan (KKK or Klan) as American saviors. The film started with white actors in blackface depicting shoeless black elected officials during Reconstruction eating fried chicken, lynching white women, and passing laws challenging the Old South. The KKK was formed to protect white women; restore the South to pre–Civil War times; and to confront these ignorant, lustful, uneducated blacks as depicted in the film. In the movie, we witnessed Klansmen riding on horseback, lynching blacks to the cheers of white citizens of the South.

After each scene, Jim and I sank deeper into our seats. In my case, I started sweating profusely and had only one goal—get out of the auditorium as quickly as I could. I was embarrassed but also furious. Little did the well-intentioned teachers at Francis W. Parker realize that my grandfather was forced to leave Mississippi to escape the hangman's noose of the KKK, the heroes of Griffith's movie.

I am sure the organizer of the event at our esteemed private school had good intentions, trying to educate the students, but they were utterly insensitive to the few blacks in the audience and the scars that movie would have on me. We never complained about the film or even discussed it with our teachers, the administration, or our classmates. The event was just too painful and impactful and would be only one of many to come where I would be forced to suffer in silence.

The movie also had another impact on me. It gave me empathy for my Japanese classmates who were forced to view thousands of World War II movies featuring John Wayne winning against the "despicable Japs" and my Native American classmates forced to watch thousands of movies of John Wayne saving the West from the lustful "red savages." They too remained silent. We were expected to remain silent because we were among the first generation opening doors to allow others to enter. We had to be model students, hardworking, respectful, friendly, and willing to turn the other cheek. The fifties were painful times.

Another major challenge for me at Parker was the realization that I was considered lower class. I guess I was in denial of the fact that while the combined salaries of two postal workers may indeed have provided for the necessities of our day-to-day existence as children, they failed to elevate my family to middle-class status. While I stayed on the South Side of segregated Chicago, my status did not affect me, but being a student at Parker was a different story. Every day, I would see limousines drop students off and read about their wealthy parents in the newspapers. Occasionally, when I visited classmates, I was forced to enter through the back door of prestigious apartment buildings by the doorman. I will always treasure the Wallerstein family and other Parker parents who demanded that Jim Simmons and I be granted entry through the front door.

On June 12, 1957, Jim Simmons and I joined seven of our classmates at the Francis W. Parker commencement ceremony. My proud parents were there, along with Jim's mother, Phyllis. Unfortunately, Jim's dad was killed in Italy during World War II. We both had a sense of pride in our five years at Francis W. Parker, with what we had achieved during our school years and life in general. We won private school championships in football and basketball; we were both student body officers; we did well academically; and we made many friends among the student body, the administration, faculty, and other parents. We were considered a credit to our race. Our acceptance and success widened the doors for other blacks to enter, even those with low standardized test scores.

I lived in two different worlds: one with rich, smart white kids on the North Side; the other returning to my "village" on the

South Side with black peers of equal status. While this bothered me, it fortified me for my future and cemented my lifetime goals. When I graduated from Francis W. Parker, I was determined to leverage this unique experience, to enroll in a good college or university, distinguish myself, and become a multimillionaire.

During my five years at Francis W. Parker, I accumulated many friends and allies. I was able to develop unique and robust relationships with the students of color and the admiration of nonminority students, teachers, and parents. The esteem I gained was not only because of my exploits on the athletic field but also for the academic progress I had made, the leadership roles I played, and how I purported myself. I will always remember the kindness of Carolyn and David Wallerstein. When I returned to Chicago in the seventies, I went on the board of the Chicago Youth Center at Carolyn's request and was the chair of the annual CYC big fundraising event. My involvement with CYC was a small price to pay for the role these two supporters and friends played in solidifying my acceptance at Francis W. Parker and getting my career started.

During those five years, I wanted to make my parents proud and make it easier for blacks and students of color coming behind me. I was challenged in many ways, but I survived it. Being exposed to affluent students and their parents, who at times were our most stalwart supporters and advocates, taught me that there were outstanding people of goodwill at all levels of our society. I remember fondly one parent, Eppie Lederer, who was very supportive of me at Francis W. Parker; she later became the iconic columnist Ann Landers. Many others eased the transition from a segregated black community to a practically all-white education community, and I will forever be grateful to them.

I would not have survived my five years at Francis Parker had it not been for my mother, Jimmy Simmons, and athletics. Their support and inspiration meant everything to me. To use Reverend

Jesse Jackson's favorite chant, "I am somebody," in the eyes of others, and more importantly, to myself, I was somebody. When I later became a successful businessman, I had the same strong feelings I did about Jack and Jill that I did when approached to join the Boule, the Guardsmen, or similar members-only groups, for different reasons. In hindsight, this was a mistake because many of my close friends did join these prestigious black private clubs, and they enjoyed such affiliations immensely.

These organizations, along with Greek fraternities and sororities, have provided invaluable support for blacks socially, politically and civically. Within these very strong organizations are the greatest minds and intellects in the black communities. It was always my dream that, in addition to supplying civic and social support, these same institutions could be utilized to create large businesses capable of empowering communities and helping those less advantaged.

Historical Background 1957–1960

Mainly because of the nation's daily focus on the events of the civil rights struggle in the South, doors were being opened for blacks and other people of color. Even Mississippi, Alabama, and Georgia were allowing a few blacks to enter their universities:

- Ernest Green and the students named the Little Rock Nine in 1957 were the first black students to attend classes at Little Rock Central High School, and they had to be protected by the National Guard.
- Hamilton Holmes and Charlayne Hunter Gault were the first black students admitted to the University of Georgia. Hamilton Holmes also was the first black student admitted to Emory University School of Medicine years later.

The South was changing—in the eyes of some, too rapidly, and in the eyes of others, not rapidly enough.

- 1958: The US Supreme Court ruled in *Cooper v. Aaron*,[12] that states may not use evasive measures to avoid desegregation. Subsequently, a federal judge in Harrisonburg, Virginia, ruled that for schools that are funded wholly or partially by public money, those school must not be segregated.
- 1960: Four black college students from Greensboro, North Carolina, sat down at a whites-only lunch counter and ordered coffee. This act of defiance ignited the sit-in movement in effort to desegregate department store restaurants throughout the South. The Freedom Riders movement took place shortly after in 1961 to protest the segregation of interstate buses.

---

[12] *Cooper v. Aaron*, 358 U.S. 1 (1958).

CHAPTER 3

A BIG FISH IN A SMALL-TOWN POND— GRINNELL COLLEGE

There was never a question that I would go to college. I was a B student at Francis W. Parker and an athlete. I knew I was going to get a scholarship somewhere. Jim Simmons and I decided we would go to the same school, which worked in our favor since whatever college we finally decided to attend would get two star athletes instead of one. After lengthy discussions with the principal of Francis W. Parker, Jim and I produced a shortlist of three schools to consider: Lawrence College, Grinnell College, and Kenyon College, where my brother had a brilliant career. My brother, Bill, had continued his success from Francis Parker and was the same trailblazer at Kenyon College. He was a standout in baseball, basketball, and football. He also became the first black accepted at a national white fraternity. He served on the Kenyon board of trustees and was later inducted into the Kenyon Hall of Fame.

The criteria Jim Simmons and I established for our college choices were outstanding academics, progressive environment, and acceptance of our desire to participate in three sports. We visited all three schools and quickly eliminated Kenyon because at the time it was an all-men's institution, and I did not want to compete with my brother's fame. The choice was then between Lawrence and

Grinnell, but we were leaning toward Grinnell. In our junior year at Parker, our football and basketball coach, Don Boya, an alumnus of Lawrence, took us to visit Lawrence but at the time advised us not to attend his alma mater because of the town of Appleton, where Lawrence was located. Appleton had a law on their books stating that blacks could not stay overnight in town. So, going into our senior year of high school, we were confident we were going to Grinnell. After we won both private school championships, things changed.

First, Don Boya was offered the head basketball job at Lawrence, assuming he would bring Jim and me to Lawrence, and the sage advice he had given us the year before was retracted. He insisted on another trip to Appleton to allay our fears about the community, and this time we were treated like royalty. It was almost comical as Don, this intimidating former FBI agent turned Appleton businessman, took us from store to store. When we eventually stopped at a barbershop, entering with the businessman's arms wrapped around us, he stared the barber down and asked forcefully, "Joe, you *will* cut these boys' hair, won't you?" For the first blacks at a basically all-white university in a small, all-white town, getting a decent haircut was a major concern. Still, to parade us down Main Street, Appleton, to get the right answer was embarrassing, to say the least.

We loved our coach, Don Boya, but Jim and I both knew the law against blacks staying overnight was still on the books. So despite the two trips to Appleton, Jim and I were confident we would attend Grinnell. That is, until we visited Grinnell. On our recruiting trip to Grinnell, we were introduced to head basketball Coach John Pfitsch, who uttered, "Damn, we have been waiting for two Watusis like you for years."[13] I looked at Jim, and Jim

---

[13] "Watusi" is a former name used for the "Tutsi" population who were originally located in the African Great Lakes region, a region that encompasses Burundi, Democratic Republic of Congo, Kenya, Tanzania, Rwanda, and Uganda.

looked at me, and simultaneously we both decided maybe we should consider a third visit to Lawrence. We wondered what would be worse—a racist town with a liberal coach, or a racist coach in a liberal town? After an extensive debate, we opted to go to Grinnell, one of the wisest decisions I ever made. Over the next fifty years, John Pfitsch became my coach, mentor, promoter, and one of my closest friends.

In many ways, Grinnell College, located in the middle of the Iowa cornfields, was an extension of Francis Parker. The college was started by Josiah Bushnell Grinnell, and it was the oldest college or university west of the Mississippi River. When we enrolled at Grinnell, the three most famous alumni were Gary Cooper (who did not graduate); Harry Hopkins, the closest advisor to President Franklin Delano Roosevelt; and Judge Joseph Welch, who was responsible for bringing down Senator Joe McCarthy. When we started as freshmen, Grinnell had an endowment of $26 million and was beginning to be recognized as an outstanding small liberal arts college. It had a lovely campus with the men's and women's dormitories separated by a railroad line running through the campus. The school did not have Greek fraternities and sororities, so we were assigned to residence halls for four years. Each dorm had its own name, and Jim Simmons and I were assigned to Smith Hall.

As freshmen, we were not allowed to participate on the varsity teams, so we focused almost exclusively on academics. Because we were two of only eleven blacks on campus, our social life was limited. Being isolated in the middle of Iowa with no social life was difficult, and I must admit there were times I thought about leaving. I would have left if it had not been for Jim Simmons and our third roommate, Allison Davis, our friend from Chicago. Allison was the son of famous black sociologist Dr. William Allison Davis, a highly esteemed professor at the University of Chicago. Young Allison was not an athlete, but every day he brought laughter, unique insights, and a degree of sophistication he had developed at an eastern prep school.

Even before we set off for Grinnell, Jim and I had decided we wanted to be roommates. The admissions office also added Allison as a third roommate, probably not thinking he was black too, which was understandable because unless one knew otherwise, people had no idea looking at Allison that he was black. Although Allison could easily pass for white, he never chose to and instead always identified his ethnic background.

From day one in the three-bedroom suite, we were inseparable. However, unbeknownst to us, another friend from Chicago, Don Stewart, wrote a letter to the admissions office suggesting we be separated because it did not seem appropriate to have three blacks in the same suite. He felt these were the days of integration, not segregation. We thanked Don for his obviously good intentions but informed the admissions office that we were indeed happy in our segregated little environment. Besides, I had to wear my stocking cap at night and never really felt comfortable letting my white residence hall mates see me wearing it. For clarification, in the fifties, many young black men would ask their mothers or girlfriends to give them their old stockings with runs in them. We would cut off the ends, tie a knot, and wear the stocking cap while we slept. The next morning, due to the eight-hour press of the stocking cap, our hair would be neat and manageable. Eventually, I got over my fears and openly started wearing my stocking cap in front of my white friends. One of my close friends, Jim Taylor, a white boy from Boone, Iowa, started wearing a stocking cap and continued wearing it until we graduated. God bless him. I hated to admit it, but that white boy's hair looked better after the eight-hour pressing from the stocking cap.

My freshman year was another year of transition with many highs and lows. Academically, I did well and received an academic scholarship my sophomore year. I had initially received a grant and aid because of my low board score. I supplemented my scholarship by working in the dining hall, so money was not a problem. The problem was my lack of an active social life. Because there were only three black girls on campus and I did not know if Grinnell or the town would accept me dating someone of opposite race, I basically didn't date. This was difficult because Allison had fallen in love with Karen, whom he eventually married, and Jim's girlfriend, Joan, from Chicago would often visit him. My freshman year was tough, but things would drastically change in my sophomore year when a beautiful, intelligent, and talented daughter of a Washington, DC, doctor arrived on campus by the name of Suzie Brown.

Suzie Brown was the perfect campus sweetheart, walking by my side around campus, waiting for me after the game, and helping me show off the latest dance moves at the student union. I was a good dancer but paled in comparison to my cousin Ron Gault, who was so good everyone would form a circle and watch Ron do his thing. Suzie came to Grinnell as a premed student but truly wanted to be a professional dancer. Suzie was good, even better than Ron, although Ron would never admit it. After graduating from Grinnell, she later attended the Juilliard School, majoring in dance. After graduating from Juilliard, she tried to have a professional career in dance, but at the time, white dance companies were not hiring black dancers. There were only two black dance companies, namely Don McKayle and Alvin Ailey, so the competition to get in was extremely fierce. Unfortunately, because of prejudice and tough competition, Suzie was forced to give up her dream of a dance career. She later followed in her father's footsteps and became a highly successful doctor in Kansas City.

My social life became a bit complicated my junior year when Mickey Clark came to study at Grinnell. Mickey, as we called her, was a beautiful, intelligent, and talented black coed I had known from Chicago, because she had attended the University of

Chicago Lab High School before coming to Grinnell. At the Lab School, Mickey was a cheerleader, and the daughter of Mr. and Mrs. Harvey Clark. Mickey's mother, Mrs. Clark, who had a very fair complexion, could have passed for white and had purchased a home in Cicero, Illinois. When her husband and children arrived on the scene, riots ensued, crosses were burned on their lawn, and snakes were put in their mailbox. They were forced to leave Cicero and were escorted out by the National Guard under the orders of President Dwight Eisenhower. I remained friends with Mickey and her parents after Grinnell, and not once did they discuss those scary days in Cicero.

Upon graduating, Mickey began work as a reporter for WBBM-TV, a CBS-owned station in Chicago. In July 1972, she was named as a CBS news correspondent and later the first national black female correspondent, inspiring other young black female journalists to be in front of the camera, like our own Chicago local reporter Dorothy Tucker. Mickey's major responsibilities involved coverage of the 1972 presidential primaries. Tragically, she was killed on December 8, 1972, in a plane crash at Chicago's Midway Airport. She was twenty-nine years old. After Mickey's death, the Columbia Graduate School of Journalism created a special program in her name funded by the Ford Foundation to recruit, train, and place minority journalists. The program was designed by Fred Friendly and Eli Abel, both icons in the field. Geraldo Rivera was in the inaugural class of the program. Also on the plane was the wife of Howard Hunt of Watergate fame and black Congressman George Collins.

In our sophomore year, both Jim and I started for the football team, he as a wide receiver and I as a fullback. Grinnell's football team was highly competitive. We did not win the championship trophy, but Jim and I both received All-Conference honors. After the season ended, we had a short break, and immediately after the Christmas break, we started our basketball season. Jim was put on the first team, and I on the second team, along with All-State player Jon Groteluschen from Manning, Iowa. Jon and I became very close friends, and neither of us appreciated not starting. One day, I boldly confronted Coach Pfitsch, and I told him if he put me in the starting lineup, I would give him 10-10-10. Translated, I would average ten points a game, get ten rebounds, and hold the opposite team's player to ten points. He looked at me sort of funny and said, "Okay, you are starting." I backed up my promise, and for three years I was a starter. In my senior year, I received All-Conference honors and was voted the most valuable player by my teammates on the basketball team. The same year, I was named the most valuable backfield player on the football team and received the G. Lester Duke award for being the school's most outstanding athlete. I guess I got the award because I was the first nine letterman in thirty years, but Jim Simmons really deserved it because he was first team All-Conference in both football and basketball. Jim and I competed as close friends and brothers. Over a seventy-year period, we have never been jealous of each other's achievement and have never had an argument, and every time we meet, the time is filled with positive thoughts and fond memories of A.O. Sexton, Francis W. Parker, and Grinnell College.

Looking back, I accept I was greedy, going from social starvation to now dating two beautiful girls. Yes, I dated both, mostly Suzie on campus and Mickey during the summers in Chicago. I had a great experience at Grinnell. I participated in three sports, was the captain of the basketball team, and was a B student and president of the letterman club. Everything was perfect until the last semester of my senior year. At the beginning of the year, the third beautiful Grinnell coed girl came into my life, Suzie Jean Gustafson. You can tell by her last name she was not a routine member of the Jack and Jill club. Not only was Suzie Jean beautiful, she was blonde, extremely smart, and always positive—but also a white "townie." In fact, in her last year at Grinnell High School, she had been the homecoming queen. Initially, recalling my Francis W. Parker experience, I had a certain degree of trepidation upon meeting her parents, Sid and Lenora. My fears proved to be unwarranted because her parents were the most gracious and open-minded people I had ever met. Even after Suzie Jean and I broke up two years after my graduation, the Lowrys and Gustafsons have remained friends for more than thirty years, with my mother taking annual trips to visit them in Grinnell, independent of me.

No, the problem wasn't going to be with the Gustafsons but with the townies from the other side of the tracks who did not like me dating their Grinnell High School homecoming queen. One day I got a call from one of my young Grinnell basketball fans who told me that his uncle was part of a vigilante group that planned to lynch and castrate me. I did not respond to the initial call, but when I got five more calls, all indicating the same potential horrendous event, fearing for my life and loss of my manhood, I decided it was time to take action.

With the backing of the football team and hundreds of others, we staged a march down Main Street near Grinnell. In addition, for the rest of the semester, I carried, for the first and only time in my life, a gun that I purchased for one dollar from the star of the cross-country team. I never did have any encounters with the townies, but I remained vigilant. I did not have any incidents on campus, but once when I took Suzie to Chicago and she called her parents to say she arrived safely, the telephone operator gossiped to others in town that Suzie was staying with the Lowrys. When Sid Gustafson heard the operator had violated the public trust with this action, he marched into the office of the president of the local telephone company and said if this happened again, he would sue him personally along with the telephone company. I will always have a special place in my heart for the Gustafsons. They strengthened my belief that there are good and honest people irrespective of race, gender, sexual preference, religion, and economic status. One of the highlights of my four years at Grinnell was having the Gustafsons in the audience when I received the award for being Grinnell's most outstanding athlete.

During the last semester of my senior year, a student approached me to go to the office of one of my professors, who, unbeknownst to me, was in a tough battle to retain the position of head of the Political Science Department against my mentor, Dr. Harold Fletcher. I went to his office, and he immediately requested that I remain silent about this secret meeting. I told him I would not commit to that because I did not know what the meeting was about. As it turned out, the group led by the other professor was alleging Dr. Fletcher was a Communist and he was influencing students with his views. Upon reading this petition, I immediately excused myself and went directly to the office of President Howard Bowen and informed him of the nature of the meeting. Within two months, that tenured professor was removed. I was told my actions on this incident got me more respect with the faculty than any of my athletic accomplishments and helped me later to be selected as the first black trustee of Grinnell College at the age of twenty-nine. I was not trying to be a hero; I was just trying to protect my friend Dr. Fletcher.

The four years went by very fast at Grinnell. They were fun-filled, at times challenging, but in the end very enriching years. Like Francis W. Parker, college changed my life in many positive ways. I became a good but not an outstanding student, I bonded with teammates and dorm residents of all races, creeds, and religions, and I grew to truly appreciate Iowa and its uniqueness. I became more politically aware and was embraced as a campus leader. I fondly remember world-renowned jazz musician Herbie Hancock (class of 1960) accompanying Jimmy Simmons and me singing old Everly Brothers hits at the talent show. I also have fond memories playing baseball and basketball three years for John

Pfitsch, the coach I felt was a racist when I first visited Grinnell. John was not a racist, just a middle-aged white person from Kansas going through his own learning period about social issues.

Over the years, during and after Grinnell, John was my confidant. When I later went on the Grinnell Board of Trustees, I never failed to visit John Pfitsch and his lovely wife, Emily. In the last years of John's life, we had long and open discussions. He confessed how Jim Simmons and I had changed his life and his views and how much he appreciated us. At my last meeting with John, we both cried, and I thanked him for his support and guidance. Both Jim and I spoke at his memorial service at Grinnell, reminiscing over our shared decades of experiences. I was the last speaker, and I shared our journey of discovery and mutual respect to those in the chapel. After I finished delivering the eulogy, many others in the chapel joined me in letting our tears flow.

While my freshman year had been difficult and socially challenging, I knew I had to be a positive role model not only for the black students on campus but hopefully the hundreds who would be coming after I graduated. I was a big fish in a little pond, and as such, I had to represent myself in the appropriate manner. This was true for me and other young blacks who had enrolled at majority white colleges and universities in the fifties and sixties. It was true for Vernon Jordan at DePauw University in Indiana; Ron Brown at Middlebury; Ann Cook at Vassar; and of course our civil rights champions Charlayne Hunter-Gault[14] at the University of Georgia and Ernie Green at Michigan State University. On campus, special demands were made of us. It was a stressful existence, but it was also a learning experience that helped us later in life as we ascended to positions of power and, more often than not, became the trailblazers in our companies,

---

[14] Yes, she married my dancing fool of a cousin Ron Gault.

our various fields of endeavors, or as public officials dealing with powerful people of the opposite race, both domestically and internationally.

Grinnell is where I also started my journey as a young entrepreneur. I ran a cleaning agency that generated substantial monthly revenues. I had cut a deal with one of the local laundry owners to install laundry machines on the men's campus. In addition, I had a flower concession to supply flowers for all the dances. Realizing most male students were embarrassed to buy prophylactics in the town pharmacy, I would buy them in bulk then turn around and sell them retail on an individual basis around the campus. With those multiple ventures, I was always flush with cash. I had so much cash I was soon offering payday loans to both students and professors. On campus, I was known as Jim Lowry the entrepreneur.

Interestingly enough, after graduation, not one of my professors recommended I should go to business school. I guess for them and for me, a black going to business school was an alien concept. Later in life, the fact that none of my professors even suggested I should go into business bothered me. I was a born salesman and entrepreneur. I am confident if I had mentors and sponsors like so many of my white counterparts, I would have been a highly successful businessman by the time I reached my thirties or forties. Deep down, I feel that is one of the reasons I devoted so much of my time to mentoring young people. I wanted to support and motivate them so they could get the early start I did not receive.

The experience at Grinnell where I almost was abducted by a mob had a profound impact on me. In Chicago, I was aware of the dangers of going into the wrong neighborhoods. Almost daily we were getting new bulletins of people being lynched and other brutalities in the South, but now I was confronted with the same kind of injustice. The threat was scary, but during my tenure at Grinnell, it was an isolated episode, with the exception of the time Jon Groteluschen and I went to a bar in Omaha over winter break after a basketball game against Creighton University. We ordered a drink at the bar, and the white barmaid refused to serve us. She looked right at me and said, "We don't serve drinks to black monkeys." Jon, without hesitation, spat in her face, and we hightailed it out of the bar without saying a word, thus cementing the bond I had developed with Jon on the basketball court.

The majority of experiences, however, were extremely positive, with lifelong friendships being formed with Professor Fletcher and Pfitsch, teammates from baseball and basketball, and the Gustafsons. Sid Gustafson was head of a typical Iowan family. We bonded as friends, the urban black student and Sid, a hardworking salesman who sold for Pioneer Feed. At Grinnell, I was able to get my hair cut. More importantly, I was able to appreciate the bonds of friendship created and the life lessons learned.

My Grinnell college experience was so positive in fact that, with dedication and honor, I served forty-three years on the board of trustees and watched its endowment grow from $26 million to $1.2 billion. I never was able to write the big checks like my other board members, but I did contribute as a trustee and on occasion debated fellow trustee Warren Buffett when I disagreed with him. And yes, Grinnell College and Francis W. Parker are both in my will.

Historical Background 1961–1962

In 1961, black students known as the Freedom Riders planned a bus trip to test and implement the *Boynton* decision. Once in Rock Hill, South Carolina, some of the riders, John Lewis, Al Bigelow, and Genevieve Hughes, were beaten. This caused more racial tension in the Deep South, and protests and riots began. There was massive violence in Alabama when an angry mob of about two hundred white people surrounded a bus with cars and bats, injuring both white and black Freedom Riders. The sad thing was that the Birmingham public commissioner knew the bus was coming and violence awaited, but he posted no police protection.

Also in 1961, John F. Kennedy was elected the thirty-fifth president. He was the youngest to ever be elected. With his election, the New Frontier was created, bringing the best and brightest to Washington, DC. The Peace Corps was created, and soon the US was sending idealistic young Americans to work with the poor in emerging nations across the globe.

Attorney General Robert F. Kennedy committed to ensuring and protecting equal rights for all Americans in a speech to University of Georgia Law School. It was the Kennedy administration's first formal announcement endorsing civil rights.

- Roughly $25 billion was spent in the Kennedy administration's total procurement program. President Kennedy committed to a fair portion of the procurement budget going to people of color.

President Kennedy signed Executive Order 10925,[15] which created affirmative action. This order ultimately led to the Equal Employment Opportunity Commission (EEOC). The order required government employers "not to discriminate against any

---

[15] Exec. Order 10925 (1961).

employee or applicant for employment" based on race and required employees to "take affirmative action to ensure the applicants are employed, and that employees are treated during employments without regard to their race, creed, color, or national origin."

CHAPTER 4

THE STRUGGLE FOR FREEDOM AND CIVIL RIGHTS

As graduation loomed, I began to wonder what I was going to do with my life. My two roommates had their plans in place. Jim Simmons was to marry his girlfriend, Joan, and pursue a master's degree at the University of Chicago in social work. Allison Davis was accepted to law school at Northwestern University and was planning to marry his college sweetheart, Karen. I thought about applying to law school, but my heart just wasn't in it.

Out of the blue, my favorite political science professor, Harold Fletcher, suggested I apply for the fifth-year abroad scholarship. The scholarship fund was created by a wealthy alumnus to send students to live in China, but once China turned Communist, the funds were placed in a trust. Thus, after many years, the college decided to use the funds to send students to live in developing countries. In many ways, Grinnell was funding a program that would become a model for the Peace Corps.

I thought getting the scholarship was a long shot. My résumé was not like the résumés of previous winners. I was neither deeply religious nor an A student. In short, I was a jock with a B average and a very active social life. Still, Dr. Fletcher insisted I apply and mentioned they had never had a student go to Africa. While I had a strong desire to get deeply involved in the civil rights movement, like many of my friends from Hyde Park and Woodlawn, the thought of working in Africa in the early sixties was very appealing. So when he asked where would I like to serve, I immediately said Africa, and the scholarship was mine.

A mere three weeks after graduation, with plane ticket in hand and a $750 stipend, I took off for a teaching position at Kivukoni College in Dar-es-Salaam, Tanganyika. Had I known more, I might not have gone, because I found out quickly that a check for $750 was not enough money to last twelve months. But at the time, I was extremely excited as I boarded the plane to Africa. I'd done my homework on its outstanding leader, Julius Nyerere, the history under German rule and its president's status as an African leader, and how the country was moving quickly to independence on December 9, 1961. I even conducted research on the island of Zanzibar as the residence of the Turkish sultan and port of departure for boats carrying slaves.

Upon my arrival, the school driver dropped me off at the New Africa Hotel. I was to be picked up by the headmaster, who was going to drive me to Kivukoni College. Fortunately for me, the headmaster was late. This gave me the opportunity to take in the nuances of this historic boat city. I breathed in the unfamiliar scents wafting from the food stalls, and all around me, I heard sounds of activity. It seems like yesterday as I remember the capital and the diversity of its residents. It was easy to pick out the white British civil servants. They casually strode about in their crisp, white, pressed shirts and pleated shorts with an air of prominence. The black Africans, on the other hand, seemed to forever be late, hurriedly bustling around as messengers and laborers, with their heads cast downward so as not to draw attention from their colonial oppressors as they carried their heavy loads. Then there was the mahogany-toned Indian civil servants, who were shopkeepers and plantation owners. The port itself was majestic and chaotic at the same time, with a steady flow of tall ships making their way into and leaving stocked with raw materials on their way back to England and other European ports.

Although Dar-es-Salaam was so very different from my Woodlawn neighborhood in Chicago or Grinnell, Iowa, or any other city I had ever visited, I still felt strangely comfortable and at home in no time at all. I was pleased I had accepted the scholarship. I was in Africa! How many of my friends could say that?

Kivukoni College was a postsecondary school designed to train future leaders. The president of the college was a young British scholar who was an expert in African history and a former don at Oxford. He was very bright and extremely arrogant. My sponsor for the program, the African-American Institute, was a sponsor in name only. They provided no financial support or real guidance. The institute informed the president simply that he was going to receive an unpaid American volunteer from Grinnell College. He had never heard of Grinnell College and initially had little respect for me or what I might offer. As a result, when I arrived, I was not prepared for the one-year assignment, nor was the president of the college prepared for me.

My first month in Dar-es-Salaam was very depressing. I went from being a campus hero to a having a job with no description, living on an island accessible only by ferry. To make matters worse, I had spent the last four years feeding myself grandly off the Grinnell athlete meal table. I would now have to subsist on rice, beans, and stew. I was isolated, literally, and had no social life. My academic assignments were very limited in the classroom. The president assigned me simple administrative tasks and other menial tasks, such as putting chemicals into the water system to ensure the safety of our drinking water.

Not to be defeated, I decided to make the best of a bad situation because I had committed to the position for one year. My plight was improved both financially and spiritually when I met Ron and Jacqueline Springwater, a young couple who worked at the US Information Agency (USIA) and the African-American Institute, respectively (Ron later went to work for the African-American Institute as well). The Springwaters were a marvelous couple. They had met at UCLA and decided they wanted to explore the world together. During the first few months, I don't know how I could have survived without their constant laughter, warm hospitality, Jackie's great cooking, and the alcohol they could cheaply buy at the USPX. I was in their home when Jackie was rushed to the hospital to deliver their firstborn child, Adam, and eighteen years later, I repaid their friendship and hospitality by assisting Adam gain admittance to and graduate from Grinnell College.

Two months after connecting with the Springwaters, another couple arrived that would also smooth my transition and end up becoming lifelong friends. Distinguished visiting professor and Fulbright scholar Dr. Hugh Gloster, a professor at Hampton University, and his new wife, Beulah, arrived. Hugh had a teaching position at Kivukoni College. Hugh was also the one who one day pulled me aside and told me the menial tasks I was being assigned were beneath me and that I needed to have more pride in myself. He would say to me and countless others over the years to always be proud of who you were and never, ever allow anyone to belittle you. He passed along this same mantra to the students of Morehouse College when, three years later, he became the president of that outstanding historically black college.

After that initial period of evaluation of my intellectual abilities, and a reduction in menial tasks as I learned to stand up for myself, the president allowed me to assume more responsibility teaching American history and political science. I thoroughly enjoyed the teaching experience. I also enjoyed the students and the opportunity to meet the new and future leaders of the country, including President Julius Nyerere, who was the president of Tanzania from 1964 to 1985. Over ten months, I met Nyerere on numerous occasions at the school and US embassy functions. He was intrigued that I, this young African American, would volunteer to assist his country during its transition phase. It did not hurt that I was well liked, respected, and accepted by the students. The same students he had handpicked to be in this inaugural class at Kivukoni College later became leaders in the independence movement and executives in the Tanzanian government. I found out then (and it is still true today) that African Americans were accepted and trusted more readily than their American white counterparts.

My attachment to the students extended beyond the Kivukoni College classroom. We ate three meals a day together six days a week, getting to know one another on a highly personal basis. I shared much about my family, the US culture, and the problems besetting individuals living in communities like Woodlawn. They reciprocated by educating me about African culture, the history of the country, and the number of colonies rapidly gaining their independence from Britain, France, and Portugal. I augmented these insights with excessive reading. Without a TV to distract me, I invested many hours in our well-stocked, donated library, reading about African history, British colonial rule, the civil rights movement, and other significant events occurring globally. Admittedly, I read more daily at Kivukoni College then I did at Grinnell College.

It was not all work. Often, I would drive the students to the dance hall in Dar-es-Salaam, where we would share bottles of beer while listening to Tanzanian and Congolese music. I had never been exposed to Congolese music, but after going to the dance halls, I got hooked on it. The music had beautiful African rhythms, similar to African-inspired Cuban music, with the electric string guitar being the dominant feature. After two or three beers, I usually found myself in a trance, standing next to the giant speaker, surveying the many happy faces who also were deep into the music. I could not fake the warmth that was in my heart as I watched and danced along with the Kivukoni students and their families. This South Sider from Chicago felt at home, and my joyful, exuberant dance moves were appreciated by all.

I not only hung out with the Kivukoni students in town, I also visited their village near the school. The first visit to the village was exciting and challenging. First, the student leading us to the village never used the flashlight as we walked through tall grass infested with many dangerous animals. When we arrived, the chief of the village met me warmly, supplying me with copious amounts of pombe, their native wine. After many jugs of pombe, and as we were about to return to Kivukoni, he embraced me with another gift … his daughter. I was shocked and embarrassed by the chief's unexpected generosity, but I had to decline the offer, and I started my trek back to the school. Five hours later, as I lay in my bed thinking about my fun experience, I heard a knock at my door. To my utter surprise, there stood number one daughter. Once again, in true Peace Corps spirit, I declined the invitation, but it was a night I will never forget.

I always loved getting to know and enjoy people of different backgrounds. In addition to my African friends, I also established a very close relationship with the Tanzanian citizens of East Indian descent. Almost weekly, I would hang out with a group of Indian merchants drinking beer, playing darts, and watching Indian movies without subtitles. Although I did not understand the language or what was being said, the movies were enjoyable because they all had a mix of dancing, violence, comedy, and romance. Many of my Indian friends were third- or fourth-generation Tanzanian citizens. They were the merchant class who owned many of the local businesses. They were also the midlevel bureaucrats in the British civil service who served a critical tier between the British and the broader African population.

To earn additional money, I started teaching social dance to African leaders at the USIS, using Fred MacMurray records and a small record player. I taught them the waltz, foxtrot, and other popular dances that I had learned growing up. Not only did I earn more money, but it also gave me an invaluable opportunity to get to know the Tanzanian political leaders and their spouses. My friend Ron Springwater also got me a USIS contract visiting secondary schools across the country and presenting movies depicting life in America. I accepted that I was part of the US propaganda machine and that having a black American spokesperson looked good for USIS's image, but I did not care. It was an excellent opportunity to see Tanzania outside of Dar-es-Salaam. I loved the movies and loved traveling across the country on a per diem, and most importantly, I got to know the Tanzanian high school students. Thirty years after leaving Tanzania, I had just finished presenting a lecture on minority business enterprise development in Detroit, Michigan, when a person in the audience said, "I remember you. You were the person who came to my secondary school in Tanga and showed us movies."

My best friends in Dar-es-Salaam at this time were Piloo and Maroon Mawjis. Piloo owned a dairy company, and both were third-generation Tanzanians. He introduced me to the richly diverse Tanzanian culture and history but also provided me with a deeper understanding of the different Indian sects. They were followers of the Aga Khan and were Muslim. He and the Tanzanian students also educated me on British colonial rule.

Another group of individuals I got to know well were the South Africans. One of the Kivukoni College professors was a South African economist by the name of Ethan Mayisela. He took me to the refugee camps where they educated me about what was happening in South Africa and the horrors and reality of South

African apartheid. While at the camps, he cautioned me to be careful with what I said, and to whom I was speaking, because there were often South African spies who lived in the camps. He also educated me about the Cold War competition between the West and the Communist bloc to capture the continent of Africa. He introduced me to South African leaders in the camp who were recruiting young African exiles to study for indoctrination in Russia and China.

Today, a lot is written about the influence China is having on the African continent. In Tanzania, I saw the beginning of this struggle when the Chinese government outbid the United States to build the railroad across the country in 1961.

One of my proudest moments was being the guest of the president to watch the lowering of the British flag and raising of the Tanzanian flag. At twenty-two years old, I was part of history not only for Tanzania but for all of Africa. I was proud as an African American and felt a genuine bond with the continent. Not to say I didn't have a bond with Africa before, but now it was deeply personal; it was a deep connection that would stay with me for the rest of my life.

The year in Tanzania went by very fast, and after a slow and depressing start, I left with nothing but feelings of warmth for its people, culture, and leadership and sincere gratitude for the kindness shown me as a US citizen from Chicago and Grinnell College. I enjoyed my many social exchanges with the secondary students, the Kivukoni students, and other visiting volunteer undergrads spending the summer in Dar-es-Salaam, especially the group from Vassar. Under the tutelage of Professor Gwendolyn Carter, also an alumna of Vassar, each summer fifteen to twenty coeds would join her on her return trips to Tanzania. Many of these Vassar students became my friends, and one in particular, Marnie Linen, was a close friend for years. Her father was the

CEO of Time Life, and her brother later became my client at American Express.

I also enjoyed the railroad trips to Kilimanjaro, Lake Victoria, and the vast and beautiful country I would witness on those journeys. My USIS contract allowed me to experience travel on the colonial railroad system and stays at old British colonial hotels. This experience was educational and memorable, especially the times I shared the train with Masai warriors. On one occasion, I recall sitting in my seat, with three Masai standing in front of me wearing their native dress. Whenever the train would come to a sudden stop or a gust of wind would enter the train, their native dress would shift, exposing their bodies and leaving nothing to the imagination. The other passengers and I would feel united in our discomfort. But I got used to it, and in the end, we would strike up conversations and discover our commonalities while I practiced using my limited Swahili on the long trips. It was just another experience in Africa to write home about.

Most importantly, I enjoyed my new friends, the Glosters, the Springwaters, the Mawjis, the locals I got to know at the ferry and the local markets, and the many other people I met while living in Dar-es-Salaam. Every day, there was love, friendship, and a growing permanent commitment to helping individuals poorer than I. Life was tough for the average Tanzanian, but they always wore a smile and carried hope for a better future. I came to Tanzania a naïve, recent graduate. I left as a man, wiser, worldlier, and with greater insight on the challenges of disease, ignorance, poverty, and how such problems impacted decisions that a new government would face. I told my friends I would return one day and hopefully be better equipped to aid them in their struggles.

My time in Tanzania had a profound effect on my life. Africa had real meaning for me now. I was not only attracted to Tanzania and its future, but now countries like Kenya, Nigeria, Ghana, Uganda, Ivory Coast, and more were also more meaningful to me. I saw Africa as a sleeping giant with natural resources and the potential to be a significant player on the world scene. In many ways, I recognized that the challenges facing Tanzania were not unlike those in the inner cities of Harlem, Woodlawn, and Watts. Unbeknownst to me, my life was moving in a direction I could not have anticipated but one that felt good.

The biggest lesson I learned in Tanzania was that people are just people. This lesson would lead to another learning experience on the importance of valuing diversity—an experience I would later utilize as a professor and consultant on diversity and inclusion at the Kellogg School of Management. My life was impacted by many people from diverse cultural, economic, and ethnic groups from this newly independent country. After a year in Tanzania, I had a deep understanding and appreciation of the concept of black diaspora, which is still valid sixty years later—a concept that has not been embraced to the maximum but hopefully will be for the betterment of all the people in countries around the world.

I was now an international traveler looking at events and people through different lenses. Little did I know that this new insight would be tested to great lengths on my return trip to the United States. I was advised by world-renowned pacifists Baynard Rustin[16] and Bill Sutherland that before returning to the United States, I should stop in Rome. Upon my arrival in Rome, Bill had a friend who was one of the famous Peters sisters. Edith and Joyce Peters had gained fame while performing as a duo across the European continent. Edith, the more famous of the two, married her Italian agent, Silvio Catalano, and went on to appear in movies, commercials, and TV dramas in Italy.

Following Bill Sutherland's advice, I booked a ticket back

---

[16] Bayard Rustin was an American leader in social movements for civil rights, socialism, and nonviolence and fought openly for gay rights. He organized the Freedom Rides and the Southern Christian Leadership Conference strengthening Martin Luther King Jr.'s leadership.

to the USA via an extended stopover in Rome. There, Silvio introduced me to yet another Peters sister, who had gained a bit of celebrity in the Italian movie industry as a comic in the sixties' *Hercules* movies. I enjoyed escorting this mini movie star to fancy restaurants and nightclubs on Via Veneto frequented by the rich and famous. During this time, Joseph L. Mankiewitcz was producing the epic film *Cleopatra,* starring Elizabeth Taylor, Rex Harrison, and Richard Burton. Elizabeth Taylor was married to Eddie Fischer, and Richard Burton was married to Debbie Reynolds, but anyone with eyes could see the open and notoriously hot love affair between the two stars.

And there I was, a mere thirty days later after leaving my simple lifestyle at Kivukoni College, rubbing elbows with Hollywood and Italian movie stars on the Via Veneto. The only problem, I was running out of money. One day at my favorite nightclub, I stumbled up to a table of six African American former Katherine Dunham dancers. As we got talking, I candidly told them that while I loved the excitement of Rome, I was running out of money. The leader of the group said, "Why don't you do what we do to earn additional money and be an extra on the movie *Cleopatra*?" I thought it was a great idea and agreed to meet him at the Piazza Barberini the next day, and he would get me a job. True to his word, he did get me the job.

Every day, I would go to Cinecitta and hang out with other extras, leave to take a nap, and then hit the town later to watch highly trained and talented dancers perform at their Via Venite review. You won't see me in the film because I decided to leave Rome before my scene was shot. However, before I left, I was asked to model the costume of a Greek slave. The costume designer was Irene Sharaff. I modeled it in front of Irene, along with Oscar winners Elizabeth Taylor and Richard Burton. The thirty days in Rome were fun, but it was time to go back to Chicago and Suzie Jean Gustafson.

I loved hanging out on the set of *Cleopatra*, listening to endless stories about Rome, their careers, and being asked to come on stage to participate in my friends' finale dancing the twist at their review. I was so tempted to remain in Rome, as 1,500 lira as an extra went a long way during the sixties, and I often wonder what my life would have been like had I remained in Rome. Many of the African American *Cleopatra* extras who returned to the US found stardom in black exploitation movies, while others stayed in Rome, finding a place in Italian or spaghetti westerns. I was tempted, but at the time, I didn't think being a B movie star would be an acceptable career choice for a Grinnell graduate.

Historical Background 1963–1968

The nation was going through some very challenging times with young radicals testing the American power elite in both violent and nonviolent ways. In these turbulent times, ambitious young minorities were often caught between competing worlds. On the one hand, for the first wave of black executives, these were exciting times. Yet, because of the complexity of the situation, it could be extremely anxiety provoking. Often, they were criticized by blacks in the community for accepting the corporate life.

The year 1964 was important for the civil rights movement. President Johnson, knowing the importance of the Civil Rights Bill after President Kennedy's assassination, made the bill his top priority in the first year of his administration. With the head of the NAACP, the CORE, the Urban League, and key members of Congress, they worked to make the bill a law. Many senators were opposed to the bill. Republican Senator Dirksen introduced the bipartisan Dirksen-Mansfield- Kutcher-Humphrey-comprised bill as a substitute for the original version. On June 19, 1964, the bill was passed in the Senate by a vote of seventy-three to twenty-seven.

- 1963: President Kennedy was assassinated in Dallas, Texas, shocking the entire nation.
- 1963: President Lyndon B. Johnson becomes the thirty-sixth president of the United States.
- 1964: President Johnson announced his War on Poverty campaign, which ultimately had little program impact, but it did train leadership in the inner cities.
- 1964: President Johnson signed the landmark Civil Rights Act of 1964[17] outlawing any form of discrimination in

---

[17] Pub.L. 88–352, 78 Stat. 241, enacted July 2, *1964*.

public places or employment processes on the basis of race, color, gender, or religion, finishing what President Kennedy hoped to accomplish prior to his death.

- 1965: Malcolm X was assassinated in Harlem at the Audubon Ballroom. The *Autobiography of Malcolm X* was published shortly after his death and was considered one of the most influential books of the twentieth century.
- 1965: The Voting Rights Act of 1965[18] was signed by President Johnson, outlawing racial discrimination in voting.
- 1965: The Equal Employment Opportunity Commission (EEOC) was established.
- 1965: President Johnson signed Executive Order 11246, which abolished discrimination in hiring and employment by US government contractors.
- 1967: In the case *Loving v. Virginia*,[19] the US Supreme Court ruled laws prohibiting interracial marriage as unconstitutional.
- 1967: Thurgood Marshall became the first black US Supreme Court Justice.
- 1967: Julius Nyerere was elected president of newly merged Tanzania, and his agricultural-based socialist concept named Ujamma was the basis for a national development project. He had been elected president of Tanganyika in 1961.
- 1967: Carl Stokes was elected mayor of Cleveland, becoming the first African American to serve as mayor of a major city. He served from 1968 to 1971. Richard Hatcher was also elected the same day, as the first African American mayor of Gary, Indiana, serving from 1968 to 1987. Other black mayors to follow have been Maynard

---

[18] *Voting Rights Act of 1965*, Pub.L. 89-110, 79 Stat. 437.
[19] 388 U.S. 1 (1967).

Jackson in Atlanta, serving from 1974 to 1982, Coleman Young in Detroit, serving from 1974 to 1994, Kenneth Gibson, mayor of Newark, serving from 1970 to 1986, Harold Washington in Chicago, serving from 1983 to 1987, and Walter Washington, mayor in the District of Columbia from 1973 to 1979. Mayor Walter Washington was the first and only black mayor-commissioner.

- 1967: Martin Luther King gave the speech "Beyond Vietnam: A Time to Break the Silence" in New York City, which spoke out about the Vietnam War crippling young black men fighting eight thousand miles away for liberties in Southeast Asia that were still not found in Georgia and East Harlem. Many felt because of Dr. King's strong anti-Vietnam speech, he lost a significant amount of his northern and southern support.

- Lew Alcindor (Kareem Abdul Jabbar) and other basketball players rejected the opportunity to play in the 1968 Olympics. Martin Luther King Jr. supported this boycott.

- 1968: Martin Luther King Jr. was assassinated at the Lorraine Motel in Memphis.

- April 1968: Some of the biggest riots that ever took place in Washington, Baltimore, Chicago, and Kansas City following the death of King. In Chicago, violence was over a twenty-eight-block stretch, and the majority of destruction took place on the West Side and the Woodlawn neighborhood on the South Side. Rioters broke windows, looted stores, and set buildings on fire. On April 6, Major Daley imposed a curfew on anyone under twenty-one, closed the streets to traffic, and halted the sale of guns and ammunition. More than 6,700 National Guards were called to Chicago. President Lyndon Johnson also sent in five thousand troops of the First Armored Division to the city, also authorizing the use of tear gas to control the rioters and the police order to "shoot and kill" any arsonist or anyone with a Molotov cocktail in hand, as well as to shoot to maim or cripple anyone looting any stores in the city.

- 1968: Robert Kennedy was assassinated in California while on the campaign trail. His killer, Sirhan Sirhan, was arrested.
- 1968: President Johnson signed the Civil Rights Act of 1968,[20] also known as the Fair Housing Act, prohibiting the sale and rental of housing based on race, religion, or sex.

---

[20] Civil Rights Act of 1968, 82 Stat. 73.

CHAPTER 5

FROM THE PEACE CORPS
TO INSIDE BEDFORD-STUY

I returned from Tanzania at twenty-three years of age. I felt stronger as a person, intellectually stimulated, and convinced I wanted to spend the rest of my life working around the world in the field of economic development. I had just spent twelve months watching a country gain its independent status, I had become friends with the country's first president, and even more importantly, I gained a very strong attachment to the continent of Africa. That was the good news. The bad news was that now that I was back at home in Chicago, I found myself living with my mother (my parents were now separated), without a job, and with no clear game plan for my career. The only available job I found was my old summer job working as a janitor in my mother's building. I had to take it because I needed the money to survive, but I was frustrated with my current predicament and soon became very depressed. Fortunately for me, my depression and lack of employment were quickly rectified when I received a call from the US Peace Corps.

Evidently, my name had been given to the Peace Corps by a young staff person from the New York office of the African-American Institute named Isabel Stewart. Later, Isabel met and married my Grinnell friend Don Stewart—the same Don Stewart who had advised against Allison Davis, Jim Simmons, and I being roommates back at Grinnell College. Upon receiving the call from the Peace Corps, I quickly accepted the opportunity to fly to Washington, DC, to interview for the newly created position of Peace Corps escort officer. The position was too good to be true—escorting recently trained Peace Corps volunteers to their host countries and staying with them for three weeks until they got settled in their communities. I was interviewed by Pat Kennedy (no relation to the president). Pat was a great person who, in many ways, typified the young idealist professionals who joined the Kennedy administration, especially in the Peace Corps organization. I liked him. Unfortunately, he did not think I was qualified for the position, and my application was rejected. Instead, he thought I was better suited to be an Outward Bound training officer at the Peace Corps training camp in Puerto Rico.

Outward Bound began in 1941 as a one-month course that would foster "physical fitness, enterprise, tenacity and compassion among British youth." The key method was the distinction of training *through* rather than *for*. This was and still is at the essence of the Outward Bound dynamic. The sea, mountains, and desert provide training that no institute or university can offer. These landscapes, in tandem with Outward Bound principles, teach the hard, technical skills necessary for survival but also teach the relevant skills necessary for life. Outward Bound has evolved but never departed from its original concept of an intense experience surmounting challenges in a natural setting, through which the individual builds their sense of self-worth, the group comes to a heightened awareness of human interdependence, and all grow in concern for those in danger and need.[21]

I quickly gathered a few belongings and flew to Puerto Rico to a training camp outside the town of Arecibo. There were two training camps, Camp Crozier and Camp Radley. The camps

---

[21] 4 www.outwardbound.com.

were named after the first two volunteers who lost their lives in service to the Peace Corps. When I arrived, I was assigned to Camp Crozier, where I was met by a wonderful and idealistic team of training officers. The head of Camp Crozier was Manny Rivera, a former Columbia University All-American football player of Cuban ancestry. He was a great leader, mentor, and, later, friend. Manny later had a long and distinctive career as the athletic director at predominantly black Lincoln University. In addition to Manny, we had a group of highly talented young staff members, including Andrea Swanoe. Andrea (who just happened to also be a Rockefeller) had to have been tougher than almost any of the other Outward Bound instructors. There was also the young rock climber and his wife from Oregon, and Ivy League All-Conference swimmer Alan Hale and his wife. We were organized and supervised by a forty-four-year-old, superbly conditioned, black ex-football player, Lennie Clarke. Len taught me all I needed to know about being an Outward Bound trainer and life.

Lennie had lived a full life before joining the Peace Corps, and he had what we would call street smarts. One day, he pulled me aside and said, "Young blood, you have to raise your antenna." Being my naïve self, I asked what he meant, to which he replied, "Jim, while you are about to enter the pool, you have no idea the effect you have on the female volunteers. They are sending you signals, but your antenna is not picking up on them." From that day forward, I always kept my antenna up, which served me well the rest of my life. I guess I could blame Lennie Clarke for making me an even bigger player.

In many ways, my year in Puerto Rico was perfect. Every month we would receive a new group of bright-eyed, idealistic Peace Corps trainees, the majority going to Central or South America, carrying hope and dedication with them. Every morning we would get up and run a mile, have a Spanish lesson, and undergo challenging tests of rock climbing, trekking, and swimming. The latter was my responsibility, which was kind of a joke because when I was a senior at Grinnell, I almost didn't graduate because I could not pass the swim test in gym class. Back in the fifties and sixties, many colleges had that as a prerequisite for graduation. You had to demonstrate you knew how to swim or take two classes of swimming lessons. I chose the latter option and learned the basics, then perfected my skills in Dar-es-Salaam. But in Puerto Rico, we taught drown proofing, a concept developed by one of our instructors who had been the swimming coach at Georgia Tech. Drown proofing was another component of Outward Bound.

We wanted to challenge the volunteers by pushing them to overcome their fears and discomforts. The first day, the group had to swim two laps underwater without coming up for air. Most of the trainees failed. Then, after watching me successfully swim the two laps without coming up for air, the group would all try again, and almost all of them would pass. It went on like this with each test. The second day, we added the challenge of your legs being tied, with the failure rate improving to success after seeing me do it. On day three, our arms were tied. The key to this test was that psychologically, once the trainees saw the possibility, they had the faith to help push themselves through the pain spot. Before knowing it could be done, most of the trainees would come up for air before finishing, feeling like their lungs would explode. But the knowledge that is was possible, albeit with a little pain, changed their mind-set. I carried this lesson with me throughout my career as I faced many challenges. When faced with adversity, I would pull from within and believe I would win if I could just push through the pain spot. High school and college athletics challenged me but not to the depths of my Outward Bound training.

Camp Crozier was not all pain. After a long day of Outward

Bound activities, we would all retreat to the small tienda and drink beer. In fact, quite different from my time of isolation on the island off the coast of Africa, this island experience offered a party almost every night. Over many beers, lifelong friendships were established. Because the camps were popular with Peace Corps Director R. Sargent Shriver, we were often visited by dignitaries such as Senator Ted Kennedy and his then wife, Joan, and we also entertained the niece of Lyndon Johnson, who I tried in vain to teach the twist (she had no rhythm). We also had visits from Harry Belafonte and many more celebrities. I was having so much fun that at one time I thought about making a career as an Outward Bound instructor.

As much as I was loving the life in Puerto Rico, I knew deep down that I had to return to the States and get another degree. It was a sad day when I formally handed in my resignation. The Peace Corps asked if I would identify my replacement, and I immediately thought of Jim Simmons, but he was in graduate school at the University of Chicago and married. My second choice was Jon Groteluschen, my basketball teammate. Jon immediately accepted, and I extended my employment to orient Jon to the job. While training, we also got to play together again on the court as teammates, beating the Peace Corps trainees on a daily basis.

I knew I wanted to get a degree in international affairs, so I applied to Georgetown University, George Washington University, Cornell University, and University of Pittsburgh. I selected University of Pittsburgh because they had an established graduate program in public and international affairs under the leadership of Dr. Don Stone. I had a good two years at Pitt, and I learned there was a big difference between going to a small college in Iowa with a thousand students versus a large, urban university in Pittsburgh. Pittsburgh, like Chicago, was very segregated, with the majority of blacks living in the Hill District.

The year was 1963, and change was occurring under President Kennedy and his liberal administration. Laws and policies were being passed that inspired me and many others in the nation. There was so much hope for the future, but for people of color, many barriers still existed; prejudice and overt discrimination were still apparent every day of my life. Like many of my peers, I will never forget the day when I heard President Kennedy had been assassinated. I was at the dining hall at Pitt with my old Grinnell basketball teammate Jon Groteluschen, who happened to be visiting. With his death, that night I felt like a little bit of me died along with him. For me, President Kennedy represented so much hope for the United States and developing nations. I continued my educational pursuits at Pitt but was often depressed and confused about what was happening in the country.

The midsixties were, for me and the nation, probably the most turbulent and impactful period of time in the history of America. I, like the thousands of young Americans, was fearful of being drafted to serve in Vietnam, fighting in a war I did not believe in. The civil rights movement was gathering strength, and many of our societal values were being challenged. Martin Luther King Jr. and John F. Kennedy gave us leadership and hope. President Johnson provided unique leadership, and he was able to leverage his power and Senate relationships to pass the Civil and Voter Rights Bills. These bills changed America for the next fifty years.

While living off campus at Pitt, I was fortunate to have two great roommates—Calvin Sheffield, the star of the Pitt basketball team, and Howard (Bobo) Gray. I loved them both despite them having two completely different personalities. Calvin was the son of a minister and one of eighteen children. Bobo had probably never seen the inside of a church. He was a very articulate, fun-loving, and highly educated student who had attended Phillips Exeter Academy and Harvard University. Bobo had also been an outstanding athlete at Exeter but unfortunately was advised not to play football at Harvard because of a serious kidney ailment. He ran the hundred meter in 9.7 seconds, and with his size and other natural abilities, had he been able to compete, he probably would have been All-Ivy or All-American at Harvard.

After Bobo and I received our first B grades, we gave up hope of maintaining a 4.0 average. Instead, we retreated to watching sports together and visiting the bars on the Hill District. With our crewneck sweaters, bald heads, and both standing over six feet tall, we stood out at local bars as we drank and listened to great jazz, especially at the Hurricane Grill. We began to have our own following, and when we entered the bars, they would greet us with, "Here come the college boys." Although Pitt was a challenging two years academically, between exams and studying, Bobo and I were good students and made many friends in the community, and Bobo has remained a close friend over the years.

The University of Pittsburgh Graduate School of Public & International Affairs (GSPIA) was an excellent school. Not only were the professors and courses outstanding, but the students, comprising over thirty countries, were equally exciting. In my class, we also had Roscoe Robinson Jr., the first African American to become a four-star general in the United States Army. He was also a graduate of West Point. After an outstanding military career, he retired in 1985 and was awarded the Defense Distinguished Service Medal and two additional distinguished medals.

Between my second and third trimester, I was offered the opportunity to write a thesis on an experience as an intern. Just as I was about to start writing my thesis, I got another call from the Peace Corps asking if I would direct a special experimental summer training program. For the first time, the Peace Corps was going to invite students entering their senior year of college to participate in a summer program that would allow them to take courses their senior year to support their eventual two-year assignment. It was decided there would be two programs: one at

Dartmouth for Africa-bound trainees and the second at Camp Radley for trainees going to South American countries. Needless to say, I accepted the offer and pulled together a team of language instructors, six former Peace Corps volunteers and two professors from Grinnell College. The training took place over the summer, but my contract to support the trainees extended for another six months.

For many of those months, I had to travel to Peace Corps headquarters at 800 Connecticut Avenue in Washington, DC. It was on one of these trips to Washington that I reconnected with my hero and new friend Sargent Shriver, who on the spot asked me whether I would like to be an associate director in some country to be named later. Without hesitation, I accepted. I did not care where I would be assigned. I just wanted to continue to serve Sargent Shriver and the Peace Corps. Evidently, there was a great deal of discussion on my assignment. The deputy director of South America, Laveo Sanchez, wanted to send me to Brazil, but the director of the South American region, Frank Mankiewicz, nephew of *Cleopatra* producer Joseph Mankiewicz, wanted to send me to Peru, where previously he had served as the country's director. Frank had more clout, so soon after getting my master's degree from Pittsburgh in international affairs, I was off to Lima, Peru.

Landing in Lima, I had no idea of the future impact this country, its people, and the Peace Corps in general would have on me. By this time, the Peace Corps had been around for about eleven years, and Peru had one of the largest numbers of volunteers in the world. Peru was a country of more than 1,280,000 square kilometers, with rich history and diverse terrain within its three distinctive zones: coastal, selvas, and mountains. Because my Spanish was not on the same level as the other Peace Corps associate directors (all ex–Peace Corps volunteers), I was assigned to Lima to receive Spanish language immersion.

Peru, led by progressive President Fernando Belaúnde Terry, was in the early stages of an economic revitalization. Within the city limits, there were wealthy communities, but outside the city in the barriadas, there was deep poverty. The majority of the Peace Corps volunteers lived in the barriadas, serving as community organizers. As in Puerto Rico, it was a pleasure to support these highly motivated individuals who were, for the most part, recent college graduates choosing to live in poverty to serve the poor in these communities and villages.

I rented a three-bedroom apartment conveniently located one block away from the US embassy and three blocks away from the Peace Corps office. I had my daily lessons with my Spanish teacher here, and it turned out my apartment was also the perfect location for many visiting Peace Corps volunteers who wanted a hot shower and a friendly ear.

As a Peace Corps associate director, one of my main roles was to help ensure my many Peace Corps volunteers were healthy, safe, and in good spirits. Ever the party animal, I tried to keep their spirits up with monthly parties at my apartment, overflowing with bottles of pisco sour and rum and the latest hits from Motown.

My parties were organized by office manager Nina Burke and her staff of highly competent secretaries who were trained by Jesuit priests. These secretaries and trainees also loved Motown and regularly joined in on the parties. All of them, including Nina Burke, became US citizens, the majority of whom relocated to Washington, DC. The friendships started from my many visits in support of the volunteers and from my infamous parties remain strong fifty years later. Once a year, I try to have lunch with my ex-Peace Corps crew and the former deputy director Trip Reid and his wonderful wife, Hedy.

My Peruvian experience was made that much richer when I was asked to join the local basketball team, Club Revólver. At the time, Peru had some very competitive basketball teams.

For years, another team that represented the Yacht Club (Club Regatas) were the national champions. They had two outstanding players by the names of Enrique and Raul Duarte. Enrique went on to play at Iowa State University, and his brother, Raul, was the leading scorer in the 1964 Olympics. My teammates were not rich, but they were talented, and in the two years I played with the team, we became the national champions, beating Regatas in both finals. I was invited to play for the Peruvian national team going to the Olympics, but I would have had to renounce my citizenship. I declined, of course, but I truly enjoyed this second chance to be a recognized player of distinction, especially since I thought my playing days were long over.

During my brief time playing for Club Revólver, our team received significant publicity, often making the headlines. Tomás Sangio, one the stars on the team, was given the name "El Pulpo," meaning octopus, because of his long arms. The name the local paper gave me was "El Chalon." I did not know what El Chalon meant, so I looked it up in the Spanish/English dictionary. When I mentioned to my teammates that I was considered a leader, in unison they all started to laugh. When I asked why they were laughing, they said, "Jim, they are not calling you El Chalon because of your leadership skills." Then they asked me what color the popular little black cigars the people in the barrios were smoking. Then I got the joke, they were not calling me a leader. They were calling me a black cigar! To them, it was a term of endearment, as it was when they called me "Sambito." I never got used to it. All I heard was *Little Sambo*.

For the better part of two years, I led an unbelievably rich, exciting, and fulfilling life. I was getting paid to be part of a global movement, supporting highly motivated young Americans, and being accepted in yet another new culture and country. For the majority of time, I dated a stunning Peruvian airline stewardess (with whom I recently reconnected via Facebook). I also occasionally dated a Peace Corps volunteer who was a nurse from Cincinnati.

I was looking forward to serving in another country like my predecessor. Then one day I got a surprise call from one of the ex-Peace Corps volunteers who was now working at headquarters. He called to advise me I was going to be fired. When I asked why, he stated because I had fraternized with a white Peace Corps volunteer from Milwaukee, Wisconsin. Initially, I was taken aback, because I knew other associate directors had tried to date that same volunteer.

I was extremely moved when many of the existing and ex-Peace Corps volunteers supported me and complained to Sargent Shriver's successor, Jack Vaughn, for even considering firing me, but I accepted that I had broken an unofficial policy of dating a Peace Corps volunteer. I decided to serve out my two years and provide a smooth transition for my replacement, Tom Torres, a former Peace Corps volunteer and former associate director in Colombia. Tom had a beautiful and charming wife, who I discovered he had met while she was a volunteer serving under him in Colombia. I was reminded yet again of the double standard, even in the Peace Corps.

Soon after meeting Tom Torres and his wife, I received a letter from my mother saying she had been befriended the same Peace Corps volunteer that had necessitated my departure. After leaving the Peace Corps, she had enrolled at the University of Chicago to earn a master's degree. Living only ten blocks from my mother, she would often visit her, and they became close friends. One day they decided, without telling me, they were going to visit me in Lima. I was glad they came because it turned out to be a very special two weeks. There were trips to Machu Picchu, Peace Corps parties with my mother frying her outstanding chicken, and visiting volunteers from the coast. My mother could not speak a word of Spanish; nevertheless, she continued talking to my dark-skinned maid in English because she looked exactly like my cousin Mamie. It was both comical and painful watching my mother talking to my maid, assuming she would answer her in English.

Our near-perfect two weeks almost ended in disaster when the coaches of the national basketball team requested I return from one of our planned trips to join the team. The national team was asked to play the basketball team from Wichita State, led by All-American David Stallworth, who later became a star for the NY Knicks. Being the only black on the Peruvian team, I knew Stallworth was going to single me out and dunk on my head all night long. To make matters worse, I would be playing with my mother and dear friend watching. But that night, the gods were on my side. The game was cancelled because Wichita State's plane had motor problems. Thus, I was able to return to our planned trip and spared much embarrassment. I will always be indebted to my friend from Milwaukee for befriending my mother and escorting her to Lima. It was a great two-week vacation. My mother saw me in my professional role, and my friend and I were able to part in an amicable way. I still have such fond memories of her and the great time we all had in Lima and other parts of Peru.

While awaiting my replacement in Peru, I got a call one day from the US embassy in New York. Senator Robert F. Kennedy was in Lima and requested a visit to the barriadas. When told that no one in the embassy knew where the barriadas were located, Senator Kennedy then asked for the Lima Peace Corps director to be his guide. This call came when I was at my lowest yet would end up changing my life. For three days, I was the guide and translator for Senator Robert Kennedy and his wife, Ethel. Those were three glorious days spent listening to his challenges, his hopes for America, and his vision for Latin America.

Between that three-day experience and my departure from Peru, Senator Kennedy sent one of his aides to recruit me to work in a special program "in Brooklyn." This program, designed by his top assistants, was going to be the alternative to Lyndon Johnson's Poverty Program. In the senator's model, instead of direct federal grants to poor areas, there would be public/private partnerships to foster economic development. He and his staff had selected the community of Bedford-Stuyvesant in Brooklyn to carry out the model. Under the senator's leadership, they had formed two boards: the Bedford-Stuyvesant Board headed by John Doerr, former assistant of the US Secretary of Civil Rights Justice Department, and the Bedford-Stuyvesant Restoration Board to be headed up by Franklin Thomas, deputy commissioner of New York City.

Although I was leaning toward accepting the offer, I felt I had to first take a temporary assignment in the Peace Corps headquarters to try to clear my name. When I arrived in Washington, the first person I went to see was C. Payne Lucas, the former head of the African division and a favorite of Jack Vaughn. He was also the Peace Corps compliance officer. When I shared with C. Payne how I was being unjustly punished and there appeared to be a double standard, he loudly agreed this was awful and that he would support me. He might have tried; I will never know, because he never called me back, and my career with the Peace Corps was over.

While working in DC, a famous headhunter, Dick Clark, had me interview for a job with the Ford Foundation. At the same time, I was approached by Sargent Shriver to take a position with the Vista Poverty Program in Chicago. Shriver was going to run for Senate in Illinois, and he wanted me in his camp before he announced. I decided to take the job at the Ford Foundation as assistant to the head of European affairs because it was such a big offer. It had been a difficult decision because both Senator Kennedy and Sargent Shriver were my idols, and they were both putting pressure on me not to take the Ford Foundation job.

Even though I had accepted the Ford Foundation's offer, they were both still very persistent. But Senator Kennedy had an ace in the hole, his black assistant, Earl Graves. Earl Graves, a resident of Bedford-Stuyvesant, former federal government officer and alumnus of Morgan State University, was sent to try to get me to change my mind and leave the Ford Foundation. Within three days, Earl Graves demonstrated the sales skills that later made him a multimillionaire, an outstanding entrepreneur, and publisher of *Black Enterprise* magazine. I resigned from the Ford Foundation after only three weeks and moved to Brooklyn.

Initially, there was only me and Earl Graves's friend Lewis Douglass on the payroll of Bedford-Stuyvesant Restoration Corporation. Lewis Douglass later became a very distinguished juvenile judge. Working with Lewis Douglass and Earl Graves, we operated as the advance team creating an organization and recruiting staff. As an outsider, and because Brooklyn politics were deep and complex, I just supported Earl and Lewis (who both were longtime residents of Bedford-Stuyvesant). Brooklyn had a large West Indian population, and I quickly noticed there was competition among the different West Indians from Jamaica, Barbados, and other island countries; there were a lot of sensitive moving parts.

Then there was the ongoing political gamesmanship between handsome New York Mayor John Lindsay and Senator Robert Kennedy, who originally hailed from Boston, as both were running for president of the United States. There were also political games between the New York business establishment and the black and Hispanic local civil rights organizations. I remember going to an Urban Coalition board meeting on Fifth Avenue, representing our board. At the meeting, I thought I had made a well-thought-out, cogent statement, only to be thanked for my contributions by a Fortune 500 corporate CEO, who then added that my opinions and insights had no value because I was not a "real black." Taken aback, I thought, *What is a "real black"?* I guess my Francis Parker English and diction classes took away my black card.

On this very distinguished Urban Coalition board of directors were many of the top NYC corporate CEOs, with a handful of black community leaders, who were included because the CEOs felt they had the answers to many inner-city problems since they were from the "hood." From my personal observations at the time, I felt many of the leaders could clearly define the problems, but few had viable courses of action to solve them. Too often, the leaders from the hood had only one answer, to ask for increased federal funding. I also observed that many of the leaders were just hustlers. One of the smartest and most sophisticated hustlers was Dr. Timmy Vincent, the head of the Brooklyn Poverty Program. I would often observe Timmy take over the room at these Park Avenue board meetings with tales from the ghetto. He took hustling to the highest levels and always with a cunning smile. One day, I had the temerity to ask Timmy what he received his doctorate in, and with a smile, he stated, "Streetology." He gave me his card, and there it was in print, Timothy Vincent, Doctor of Streetology. Timmy and his card captured the times we were living in during President Johnson's War on Poverty, local black leadership, and many of the problems that still exist today.

Just as on Park Avenue, our Restoration Board was plagued with day-to-day political intrigue. Initially, board chairman Judge Thomas Jones and the other members were selected prior to our first board president, Franklin Thomas. They knew each other, but they often fought for power and control of the board. While Franklin was in a fight for power within Restoration, he was also maneuvering to gain more independence from its counterpart board. When we first started both corporation boards, Frank lacked the power to write checks, and as a result, all funds had to flow through the D&S Board's President Eli Jacobs.

At first, I got along well with my new boss, Franklin Thomas. Although only six years separated us in age, I was extremely impressed with his style, his eloquence, and the way he was able to control a room. He was a good mentor and gave me advice I would never forget, "Jim, you have to learn to smile and give them fluff." I greatly admired Frank, but over the next several months, we soon grew apart. Back then, he was the most conservative black man I had ever encountered. This was the sixties. People were rioting in the city, little children were being killed in the South, students were protesting, and President Kennedy and Martin Luther King Jr. had recently been assassinated. I was not the only person in America angry after the assassination of Dr. King. Major cities saw devastating riots, counterculture movements from students and hippies, and antiwar demonstrations. A lot of us were angry. On the surface, it did not appear to bother Frank, who continued to take the high road. Underneath that cool and friendly facade, I had to believe Frank was also suffering and angry.

Although I was struggling inside, an exciting opportunity came my way, and once again my direction would be changed in a way I could not have anticipated. President Johnson had established the National Advisory Commission on Civil Disorders and appointed Illinois Governor Otto Kerner to lead an investigation into the causes of the 1967 race riots in Chicago, as well as other major cities. The three questions the commission was to address were: What happened? Why did it happen? What can be done to prevent it from happening again? The results from their findings were known as the Kerner Report. The report became an instant best seller, and more than two million copies of the 426-page document were sold. The major findings were that the riots resulted from black frustration and lack of economic opportunity—the same lack of economic opportunities that still haunts our minority communities today.

The Kerner Report concluded that the nation was "moving

toward two societies, one black, one white—separate and unequal." Unless conditions were remedied, the commission warned, the country faced a "system of apartheid" in its major cities. The Kerner Report delivered an indictment of "white society" for isolating and neglecting African Americans and urged legislation to promote racial integration and to enrich slums—primarily through the creation of jobs, job training programs, and decent housing. President Johnson, however, rejected the recommendations. In April 1968, one month after the release of the Kerner Report, rioting broke out in more than one hundred cities following the assassination of civil rights leader Martin Luther King Jr.

Fred Pappert, a friend of Senator Kennedy and owner of a successful advertising agency, like many others, was trying to get close to Senator Kennedy in anticipation of his election as the next president of the United States. Fred was also a very sensitive person who was shocked to read in the Kerner Report that blacks and Latinos were seldom seen on television or in movies, contributing to the widening gaps of miscommunication and understanding between blacks and whites. Fred decided he wanted to make a difference and came up with an idea for a television program to close those gaps. It was decided that the show would take place in Bedford-Stuyvesant and would showcase black entertainment and give a voice to the community members and shine light on a different portrayal of the black community—one that was more than poverty and violence. With initial funding from the Ford Foundation, a handful of corporate sponsors, and his own money, Fred Pappert founded America's first black television show, *Inside Bedford-Stuyvesant.*

Fred was the executive producer, but the genius behind the direction of the program was radio producer Charles Hobson. Although Charles Hobson had never produced or directed a TV show, he had been highly successful as a writer, radio producer, and interviewer. When Charles was hired, he was given clear direction by Frank Thomas and the BSRC Board to give a positive image of the community and its residents, working families, students, artists, and professionals. They also asked that, whenever possible, he hire as many professionals as possible.

When the program was first conceptualized, Roxie Roker was instantly given one of the cohost slots. You may remember Roxie Roker from her character Helen Willis on the television show *The Jeffersons*. In that role, she was one half of the first interracial couple on national television. *Inside Bed Stuy* was the show that got her noticed. With Roxie cast, it was unfortunately proving difficult to find a cohost to appear opposite her. The auditions were organized by Lally Weymouth, daughter of Katherine Graham, publisher of the *Washington Post*. One day, while I was sitting in on the auditions, I said I could do better than the guys auditioning, prompting Lally to challenge me to do an audition. Evidently. the audition went well because Lally lobbied Frank to let me to be the cohost. Frank asked me whether I wanted to do it, and I said, "Why not?" Although I was going to be the cohost of the program, I promised Frank I would continue to give him and BSRC fifty to sixty hours a week operating as his administrative assistant, community organizer, and project leader.

Even with the terrible airing hours, *Inside Bedford–Stuyvesant* was a local success, reaching over a million households. Frank and the board were pleased with the open and positive portrayal of Bedford-Stuyvesant. We had no problem securing guests in New York City's first black TV program. We had guests like jazz great Max Roach,[22] singer/songwriter and guitarist Richie Havens,[23]

---

[22] Max Roach was a jazz musician and forerunner of bebop from North Carolina. He worked with many of music's greatest artists, such as Dizzy Gillespie, Miles Davis, and Duke Ellington.

[23] Richie Havens was an American singer-songwriter and guitarist. He played soulful covers of pop and folk music and was the opening act in the 1969 Woodstock Festival.

and superstar Harry Belafonte. Roxie and I were a formidable team on camera, and I was part of her family off camera. Her husband was an executive at NBC, and she had this darling young son named Lenny, who would often sit on my lap at tapings. Lenny and I shared the same birthday, and later, well, you may know that Lenny Kravitz went on to have a brilliant music career, even following in his mother's path with an acting career. One night when Lenny was starting his career under the name Romeo Blue, I got a call from his mother saying Lenny was performing in my neighborhood in Chicago. I wanted to see him, but it was just so late. I felt guilty for years for not getting out of bed to see Lenny perform early in his career at a time when he needed support. Often I saw him perform, but I never identified myself. Maybe out of guilt, I said to myself if I had another opportunity to support another up-and-coming star, I would do so with gusto and total commitment. Later in life, I got that opportunity.

While leading another Bedford-Stuyvesant Restoration Corporation project to train Brooklyn youths to be professional survey takers, I was approached by a young man by the name of Jerry Lawson. Jerry was a very affable young man who claimed he had a singing group, the Persuasions, and they were very good. One day, I listened to the group, and he was right, they were very good. Soon I became their nonlegal manager, getting them to appear on the Amateur Hour at the Apollo Theater. They won three weeks in a row and had the honor of being the first group to perform on our show, dressed in tuxedos I had rented out of my own pocket. The Persuasions went on to have a distinguished career singing acapella, recording twenty-five albums, and are still performing today. Jerry Lawson, the lead singer, after having a minor stroke, came out of retirement in 2007. He joined up with the acapella group Talk of the Town, who had studied the Persuasions for thirty-five years, and they released *Jerry Lawson and Talk of the Town* album. Jerry Lawson died July 10, 2019, at the age of seventy-five.

Because we were on TV, we had to join the AFTRA union. As union members, we were paid union wages as performers; that was the good news. With the additional money, I bought a new Chevy Camaro, which I proudly showed the boys on the corner. I was surprised when I saw they were not impressed. One of my friends opened up and asked me why I didn't buy a Cadillac or at least a Buick 225. When I replied I did not want to separate myself from the people, he replied, "Lowry, we know you were in the Peace Corps and you are a friend of the people, but you are very naïve, so I will give you some good advice. If you want to help people less fortunate than you, you need to remember 'poor people' cannot help 'poor people.'" After he said that, I got defensive and started a debate with him. But when I went home that night, I had to reflect on the fact that the people on the D&S Board and their friends had the power to sign the checks and to effect change in communities like Bedford-Stuyvesant. The majority of the poor people trying to lift themselves up from their bootstraps are just trying to survive. Obviously, throughout history, many poor people have effected change. However, wealth, economic power, and global alliances are what changed societies and even civilizations.

Frank was happy with the program and my performance as a cohost, but he was not happy with the fact that with my combined Bedford-Stuyvesant Restoration salary and union pay, I was making as much money as he was. For months, I was able to placate him with the fact the taping only took five hours every Wednesday night, and every Wednesday I worked five hours in the community promoting the I.M. Pei Superblock Project. The I.M. Pei project was a specially designed urban park system connecting three blocks with special lighting and green park space. But the communities wanted jobs and economic development. It was my job, working with the architects Bill Chafee[24] and Yann Weymouth,[25] to convince the community that the project would eventually be the catalyst for economic development projects to follow.

I was able to hold Frank off for months, until one day I picked up my paycheck and noticed my salary was cut in half. When I saw that, I had an idea that continuing as his special assistant was not going to be a wise decision. In all fairness, Frank was probably right, and I was wrong. I was a staff member, and he had given me the big break to make history appearing in the first black television program in New York. But these were the sixties, and I was young and impatient. If I had to do it over again, I would have accepted his decision gracefully, and we would have remained friends. Frank went on to have an outstanding career.

After leaving Restoration, he became the president of the Ford Foundation, where he served for fifteen years, and went on to serve on the boards for major companies like Citicorp and Pepsi. He was the chairman of the September 11th Fund and a consultant of the TFF Study Group, a nonprofit organization assisting South Africa. I was proud of Franklin Thomas and what he had accomplished. Later in life, I confronted John Johnson, publisher of *Ebony*, and asked him how *Ebony* could compile a list of the hundred most powerful blacks and not have Franklin

---

[24] William Chafee graduated from Dartmouth College in 1953 and received a master's in 1961 from the Harvard Graduate School of Design. He served as a lieutenant with Naval Intelligence and, during his time as an architect with I.M. Pei & Partners, was chief architect for the NY State Urban Development Corporations.

[25] Yann Weymouth graduated Harvard University in 1963 and MIT in 1966. He served as chief of design for I.M. Pei on the National Gallery of Art East Wing, Washington, DC, and the Grand Louvre Project, Paris, France.

Thomas on it. Frank played a different game than I did, and he was very, very good at it. Over the years, I would often ask myself, "How would Franklin Thomas handle this?" Nevertheless, although Frank cut my salary, which I took as my cue to leave, his image and sound advice stayed with me for more than fifty years.

The one event that brought Frank Thomas and me together, albeit briefly, was the assassination of Senator Robert F. Kennedy. JFK's death affected me deeply in 1963, but Senator Kennedy's death, so quickly after the assassination of Martin Luther King Jr., completely devastated me. I quickly saw the glorious beginning of the New Frontier and the days of America being destroyed by three terrorists. When I received the news of his assassination, I cried openly on the set of *Inside Bedford-Stuyvesant*. Senator Kennedy was my hero, who, after visiting poor blacks in Mississippi, became a changed man and a dedicated leader and advocate for the poor who helped the poor. Senator Kennedy had been my friend. Most importantly, he had the vision, power, and the loyalty of very intelligent men who surrounded him. They had a mission to change America and the world, and now he was gone.

After work that night, Frank and I shared our feelings of loss, and the cut in my monthly salary just did not seem that important. Nonetheless, Frank and I kept our distance for more than fifty years. I followed his career, and I was told he followed mine, but we never spoke. This continued until 2017, when I was asked to attend "An Evening with Franklin Thomas" in New York, hosted by the History Makers. Initially I turned down the invitation, but eventually I decided to attend. I did not know how I would be received by Frank, and to be honest, how I would feel after all these years. Upon entering the event, the first person I ran into was none other than Franklin Thomas himself. He greeted me with a warm embrace and that big, infectious Frank Thomas smile. And just like that, fifty years of doubt and fear evaporated.

We were friends again like when we started out so many years ago when Senator Robert F. Kennedy introduced us. Equally satisfying, I was warmly welcomed by the old BSRC team and his old administrative assistant, Marge Thomas. Unfortunately, too often, fifty years of separation over minor things occur in the black community, especially among proud black men. It is a shame; we have to do better because too much is lost.

While we might not have seen eye to eye on all things, I will always be indebted to Frank for affording me the opportunity to make history. The most significant contribution *Inside Bedford-Stuyvesant* made was to be the first black TV show of its kind in the nation's largest market. We were reaching millions of people daily and became the model for similar programs in New York. Charles Hobson left *Inside Bed-Stuy* to become a producer for ABC in New York and was the producer of *Like It Is*, with host Gil Noble. That program, with the themes presenting current issues of importance to African Americans and introducing personalities that were influencing the black community, ran from 1968 to 2011. Another early black interview program created by Charles Hobson was *Tony Brown's Journal*, which started in 1978 and ran for more than twenty years.

Presently, all of the episodes of *Inside Bed-Stuy* are archived at the Museum of Television and Radio Center for Media, at the Paley Center in New York City. When my daughter attended Sarah Lawrence University, she and I viewed a few of the episodes. I was proud of our historical contributions, of opening doors for others, sharing a positive image of Bed-Stuy and how the young Jim Lowry looked in his dashiki days with dark hair.

Historical Background 1969–1974

When President Richard Nixon was elected in 1968, many of the Johnson administration's laws and policies were not only accepted but in some cased expanded. This was particularly true in the field of minority business enterprise development. President Nixon should be given credit for driving the concepts of black capitalism and minority business enterprise development.

- 1969: President Nixon established the Minority Business Development Agency (MBDA)—first established as the Office of Minority Business Enterprise (OMBE). It was the first federal agency dedicated to assisting minority business owners.
- 1969: President Nixon signed Executive Order that "prohibited discrimination on certain grounds in the competitive service of the federal civilian workforce, including the United State Postal Service and civilian employees of the United States Armed Forces."
- 1971: Executive Order 11625[26] is signed by President Nixon, which "expands the scope of MBDA and its minority business programs by authorizing grants to public and private organizations to provide technical and management assistance to minority business enterprises."
- 1971: In the case *Swann v. Charlotte-Mecklenburg Board of Education*,[27] the US Supreme Court upheld busing programs that helped speed the process of school integration.
- 1973: OMBE forms a national business service network by establishing seed programs such as the National Minority Supplier Development Council (NMSDC) and

---

[26] Exec. Order 11625 (1971) 36 FR 19967, 3 CFR, 1971-1975 Comp.
[27] 402 U.S. 1 (1971).

National Economic Development Association (NEDA) to strengthen minority businesses across the country.[28]

- 1974: President Nixon resigns from office, and Gerald Ford becomes the thirty-eighth president of the United States.

---

[28] https://www.mbda.gov/about/history.

CHAPTER 6
MY MCKINSEY YEARS

I stayed on the payroll at the Restoration Corporation at half salary for a short time, but I knew I had to seek employment elsewhere. At that time, there were only two national black search firms, Dick Clark & Associates and Charles Fields & Associates. It was Dick Clark who got me my short-lived job at the Ford Foundation. About the same time that I started looking for another job, I received a call from Charles Fields. He asked if I would be willing to interview with a consulting firm called McKinsey & Company. I had only heard of the name McKinsey but was unaware of how prestigious the company was worldwide and its status in the field of consulting. I knew very little about consulting or the skills needed to be successful. Interestingly, I met a team of McKinsey consultants led by a young principal named Carter Bales while they were doing a short pro bono study for the Bedford-Stuyvesant Restoration Corporation. Little did I know at the time, Carter Bales was one of the reasons I got the opportunity to interview for the job. Carter was a very smart and ambitious young principal who was creating a public sector practice at the firm, with the hopes of leveraging the practice to become partner.

Both Carter and McKinsey were aware that the civil rights movement was effecting change and, more importantly, making institutions have a moral conscience. The firm was actively working with many federal agencies, as well as the city of New York, within a large public sector practice. But Carter and the partners were sensitive to the fact it would be difficult to grow a practice and look good doing it without minority consultants. Thus, this gap presented an opportunity for Charles Fields and Jim Lowry.

When I walked through the lobby of McKinsey on the first day of interviews, I was very relaxed. I still had my job at Restoration, I had my TV show, and I had been approached by the local CBS TV station to be one of their first black field reporters. I felt if I did not get the job, I still had many options. The first interview was a challenge, but by the fourth interview, I was in my groove, and I knew I was being well received. I followed the same advice I had offered many young professionals when going through a challenging interview process: (1) do your homework on the firm and the individuals conducting the interviews; (2) ask a few questions to demonstrate you have done your homework; (3) let the person with the Harvard degree do all the talking, because they love to talk; (4) be a good listener and maintain good eye contact; (5) be prepared to answer them with style, coolness, and in a systematic manner; and (6) never sweat.

The further I progressed in the interview process and the more research I did on McKinsey, the more my indifferent attitude changed toward wanting to get the job offer. By the time I was at my seventh interview, I was very concerned I would not get the job. However, I never lost my composure, never broke a sweat, kept to my strategy of letting the partner do all the talking, and answered all their questions concisely, logically, and always with a smile. When I got to the ninth interview with the head of the office, Richard Neuschel, I knew this was a formality and I had the job. It seemed like yesterday that Dick Neuschel reached out his hand nervously and said, "Welcome to McKinsey & Company." Even now I have nightmares recalling my response to him, "Thanks, but I don't know if I will accept your offer. I will get back to you." I thought Dick was going to die of shock.

I returned to Brooklyn to contemplate my decision. It did not take long. With my salary cut in half, I decided it was time to start the next phase of my career as a consultant with McKinsey. When I told Frank that I was going to McKinsey, I will never forget his response, "McKinsey hired you?" When he said that, he gave me all the motivation I needed to succeed at McKinsey and in life.

It was a short subway ride from Brooklyn to Park Avenue, but a significant distance culturally and professionally, from being a community organizer in Bedford-Stuyvesant to a high-end consultant at McKinsey. As soon as I walked through the doors, I knew I was in another world. This was apparent when, on the first day of work, I received a checkbook with the instruction to write myself a check twice a month for expenses. If the amount was over $500, I should write myself a second check for the difference. This was quite an improvement from my Woodlawn and Peace Corps days, not to mention the $750 check that was supposed to last a year at Kivukoni College.

In surveying the office and researching the company, I noticed all my fellow consultants were tall, physically impressive, and graduates from the top 10 percent of their classes at Harvard, Wharton, University of Chicago, or Stanford business schools. Occasionally, they let consultants from other schools in during the late sixties but not a high percentage. When I joined McKinsey, the "Godfather" of consulting was Marvin Bower;[29] he was still an active consultant with the firm. I don't recall exactly when, but he relinquished the majority of his stock in the firm to ensure the ongoing viability of the firm, so the ownership would be shared among the partners.

Making it to Wall Street was a feat in itself, and upon arriving, you had to look the part. At McKinsey, the unspoken rule was that we look well dressed. We all had to wear Brooks Brothers suits, although less expensive knock-off brands might pass. The unspoken uniform also included black socks over our calves and … hats. Wanting to fit in, I wore everything, all except the hat. I simply could not conform to that level. One day I found myself on the elevator with Marvin Bower himself. He met me warmly, but you could tell he was bothered as he looked me up and down. Obviously, I was not wearing a hat, and he finally nervously said to me, "Jim, doesn't your head get cold?" Without thinking, I responded, "No, Marvin, I have hair that protects my head." This too became a source of many a nightmare. I was talking to the founder of McKinsey & Company, the Godfather of consulting, and I gave this stupid response. Over my years with the firm, I got to know Marvin Bower on a personal basis, and he would ask me to accompany him on professional meetings and inquire how I was adjusting to consulting.

Later, in 1987, after my firm, James H. Lowry & Associates, was named one of the one hundred leading management consulting

---

[29] Marvin Bower, Marvin's leadership of McKinsey & Co., turned the business of selling management advice into a keystone of American corporate culture. In decades to follow, he helped to grow consulting, which some called a racket, into a serious and substantive industry. *Business Week* magazine in 1987 named Bower one of two people most responsible for the growth of management consulting after World War II. Marvin Bower died in 2003 at his home in Delray Beach, Florida, at the age of ninety-nine.

firms in the United States by Consulting News, I received a very personal and congratulatory letter from Marvin Bower. He said I should feel honored to be acknowledged as a leader in the field. He also added he was proud of the fact McKinsey had recruited me in 1968.

I was tall and looked the part of a McKinsey consultant, but I still felt different. I had not attended one of the prestigious schools, and my degree was in public and international affairs, not business, and from the University of Pittsburgh, not an Ivy League university. To say I was intimidated would be an understatement. It did not help that I was the first black consultant McKinsey had ever hired. In many ways, this was like starting at Francis W. Parker all over again but on a much higher and more critical level.

Unlike when I started at Francis W. Parker, I did not have my athletic prowess to give me a competitive advantage, and I did not have a Jim Simmons. As the first black at McKinsey, I could not fail. The pressure of being the first meant my success could make or break the path for those after me. Fortunately, four months later, Charles Fields worked his head-hunting magic and recruited Bob Holland to become the second black at McKinsey.

Bob Holland was the smartest, most ambitious and unique individual I had ever met. Unlike me, he did not go to an exclusive private school in Chicago. Instead, he came from a public high school in the small town of Albion, Michigan. Bob had received a scholarship to Union College in Upstate New York. He had enrolled with the goal of getting a degree in mechanical engineering and hopefully later a big job with a Fortune 500 company. While at Union College, he met the love of his life, Barbara, a student at nearby Skidmore College for women. Soon after graduation, they got married and raised a family of three outstanding children, who would go on to become accomplished professionals in their own right.

Prior to joining McKinsey, Bob had worked at ExxonMobil as

an analyst. While at ExxonMobil, he also got a graduate degree in business from City College of New York. While Bob did not attend Harvard, Chicago, Wharton, or Stanford, he did have a degree in business. As a result, he was put on various private sector studies, whereas I was assigned solely to government or nonprofit studies. At the time, this seemed fair and was fine with me, coming from my Peace Corps and Bedford-Stuyvesant experience coupled with my strong desire to work in the community. McKinsey assured me I would be able to make an impact for disadvantaged people and communities if I remained in the public sector practice. Thus, I had a perfect situation working with the world's top consulting firm, with an office on Park Avenue, making more money than I ever imagined, with an expense account, and working in the community to effect change for the less fortunate. I thought life could not get any better for me.

My first assignment was working for the Philadelphia Model Cities Program. The project leader, although not a partner, was a fellow named Ross Pirasteh. He had an MBA from Yale—not one of the top four, but it was still Yale. Under Ross's guidance, I developed my initial skill set of consulting. Although I was a new consultant, I felt I could add value to the team. Ross and I worked well together. I accepted I knew little about the field of consulting, but I wanted to be trained. Ross also accepted he knew little about the inner city and minorities, and he had to be educated. As a team, the consulting advice we gave to the client was well received, and Ross gave me a solid evaluation. Ross, who was from Iran, also educated me on his country and its rich Persian culture. He left McKinsey and became the minister of finance in Iran but later got caught between government transitions and was put in jail. After his release, he returned to the United States and had a successful career as a corporate executive.

I passed my first test at McKinsey, and as I excelled within the firm, my confidence grew. Still, for Bob Holland and me, it was difficult to get the proper staffing assignments. During our first two years at McKinsey, Bob Holland and I were a "black network of two." Every day, we came to our Park Avenue office in our three-piece suits, articulating in our best Harvard English to the clients. Almost every night, we would compare notes and motivate each other to continue the fight. In a way, we were a two-person diversity cadre. We would discuss the McKinsey culture, the key players, and various approaches to developing our careers at the firm. We were playing to win the game instead of playing not to lose. Under the surface, however, it was a dark and depressing time for us both. After hours, we would often retreat from Park Avenue and lose ourselves over glasses of beer or scotch, listening to the music of Motown, eating greasy soul food.

It was a tumultuous time for blacks, especially with lynchings still going on in the South. Deep down, we often felt hurt and angry when we read about those many injustices. We would share that pain and often escape the dark times with talk about the Knicks, Jets, or Giants. Two seasons, we bought season tickets to the NY Knicks and followed them to the first of two world championships. Unfortunately for Bob, the year the Knicks won the championship, he was assigned to the Amsterdam office. I am embarrassed to admit this many years later, but when I left the office for the seventh game between the LA Lakers and the Knicks, I sold my ticket when I heard the price of one ticket was equal to the price of the season package. This was the game Willis Reed limped onto the court and made his first shot, and Walt Frazier scored forty-four points. It was not a total loss since I ended up watching the game with my cousin Ron Gault at the apartment of Ed Bradley, who was at the time one of the first black CBS reporters and later an anchor on *60 Minutes*.

In addition to sports, Motown was the other lifesaving constant in my life. I would think about the many times Allison Davis and I would go to the Regal Theater in Chicago and watch the *Motown Review*. We would pay five dollars to get in, watch a movie, and then stay for six or seven acts of the *Motown Review*. It was intriguing to see who Barry Gordy would have as headliners and who he would have opening the show. We witnessed the Temptations, Smokey Robinson, the Supremes, Mary Wells, Martha Reeves and the Vandellas, and many others fight for top billing. This fierce competition was highlighted in *Motown: The Musical* on Broadway, the lively song and dance musical about Barry Gordy's life at Motown. I remember seeing Dionne Warwick as an opening act well before she became famous, back when she had blonde hair. I loved the *Motown Review* and followed it to the Howard Theater in DC and Apollo Theater in New York.

Bob and I continued to bond over family trips to the West Indies, intense games of tennis, our love of sports, and our families. We also shared the desire to help others join the firm at 245 Park Avenue. We were never satisfied being the token blacks. We felt it was important to open the doors for others to join us. Although Bob and I were very ambitious and had positive mental attitudes, I don't know if either of us would have made it had we not bonded at the firm during that early stage of our careers. We came from different cities, with different educational experiences. He was married, and I was a very happy bachelor. Yet we showed up to McKinsey as brothers motivated to help each other.

I got a real break early in my career when McKinsey got a contract to assist the reorganization of the Peace Corps in the Nixon administration. Although the basic foundation of the Peace Corps would remain the same, the new administration wanted the Peace Corps to be more efficient. It was great returning to DC headquarters to be one of the leaders of the team asking some valid and difficult questions of Peace Corps leadership. Most of the administration from my time there had left or had been asked to leave—with one exception, C. Payne Lucas. C. Payne had been removed as the head of the African region and delegated to a small office with no staff. When he saw me, he embraced me warmly and for the next hour bombarded me with stories of how he had been mistreated by the new administration. I listened patiently and ended our meeting saying, "C. Payne, I will handle this." C. Payne never regained his power within the Peace Corps but did go on to become a global leader and spokesperson for the poor in Africa, as the founder of the organization AfriCare.

While working on the Peace Corps assignment, I received another request for help, this time from one of my old Francis W. Parker classmates, Don Richards. After graduating from Parker, Don had received a BA from Yale and a PhD in psychology from Harvard. Don was a Peace Corps trainee at Central State University, a historic black university in Ohio, but was about to be deselected from his assignment. Don requested my help to rectify a bad situation. He was being removed because they felt he had a bad attitude. When I asked why, Don replied, "I told the psychologist conducting the psych evaluation that I knew what he was trying to get from the test but that he was doing a poor job at it." Don had book smarts, but he was insensitive to real-life experiences and dealing with professionals at historically black universities. I felt bad that I could not save Don at the Peace Corps, because in many ways his sage advice at Francis W. Parker had such a positive impact on my career. Don did go to work overseas at Vision, a Peace Corps type of nonprofit organization operating in Venezuela.

Once again, my work with the Peace Corps provided me with a strong evaluation. I was learning a lot about the basics of consulting, problem-solving skills, the McKinsey style of writing, making friends for a lifetime, and enjoying being a bachelor in New York City during the time of Joe Namath and the Jets. Still, I was in no way on the partnership track at McKinsey.

The sixties were a period of change in many ways, but it

was an exciting time in America, especially New York City. I remember fun Sundays listening to Santana in Central Park, enjoying the many acts at the Apollo Theater, and listening to the greatest folk, rhythm and blues, and jazz music ever produced. Above all, there was the feeling that with courage and leadership, our generation was going to change the world. However, despite the feeling of progress nationwide, working on Park Avenue did have its challenges.

As a young black professional, I was caught in the middle almost every day. There were intense discussions on civil rights, black liberation, and affirmative action. I was not raised to be a militant activist, so while I was angry, very angry, I still maintained a positive attitude for my career, my people, and my country. To succeed in a company, you had to perform at a high level. In addition, you also were expected to mentor and help others from your community. So, while on paper you were considered a credit to your race, it was disheartening to go home at night only to be called a sellout, Uncle Tom, or worse, or that you weren't black enough. I was frequently asked, "How can you be working for 'the man' in this capitalistic system that is destroying 'our' people?" These comments were coming not only from the youths hanging out on the corners but even from Ivy League–educated blacks.

One such Ivy League black was Bill Strickland. Bill was three years my senior and married to the daughter of the New York fire commissioner. Bill had received two Harvard degrees and was one of the intellectual leaders of the civil rights movement. I loved Bill Strickland and his wife, Leslie. We enjoyed many dinners together, but it seemed every dinner ended with insane lectures on the ills of the American free enterprise system. He respected me because I had a TV show and for how I represented black people and myself on TV, but he had a difficult time with me at McKinsey.

I learned a lot from Bill, but we could not agree on the role of capitalism and the advancement of black people, and usually after too much wine and hours of debate, I would ask him, "Bill, if capitalism is not the answer, what is?" He never came up with an answer I could accept. He also could not answer why he and other leaders could not outline viable economic programs for the masses short of government funding. At this point, I decided if the ministers, civil rights leaders, and politicians were not going to take the lead on growing minority business, I would assume the responsibility.

Young people of all colors in New York were violently opposed to the Vietnam War and the major institutions that were the foundation of our society. Our nation was going through dramatic changes, and for many, the changes were not well received. Fueling the fires in the inner cities were the frequent riots and H. Rap Brown, Stokely Carmichael, and Malcolm X all attacking whites and the white leadership. Not helping the situation were the blatant antiwhite movies produced at this time, with the lovely Pam Grier destroying the mob, Uncle Toms, and white people in general. I will not deny that I enjoyed watching the movie *Superfly* and all of the movies featuring gorgeous Pam Grier, but deep down I knew these black exploitation movies were produced to generate revenue and pride in the inner cities. In the long run, they were not helping race relations in America. There was extreme poverty in both urban and rural America. Rioting, sit-ins, and quality-produced black movies were perhaps needed to shine the light on the plight of the disadvantaged, but by themselves, they would not solve the problem.

Because I had lived in socialist Tanzania, I knew socialism was not the answer. Capitalism had not been perfect and is not perfect today, but it is still the best system in the world. We have good capitalists and bad capitalists, but our great nation was built on the foundation of capitalism and slavery.[30] Unfortunately for blacks and Hispanics, the vast majority of the educated professionals were denied access into the US free enterprise system by discriminatory practices, government laws and policies. In hindsight, this was not only a loss for black and Hispanic communities but to American society as a whole. And now we are all paying a price.

It did not help that our civil rights leaders and politicians devoted endless hours talking about the problems: inferior education, social injustice, and a poor health system. They did not focus on the fact minorities did not control wealth, and without wealth, we have no power; without power, we cannot create jobs or influence government policies for economic development. Without jobs, our youth have no hope, and so it is inevitable they will continue to fight over who controls the corner where drugs are distributed as a means to create wealth. These facts were evident to me in 1968 when the war on drugs was created. If only we had been allowed to grow businesses, create jobs, and build hope in our communities, not only would the black and Hispanic communities be stronger, but so would America.

The years between 1968 and 1974 dramatically affected not only me but our entire society. The United States was faced with many enemies that were challenging the very fabric of the nation. During this period, President Nixon was elected and also impeached, but before he left office, he established the Office of Minority Business Enterprise (OMBE). We lost the Vietnam War. The Weathermen were bombing federal buildings, blacks were rioting across the nation after the assassination of Martin Luther King and Senator Robert Kennedy, and the Republican Party was about to undergo a radical change. Prior to 1968, there were no major differences between the two major parties with the leadership of both the Democrat and Republican

---

[30] This was highlighted in the August 14, 2019, issue of the *New York Times* magazine regarding Project 1619.

Party leaders—both with very smart, patriotic, elected officials educated in Ivy League schools and residing in New York and New England. Soon, Republican leaders would change.

Being at McKinsey at this point in my career gave me an excellent frame of reference to see the business priorities and policies guiding the country. I was often asked to represent the firm when President Nixon developed his black Capitalism Initiative. I give Nixon credit, not Kennedy or Johnson, for jumpstarting minority business enterprise development in the federal government. His motive for creating the black Capitalism Initiative might have been suspect, but he was a catalyst for encouraging major public/private business programs (as did Senator Kennedy) and forcing black leaders to think beyond the welfare mentality.

The Peace Corps and the Bedford-Stuyvesant Restoration Corporation provided me the purpose for minority business enterprise development, President Nixon provided the structure and legal understanding, and McKinsey provided the in-depth business knowledge that would allow me to be a change agent. I wanted to be a change agent, loyal to my people and America. I thought I could assume this role with a minimum of anger, a solid business acumen, and a strong motivation to make a difference.

Historical Background 1975–1980

Under the leadership of Jimmy Carter, who became president in 1977 after a ten-year military career and four years as governor of the state of Georgia, the number of black businesses grew faster than ever in America. Carter had a history of receiving wisdom from three black iconic leaders—Andrew Young, John Lewis, and mayor of Atlanta, Maynard Jackson. At the same time, the Republican Party was heavily investigating ways to remove affirmative action laws.

- FY 1977-1979 - federal contracts to minority business increased from $1 billion to $2.7 billion
- 1977: President Carter signs Local Public Works Employment Act of 1977, which "mandated that minority firms receive 10% of all such contracts—roughly $600 million in new business." President Carter also set aside $100 million for minority-owned banks.
- 1977: President Carter appointed Andrew Young as first African American US ambassador to the United Nations.
- 1978: In the case *Regents of the University of California v. Bakke,*[31] the US Supreme Court upheld the constitutionality of affirmative action, however, ensured that affirmative action did not come at the expense of lost opportunity or rights for whites.
- 1979: Executive Order 12138[32] was signed by President Carter, requiring federal agencies to take affirmative action in support of businesses owned by women.
- 1979: Jane Byrne is elected as the first female mayor of Chicago.

---

[31] 438 U.S. 265 (1978).
[32] Exec. Order No. 12138 (1979), 44 FR 1071.

- 1980: President Carter signed Executive Order 12232,[33] which requires a federal program "to overcome the effects of discriminatory treatment and to strengthen and expand the capacity of historically black colleges and universities to provide quality education." Subsequently, in 1981, President Reagan, under Executive Order 12320, augmented the strength of federal support to historically black colleges.

---

[33] Exec. Order No. 12232 (1980), 45 FR 989.

CHAPTER 7

EFFECTING CHANGE IN AFRICA WITH MCKINSEY

Despite enjoying New York City and working in the McKinsey office, both Bob Holland and I realized that to succeed, even survive, we needed to take overseas assignments. Bob accepted an assignment to Amsterdam, and I was elated when New York office leader Ron Daniel asked me to take a transfer to the London office to work on a project back in Tanzania. In Tanzania, the total apparatus of government remained in Dar-es-Salaam, the capital. The goal of the project was to assist Tanzania's President Nyerere implement his vision of transforming the country from a highly centralized to a highly decentralized governmental structure. Our study concluded we could achieve this goal by reorganizing eight ministries and sixteen regions. The study was highly controversial for two reasons—one, because we recommended moving the apparatus of government into a different region, and two, for the size of our contract. With respect to the latter, the president answered the critics in his party by saying, "If you want quality, you do not pay them with peanuts." This assignment also gave me the opportunity to live up to the promise I had long ago made to my Kivukoni students, that I would one day return. I was returning to Tanzania to change government and accelerate development.

At about the same time, I ran into an old friend from Chicago,

Nettie Camille Anthony. Nettie was something special. We had dated once in Chicago when I was a freshman at Grinnell and she was a senior at Hyde Park High School. She was a doctor's daughter, Jack and Jill Club member, and a graduate of Goucher College and the University of Chicago, and frankly, she was also one of the prettiest girls in Chicago. Seizing the opportunity to invest time, money, and the most aggressive courtship I had ever undertaken in my young life, I made up my mind that Nettie was going to be my wife. A short seven months later, she agreed, and we got married in a beautiful, romantic ceremony at the Great Barrington, Massachusetts, home of my good friend Bill Chaffee, the architect with the I.M. Pei firm I'd met during my time at the Bedford-Stuyvesant Restoration Corp. Soon after, I was planning my return to Tanzania, with Nettie by my side.

When Nettie and I arrived in Dar-es-Salaam, only a skeleton McKinsey team remained, as most of the team was already being sent home after presenting our team's final recommendation to President Nyerere on how to decentralize the government. The McKinsey team was truly outstanding, all graduates from either Oxford or Cambridge, with one being a relative of the prime minister of the United Kingdom. We worked well together professionally and socially.

One of the first things I did upon arriving was try to reunite with my students from Kivukoni College. Ten years had passed since I was an instructor at the school, and I wondered what had happened to my students and if the friendships I had established would still be intact. I was greatly moved when one of my former students said, upon seeing me, "Jim, you kept your promise. You returned to help us build our country." I soon discovered my friendships were real, and those friends had graduated to powerful positions. One of the former students was the Tanzanian ambassador to China; another was the head of the Tanzanian banking system; a third, whom I had helped get a full scholarship to Princeton University, was now the finance minister. There were many others who held senior positions in various administrative trade unions and regional governments.

When our daughter, Camille Aisha, was born, all the other wives were very supportive and often babysat for one another. It was also an exciting time for my wife, Nettie. In fact, the wife of the UK senior partner drafted Nettie to be a model in her special project to develop Tanzania's textile industry. For years, we kept this beautiful photo of Nettie modeling a Tanzanian textile dress. She had been a Wilhelmina model, so it did not come as a surprise to me that hundreds of photos of her were on display throughout Dar-es-Salaam.

While I got along well with my team members, I was troubled by the team's new leader. He was a senior associate educated at Oxford and Harvard School of Business. He was a nice man with a lovely wife and very intent on becoming a partner. He was a solid consultant but an uninspiring team leader. What I found most troubling was his style and insensitivity relating to the locals. I made the mistake of sharing my feelings to one of my British team members, who immediately relayed my misgivings directly to the leader. It should have come as no surprise that my next evaluation was negative. When a senior partner from the UK visited Tanzania, I complained that what really irritated me about my evaluation was the mention that I had not learned Swahili fast enough. Damn, my Swahili was not great, but none of my team members could even order breakfast in Swahili, including the project leader critiquing me. I was honestly trying to protect McKinsey's interest and brand by warning them about this insensitive team leader, and I was punished for my honesty.

Part of me wanted to quit after that, but we had become pleasantly engaged in Tanzanian life. Nettie had adapted well as a McKinsey wife, a supporter of young professionals working in an emerging country, and being an excellent mother to our daughter, whose middle name, Aisha, was given her by President Nyerere himself. During a visit home for Christmas, I went to see my friend Ron Daniel to complain of my unfair treatment. I thought I had built a strong case in my defense, but I was shocked to hear my friend and mentor say, "Jim, I will not go against another partner. My advice for you is go back to Tanzania and prove to them they were wrong." Thus, being a very young professional with a newborn baby, I had a choice to make. I could quit on principle or take my mentor's advice and prove them wrong. After talking to Nettie, we decided to return to Dar-es-Salaam and once again play the game to win, instead of playing not to lose. I said to myself, rationalizing and making excuses for failures was for losers, and I was not going to fail; the stakes were too high.

Fortunately, I soon got an opportunity to distance myself from the team in Dar-es-Salaam in terms of performance and geography. President Nyerere had asked McKinsey to lead a series of one-week training sessions for high-ranking Tanzanian officers in the town of Dodoma. He didn't want the officials to be distracted in the capital of Dar-es-Salaam. Dodoma was a small town with one hotel and no main attractions and thus was considered a hardship location for both McKinsey consultants and our Tanzania clients. Since no one on our team or their wives wanted to spend the next six months in Dodoma, I volunteered. I accepted the responsibility of leading the training program assisted by a young Australian Harvard MBA, Ralph Evans.[34] So for six months, I would fly to Dodoma, leaving my wife and child in Dar-es-Salaam, and come home only on the weekends. Nettie would pick me up with Aisha in the front seat with a big

[34] Ralph Evans Evans received his MBA from Stanford and joined McKinsey in 1971. He would later return to his native Sydney, Australia, and open management consulting firm PCEK with three other partners. The firm grew to about eighty professionals by 1990, when it was acquired by the Boston Consulting Group.

smile on her face. After two days, I would kiss them goodbye and return to the classroom and the small hotel, where I slept under a mosquito net.

Over that six-month period, three major things happened: I became a trusted advisor to President Nyerere and his top officials; we completed the decentralization of Tanzania; and, because of too many insensitive comments about Tanzania, our team leader was asked to leave the country. The president praised my work in Dodoma and requested that I be the one to head up the McKinsey team until my replacement arrived.

While waiting for my replacement, Nettie and I became immersed in Dar-es-Salaam culture and society. This city was unique because of President Nyerere, and Dar-es-Salaam became the mecca for leaders of emerging nations. Every week, there would be visiting heads of states from India, South America, and Africa. Often, we were invited to official Tanzanian government and US State Department affairs. One of the most memorable cocktail parties we attended was given by the US embassy in honor of the 1971 NBA championship team, the Milwaukee Bucks. The Bucks were represented by Coach Larry Costello and two of the team's greatest All-Star players, Oscar Robertson and Kareem Abdul-Jabbar (Lew Alcindor). Oscar had always been my idol since his playing days at Crispus Attucks High School in Indiana and the University of Cincinnati. When they won the championship, Oscar was thirty-two years old and his best playing days were behind him. When he was younger, he was one of, if not the, best players in the NBA's history. Even now I would rate him as one of the all-time greatest players in the history of the game of basketball.

I could not wait to meet both these superstars and their wives, especially Oscar Robertson. At the cocktail party, Oscar was outgoing and dominated the room, but I could not keep my eyes off of Kareem. Here was this 7'2" basketball player who had this regal presence about him. I also knew that even as a high school student, he was a highly intellectual young man who had a strong commitment to fight against social injustice and for those less fortunate. In high school, he, along with Jim Brown, Bill Russell, and others, stood behind a young Muhammad Ali (Cassius Clay) when he refused to be drafted into the army.

I watched Kareem, sitting in the corner of the room with his young Muslim wife, Habiba, seemingly bored. To my surprise, he got up from his chair, approached us, and asked, "Hey, do you have any jazz?" When I said yes, he said, "Let's get out of here and go to your house." So, we retreated to my house to listen to Herbie Hancock, Miles Davis, and John Coltrane for hours. We kept in touch with Kareem until he was traded to the Los Angeles Lakers.

I felt bad leaving the cocktail party and Oscar Robertson and his lovely wife, but over the next forty years, I maintained a relationship with Oscar and his daughter. His daughter was in one of my classes at Kellogg business school. Over the years, Oscar became an outstanding leader and model for the black community.

During our two years in Dar-es-Salaam, we entertained many family members, young recent graduates such as Ruth and Cliff Darden; Terry Jones; Ron Hamilton; and others. Soon after the birth of our daughter, Camille Aisha, Bill and Leslie Sutherland and Bob and Barbara Holland joined us. On the day she was born, her godmother, Sandra Forney, was there. At the time, Sandra was working in the Los Angeles office of Motown. Upon her return to the States, she was having lunch with Stevie Wonder, and Stevie asked her where she had been. She told him that she was the godmother of a newborn whose parents were in Tanzania and named her Aisha. He replied, "That is a pretty name." Twelve months later, he named his daughter Aisha and produced the hit song "Isn't She Lovely." Years later, I met Stevie at a charity event at the house of John Legend. I asked him about his conversation with Sandra, and he said it was accurate. I then replied, "Stevie, you and I are responsible for thousands of babies in America being named Aisha, Moesha, Kenisha, and fifty other versions!" He laughed and said, "I think you're right."

With President Nyerere's request that I lead the team, I felt vindicated and proud that I had made the right decision not to quit. I was also proud of the fact that the previous team leader never made partner at McKinsey and was later asked to leave the firm. The London senior partner who had relied on the complaints of that team leader and given me a bad review tried to be my friend, but it was too late, and I'd moved on. This time, he gave me a strong evaluation, and I was treated as a hero for having saved a very important project.

This period represented a true crossroad for me, my family, and America. I had done well enough but not well enough to become a partner at McKinsey. I wanted to become a partner for many reasons, but often I would ask myself, was I driven and focused enough to achieve this goal? I was willing to sacrifice six months living under a mosquito net in Dodoma, but was that enough to drive me to the top? Over the years, I have realized that those who were fortunate enough to make partner were not only able to take advantage of McKinsey's excellent training and mentoring, but they also had focus. Most of the potential partners did just that; they were focused on family and the goal of making partner.

I never had the pure focus because my mind would always take me back to the civil rights struggle, the need to educate blacks on the free enterprise system, economic development, and the unification of black leadership. Maybe I was naïve, but I thought I could achieve all three goals and make partner at McKinsey.

CHAPTER 8

LEVERAGING THE HARVARD NAME

Upon my return to the United States, my mentor Ron Daniel asked what I wanted to do during the next phase of my career. In thinking about his question, I realized I could not envision making partner in New York. For one, the public sector was going through some difficult times. To make matters worse, McKinsey's image had suffered a bit due to some unfair negative press around a close relationship between the mayor of New York City and the head of McKinsey's public sector practice. In the consulting world, without a strong leader, you have no clients. Second, although I had achieved moderate success through my Tanzanian engagement, I still did not feel like I belonged and I lacked a formidable sponsor. The fact that most of my peers had MBAs from prestigious business schools left me feeling insecure. Confronting those feelings and accepting that I was negotiating from a position of strength based on my success with the Tanzanian assignment, I asked the firm to send me to the four-month Harvard Program for Management Development (PMD). My request was accepted, and in May 1972, I went to Harvard.

Like many other midcareer business professionals, once you stepped on the Harvard Business School campus, you sensed your life would never be the same. Harvard Business School (HBS) represented history, prestige, and, let's not forget, global power. Within PMD, we got the same high-quality instructors as the regular programs, mainly because the best professors desired to teach business executives. In my class, we even had the dean of the school, Larry Fouraker, teaching a course on international economics. My classmates were on average five years older than I and highly-esteemed executives on desired career paths with companies from all over the world. In my housing cluster, I had three roommates: one from Turkey, one from Amsterdam, and one from England.

We received instruction in the same classrooms as the MBA students and used the same cases. The biggest differences were that our program lasted only four months and we received no grades. The fact we did not receive grades did not deter me or my fellow classmates from investing many hours of preparation for our classes. Prior to going to Harvard, I asked one of the McKinsey friends who had attended HBS and was a Baker scholar (top 10 percent of her class) what advice she could offer me. She said, "First, do not be intimidated by the number of pages you have to read. Second, budget your time to read each case three times. The first time to get a general understanding of the problem or opportunity, the second time to develop your hypothesis and the key elements of the problem, and the third time to structure your argument to prove your case. Lastly, be bold and aggressive in the classroom."

I followed my friend's advice and in the eyes of the professors and my fellow participants quickly rose to the top of my class. I do not know if I deserved my classmates' admiration because the fact that I was a McKinsey consultant might have biased their option. But deep down, I felt I was cheating. I had just spent four and a half years at the world's most prominent consulting firm, competing against and working with some of the smartest people in business, and was the recipient of hundreds of hours of exhaustive and brilliant training, the best any young professional could receive. In a way, it was like going backward. Attacking a Harvard case was like solving a problem for a difficult McKinsey client. I soon realized my professors, however aggressive I might be in the classroom, would not call on me. This was frustrating because, following my friend's advice, I was prepared for each and every class, but I was not getting a chance to participate in the classroom. It was only when I stopped raising my hand that the dynamics shifted. Instead, I started waiting for the professor to call on me if the logical answer was not forthcoming from my classmates.

One day we were in a class titled The Family and Business. The case was about a successful three-year-old business that was losing market share because the two partners had stopped communicating. The professor on the case was going around the class asking for probable causes of the disagreement. Some said market share, others said lack of capital, others offered poor management. After twenty minutes of not getting the correct answer, I finally did raise my hand, and this time he called on me. I paused, then told him I didn't think the impasse had anything to do with business. Instead, I thought it was a breakdown in the partner's romantic relationship, citing jealousy and a scorned heart as the reason for failure. He looked at me, then around the room, then said, "You are absolutely correct. Class dismissed." Two days later, we had our class elections, and I was elected the president of the PMD Class 25. The head of the program approached me and told me I had just made history. I thought he meant the first black elected president; instead, he said I was the first nonastronaut to be elected president of a PMD class in the last five years.

During my PMD experience, I spent a lot of time with Professor Jim Cash, a giant of a man in more ways than one. A former TCU All-Conference basketball player, Professor Cash was one of the first black basketball players in the Southwest

Conference. He later attended and received his doctoral degree in management information systems from Purdue University's Krannert Graduate School of Management. While a professor at Harvard Business School, Jim was an outstanding faculty member and later became the dean of the MBA program. Like his counterparts Charles Ogletree and Derrick Bell at Harvard Law School, Jim Cash was brilliant in the classroom and a mentor for many inspiring young professionals irrespective of race, gender, or religion. These men were models for being sensitive to the unique challenges faced by people of color. They personified individuals who were brilliant and outstanding in their fields, supporting us in our journeys but never forgetting where they came from.

Another friend was Naylor Fitzhugh. Despite being the first black recipient of a Harvard MBA, due to the times, he couldn't get a job in the private sector upon graduating. Instead, he became a distinguished professor at Howard University. Naylor, like Cash, Ogletree, and Bell, operated in the world of business very effectively but took great pride in advancing the careers of people of color, which at the time was considered a courageous thing to do. I often wondered why more blacks weren't doing the same, while so many leaders from other ethnic backgrounds did it for their members.

The four-month program at Harvard had a profound impact on my life. I was able to demonstrate the skills I had acquired at McKinsey; I developed friendships with classmates from around the world; I gained the respect of elite groups of professors; and, most importantly, my confidence was the highest it had ever been in my life. The Harvard experience provided me with solid credentials and a very strong positive outlook on life. In essence, I was ready for the world, believing there were no mountains I could not climb, no rivers I could not cross, no task insurmountable.

Being at Harvard, around so many brilliant minds that were

making a difference, I started to question my place at McKinsey. I also began to feel that maybe a long career at McKinsey was not going to happen. I truly loved the place, the leadership, and the esteemed feeling of being a McKinsey consultant. I used to love flying first-class, quietly working and reading in my seat. The person next to me would wonder, who was this person in the blue pin-striped suit? I was too old be an athlete, so how could I afford to be in first class? Hesitantly, they would ask, "What do you do?" I would answer, "I am a consultant," milking the situation, knowing he or she would have to ask, "With what firm?" and I would say proudly, "I am a consultant with McKinsey."

I maintained my connection to Harvard for many years. Soon after starting my firm, JHLA, I served for six years on the Harvard African American Alumni Board. After that, I served on the Harvard Alumni Board for four years. Later, I was asked to serve on the prestigious HBS Visiting Board for six years. During my tenure on this board, some of the other board members were John J. Nevin, CEO of Firestone Tire and Rubber; Lou Gerstner, former McKinsey partner and later CEO of American Express, RJR Nabisco, and IBM; Earl Graves; John Clarkson, who at that time was president of the Boston Consulting Group; Mitt Romney, founder and managing partner of Bain Capital; and many others. Also, over this six-year period, I spent a lot of time with John McArthur, the new dean, who at one point asked me to join the faculty. I was flattered by the request but opted out because of the salary range for Harvard professors at that time. I would later question this decision based on the success of Jim Cash. Following Cash's career teaching at HBS, after he left, he demonstrated how one could parlay the Harvard reputation to be a highly successful, professional advisor to CEOs, be a valuable member of multiple major boards, and make a lot of money. It is one of the lessons I can look back upon and wonder if I had been shortsighted.

CHAPTER 9

THE POWER OF THE FIFTH FLOOR

After completing the PMD program at HBS, I knew deep down I wanted to be an entrepreneur. Unfortunately, I did not have any close mentors to advise me on what to do or not to do. When I returned to New York from Boston, I was questioning my commitment to the goal of achieving partner at McKinsey. Despite knowing my chances were not great at making partner in the New York office, I decided to give it one more chance. Bob Holland, on the other hand, was on a strong path to partnership by embracing the golden rule: he who brings in the gold enhances his chance of making partner. Bob was making a lot of money for the firm. Finally, I was getting it. I had to remind myself, "Jim, this is not the Peace Corps or Bedford-Stuyvesant. You have to proceed with a new set of rules of engagement now. You have to produce money; the more money you generate, the brighter your future will be."

I asked my friend Ron Daniel if he would help me transfer to another McKinsey office to head up a public sector practice. He agreed and placed calls to his counterparts in Cleveland, San Francisco, and Chicago. I visited both the San Francisco and Cleveland offices but determined these were not good matches. I had close black friends in both offices, and both were outstanding consultants with MBAs from Harvard. But this was a time where society allowed room for only one of us in the room, and I believed that either my or their success might be limited should we share the same office.

Dennis Hightower[35] was in the Cleveland office and was the fifth black McKinsey recruit. Dennis was a graduate of Howard University and a highly decorated officer in the army. He was hired by Xerox, but after getting a Harvard MBA, he went to McKinsey and was a senior associate and engagement manager until 1978. Barry Williams[36] was at the San Francisco office and was also one of the early black McKinsey recruits. I first met Barry in Lima, Peru. Barry had been a star basketball player at Harvard and used to compete against Princeton All-American, Knicks player and later US Senator Bill Bradley. He had been given my name by Allison Davis's brother Gordon, and he looked me up while he was traveling the globe on a Harvard Travel Fellowship. I took him to Club Revólver and had him demonstrate his basketball skills. We kept in touch when he returned to Harvard, where he got two additional degrees in business and law. Needless to say, with his résumé, he was an easy sell to McKinsey. He later left the firm in 1979. The obvious choice for me was Chicago. My Francis W. Parker classmates were now rich and famous, my brother was a civic leader, and, most importantly, I wanted to spend more quality time with my parents, who were starting to acquire senior status.

In the Chicago office, I was welcomed with open arms by

---

[35] After his time with McKinsey, Harvard MBA grad Dennis F. Hightower became the president of Disney Consumer Products for Europe, the Middle East, and Africa. Hightower later was promoted to president of Walt Disney Television and Telecommunications. In 1996, he joined HBS's faculty, and from 2000 to 2001, he served as the CEO of Europe Online Networks.

[36] Barry Williams went on to become the president of Williams Pacific Ventures, Inc., and joined the board of directors of Kaiser Foundation Health Plan as well as Kaiser Foundation Hospitals.

the office manager, Jack Cardwell[37], one of the smartest, nicest, and most supportive senior partners I have ever known. Jack received a Harvard MBA and spent many years as an officer in the Navy. In his early years, he was an officer in one of the first nuclear submarines put to sea. He was a tall man with a lovely wife, Jeanie, and their six kids. The thing I remember most about Jack was he was always relaxed and upbeat. He retained this demeanor throughout his life, even later as he valiantly battled throat cancer, which he acknowledged was probably caused by smoking cigarettes for months at a time during his nuclear submarine days.

As the office manager, Jack gave me wide latitude to start my public sector practice. Initially, I tried to start my practice the McKinsey style with the proper introductions, well-crafted decks, and marketing material. Unfortunately, the McKinsey way was not generating revenues. One afternoon over lunch with an insider friend, I was sharing the lack of success in my marketing approaches. He looked me in the eye and said, "Jim, if you want to get government business in the state of Illinois, you have to have the blessing of the fifth floor." I answered, "What is the fifth floor?" He answered, "Jim, the fifth floor is Mayor Richard J. Daley's office." I said, "I don't know Mayor Daley, and I do not know if I like or respect him after reading about the 1968 Democratic Convention." He replied, "If you want to get state business, you should first understand how the city of Chicago works. So you better get to know him."

For almost a week, I reflected on this serious career decision, and then I got a call from someone at Senator Adlai Stevenson's office, asking me if I would like to join his campaign. Because Senator Stevenson and his father promoted policies and laws I felt

---

[37] Jack Cardwell was managing director of the Chicago office at McKinsey, then left to become president and CEO of Consolidated Food Corporation, what is now known as Sara Lee Corporation.

comfortable with, I joined his campaign. Once working on the campaign, I was introduced to all the Chicago power players in both the public and private sectors. I was also introduced to all the Daley insiders. Senator Stevenson easily won, and after the experience, while I would not say I attained insider status, I was now known by the people who counted in Chicago.

After the campaign, I was asked to participate in Richard J. Daley's last campaign. At that time, Lt. Gov. Neil Hartigan was an insider who had attended Georgetown University and then later Loyola University College of Law in 1962. He and his wife, Margo, were true players, and they had formed a special organization called For Chicago, composed of young civic leaders who were not elected or appointed officers in the Daley administration. Members such as Michael Rosenberg (a member of the Francis W. Parker's class of 1953 and former fullback on my brother's football team), Paul Stepan (son of the CEO of the Stepan Company and a big donor to the University of Notre Dame), Jim O'Connor (eventual CEO of Con Edison), Jim Reilly, Nicki and Ira Harris, and Sally and Michael Berger. Realizing this could be another one of those life-changing experiences, I went to Jack Cardwell and requested a three-month leave of absence. When he asked why, I was very candid and said I wanted to get closer to Mayor Daley. He laughed as only Jack could do and said, "Go for it."

I quickly moved into the campaign offices and managed to become the coleader in communication outreach working with Sally Berger. Soon I was the lead person introducing the mayor at all the community meetings. As a result, I got to know the mayor, and I believe he came to like me. One day, he took me aside and said, "Jim, Chicago is strong because it is like a patchwork quilt; it has many patches, only in this case the patches are neighborhoods." I saw what he was saying, and I realized that this is how he made the city great. Still, it bothered me because Chicago then and even now is one of the most segregated cities in the country. The mayor could easily lead the city of ethnic neighborhoods, but in the long run, Chicago and its citizens might have been better off if he had embarked on a policy integrating, not segregating, the city.

The mayor won the election by 68.9 percent, and I realized that in Chicago, there are many Republicans in the city who, come election time, all become Democrats. After three months, everyone knew me, and I had the blessing of the most powerful man in the state and one of the most powerful politicians in the nation. I was not a Daley insider, mainly because I was not from the Tenth Ward, but I did have acceptance from the fifth floor. I think the mayor liked me because I was different. I was a global traveler returning to the city, working for a global consultant firm, and I did not come up ringing doorbells under a ward political leader. Plus, he had heard I had gone to Harvard Business School. When he asked me if I went to Harvard, I answered truthfully by saying, "Yes, kind of." Getting a certificate from the PMD Program is not the same as getting an MBA, but I was still a Harvard alumnus.

After the election, I had a private meeting with the mayor. He asked me what my plans were for the future. I explained that I was a consultant with McKinsey. He then asked if McKinsey knew anything about health and organization. I gave him an overview of McKinsey. He said, "Great, I have a couple of studies I would like some help on for the city." I could not wait to return to the office and share with Jack Cardwell how my three-month investment of time had been successful. When I shared the success with him and what the mayor had said, I was not expecting his reply. He said, "Jim, we do not want to do any work with the mayor or the city of Chicago." I then asked him the obvious next question, "Then why did you allow me to take a leave for three months of my life?" He was typical Jack and said with a smile, "I like you, and we want to keep you in the firm." It was a compliment, and I was honored by the response but not happy.

With a deep sense of embarrassment, I returned to Mayor Daley and informed him McKinsey declined conducting the studies. He then replied with a twinkle in his eye, "Good. You conduct the studies and start your own company."

I returned to tell Jack Cardwell I was going to take the mayor up on his offer. He asked if I was sure this was what I wanted to do, and I replied yes. He said okay but asked whether I would remain as a consultant to the office to assist them in recruiting persons of color for the firm. Thus, James H. Lowry & Associates (JHLA) was started with two studies from the city of Chicago and a retainer with McKinsey. Ready for the next phase of my journey, I had my exit interview with Robert Neuschel, ironically the brother of Richard Neuschel who hired me in New York in 1968. In the interview, I told Bob how sad I was to be leaving McKinsey. He said he was sad too and stated, "We truly liked you and tried to make it work, but it was like fitting a square peg in a round hole." I left McKinsey with nothing but fond memories and respect. The firm had changed my life, advanced my skill set, allowed me to return to work in Tanzania, paid for my tuition at Harvard Business School, softened my hardcore racial views of the sixties, allowed me to appreciate the strengths and uniqueness of the US free enterprise system, and gave me the title I would keep for the rest of my life: I was the first black at McKinsey. I was officially leaving McKinsey, but my McKinsey friends and allies would be with me the rest of my life. Soon after, Bob Holland would have his own lifetime title, the first black partner at McKinsey & Company.

Looking back, not making partner at McKinsey was not a life-shattering event. I had performed well and provided value to my teams and to McKinsey. In the end, I accepted that I had not generated the revenues needed to be promoted. Without my seven-year McKinsey experience, I do not believe I could have professionally and psychologically been prepared to be a consultant for Richard J. Daley. During the short period of time I worked in Mayor Daley's campaign, I learned so much about Chicago history, political leaders, and the close working relationship between the mayor's office and Chicago business leaders. The lessons learned stayed with me for many years after and contributed to my early success as an entrepreneur.

Before becoming an entrepreneur, I thought long and hard about entering the corporate world. If I had decided to go corporate, I would have received support from Jack Cardwell and his successor Phil Purcell.[38] But I did not envision myself breaking the glass ceiling there either. At that time, very few blacks were given profit and loss responsibilities. Most of the blacks, my brother as my prime example, were given administrative positions in personnel, public relations, public affairs, or procurement. We called it the "four P" black position. This changed over time, but I did not want to take a chance.

I started JHLA with two contracts from the city of Chicago and a retainer from McKinsey. On the one hand, I was sad because I truly loved working at McKinsey and working for Jack Cardwell and later Phil Purcell. Jack and Phil were not only outstanding consultants and civic leaders; they had also become my very close and supportive friends. On the other hand, I was very eager to start the next phase of my career as an entrepreneur and change agent. Like many young black professionals during this time, I was going to be the first entrepreneur in my family. Deep down, I wanted to be *the* black community leader and a national player connecting all segments of our society. Around that time, I read

---

[38] Phil Purcell is the head of Continental Investors, a private equity firm based in Chicago. As president of Dean Witter from 1982 to 1986, during Morgan Stanley's acquisition of Dean Witter, Purcell, as CEO, helped the firm to see extreme gains in league table rankings. Purcell is a graduate of the University of Notre Dame, holds an MS from the London School of Economics and MBA from the University of Chicago.

Stephen Birmingham's book, *Our Crowd*.[39] The book traced the trials and tribulations of prominent New York Jewish families during the nineteenth century. Not surprisingly, and like many cultures and institutions, the Jewish people as individuals were often judged by their family heritage; your last name could have a major impact on your future success.

I was so intrigued by the fact that in the prominent Jewish community, even when they would fight against one another, in the face of a threat from an outsider, they became a unified front. Recognizing that the Jewish community in New York and elsewhere in major US cities had survived great adversity but still had prospered for more than two hundred years, why couldn't the black community operate the same way? Why couldn't we put aside our differences and rather than infight with one another, band together, united? Why did we have to operate like "crabs in a barrel"?[40] The basic sentiment is if I can't have it, you can't either.

Initially, I did not have a detailed McKinsey-type, three-year strategic or business plan for JHLA, but I did list five things I wanted to achieve. First, I knew I wanted to train and mentor many young professionals, with a special focus on minorities as much as possible. Second, I wanted to leverage my skills, contacts, and resources to effect social and economic change. Third, I felt it was important to greatly enhance the concept of minority business enterprise development (MBED), both domestically and

---

[39] Stephen Birmingham, *Our Crowd* (New York: Harper, 1967).

[40] "Crab in the Barrel Syndrome (CBS)—a metaphor used to describe the mentality and behaviors of individuals belonging to or identifying with a particular community or culture, who 'hold each other back' from various opportunities for advancement and achievement despite incentives and expectations for collaboration (in-group solidarity)" (Carliss Denise Miller). "Interpersonal competitive dynamics in the workplace: The dark side of demographic similarity" (PhD diss., The University of Texas at Dallas, 2016).

internationally. Fourth, I wanted my firm to be recognized as one of the nation's top consulting firms. And lastly, I wanted to achieve these goals while maintaining balance in my life and being a role model for my daughter. Again, not only did I lack a finely detailed written plan to achieve these five goals, I did not even have an office or staff. What I did have though were my savings and powerful contacts. Fortunately for me, I had other assets that would prove to be invaluable. I had the support of the most powerful mayor in the country and my Outward Bound positive mental attitude.

When I started JHLA, I immediately asked one of my Chicago friends, Jack Guthman, a partner at the prestigious law firm Sidley Austin LLP, to represent me. Jack was a great lawyer, and he represented me admirably. But after Sidley made Charlie Lomax their first black partner, I felt compelled to transfer my business to Charlie, much to the disappointment of Jack Guthman. Like Jack, Charlie Lomax served me well and provided high-quality legal assistance, and over an extended period, he became a close friend.

Not just a star lawyer, Charlie was a unique character. He introduced me to the business end of boxing, the world of Don King, and Las Vegas. Often, we would go to the big Michael Spinks and Mike Tyson fights. He also introduced me to his young protégé from Harvard Law School, Tony Licata. When Charlie died, Tony Licata became my lawyer and my friend. In the end, all I wanted was outstanding legal advice, loyalty, and friendship. I got all of the above from all three; it just happened that one was Jewish, one was African American, and one was Italian.

With Jack as my lawyer, the next person I contacted was my old Grinnell College roommate Allison Davis, who had just started his own small, highly successful boutique law firm with Francis W. Parker alumnus Judd Miner. For a nominal rent, he gave me a small office in his law firm. The next thing I did was recruit my best friend, Jim Simmons, as a subcontractor. All that was missing was a secretary to do my typing. Luckily for me, soon after I moved into the firm, Grinnell alumna Dianne Jones just happened to contact me about helping her find a job. I knew she was bright, so when I asked her if she could type and she replied yes, I hired her on the spot. I told her if she supported me, I would be her mentor for life and assist her to achieve her career goals. Dianne was an invaluable asset and a loyal staff member and friend for many years. She eventually got her MBA from the University of Indiana, had an outstanding professional career as a human resource executive at Xerox, raised two outstanding kids, and retired after many productive years.

Over the years, I would occasionally hire Grinnell alumni. One year I hired Chris Hollins as a summer intern. Chris was the son of one of the early JHLA consultants. Chris graduated from Grinnell and later became a top executive at American Express and JPMorgan Chase. However, the alumni I recruited and have the most pride in is Jerome Simmons. I got a call one day in 2011 from Jerome, informing me he was a graduate from Francis W. Parker and Grinnell. I hired him immediately and trained, mentored, and sponsored him for six years. He left JHLA in 2017 and went on to receive an MBA from the University of Chicago's Booth School of Business, and he is now an executive in a top tech firm in San Francisco.

However, my most valuable recruit was Peter Bynoe. Peter was truly gifted and highly intelligent, having attended Harvard for his undergraduate degree, his master's and law degree. Before Harvard, Peter had attended the prestigious Boston Latin School and was an All-City football player. Initially, I was introduced to Peter by Barry Williams, who was his proctor at Harvard. While at Harvard, Peter had applied for a summer internship, a position in HBS's McKinsey-Tanzania Program. After his summer experience, Peter was not selected to be a consultant for

McKinsey but did receive a prestigious offer from Citicorp to be an international banker. On one of my many trips to New York, I took Peter to lunch and convinced him to join JHLA. I was very candid with him, telling him I could only match his salary, but together we would make a lot of money, have a lot of fun, and we would make history. In retrospect, we did all three.

Peter was twelve years my junior. He was an excellent writer and a natural leader of what I would later call the new generation of black leaders. These were highly qualified young blacks who were the early beneficiaries of the civil rights movement. They were the first to be accepted in numbers at prestigious prep schools, Ivy League schools, little Ivy League universities such as Williams, Wesleyan, and Middlebury, and top business schools like those at the universities at Stanford, Harvard, and Wharton. They had a different mind-set from the blacks of my generation and probably were better able to float between white and black cultures. Many were very pro-black, but unlike my generation, they did not wear it on their sleeve. And they were ambitious— very, very ambitious.

As a group, they were sensitive to the events occurring around them in our society, especially the civil rights movement. But collectively, I felt they were more focused on career, status, and money much more than my generation. Many were the first in their families to graduate, and although they would occasionally demonstrate their blackness, as with historic sit-ins at Cornell and Harvard, it seemed they easily integrated themselves onto the Ivy campuses.

Over the years, I noticed a significantly different attitude from the Ivy League graduates than with the graduates of historically black colleges and universities (HBCUs). Students from schools such as Morehouse, Howard, Hampton, and Florida A&M had more of an edge and an ongoing personal commitment to the civil rights movement. They were deeply involved with the

Greek sororities and fraternities on their campuses. I've always thought one of the many reasons they were different was they were still living in the South. Although there had been progress in the fifties and sixties, the South had not changed that much. The South in the sixties was a very challenging place to live, which created an environment that led to significant bonding on campuses among black students. That is not to say that going to school in the North was not equally challenging. I will never forget an incident when I was at Grinnell when a black student was demonstrating on the steps of a federal courthouse in Boston as a protest in support of integration within the Boston school system. A white student carrying an American flag approached the black student and impaled him with the flagpole. These were isolated incidents, but for blacks studying at HBCUs, the mere fact they were living in certain communities in the South meant their lives were threatened. Interacting with the next generations from both northern and southern universities through Peter was exciting, motivational, and educational. I believe for Peter the same was true, because from me he would hear the stories of black migration and discrimination prior to the civil rights movement.

Peter and I were a good team. Working together, we could produce McKinsey quality reports and recruit talented professionals, irrespective of color. During the early years, we focused most of our activities in the Chicago area, producing reports for Mayor Richard J. Daley and executives in his administration. On one of our first assignments, we were asked to merge two city agencies with the same mission. It was a difficult assignment because each was led by two of the mayor's favorite black local civil servants. When we completed the work, I was asked to meet with the mayor. He thanked me for producing a first-rate document and ended the meeting by saying, "Jim, I knew you had rocks in your jaws." I did not know whether I did, in fact, have rocks in my jaws, but I knew our recommendations were valid because the two departments were providing duplicate services.

Over the next couple of years, I was often invited to attend black-tie events hosted by the mayor. Although I would never say I was part of the mayor's inner circle, over time I came to believe there was a certain degree of mutual respect between the mayor and myself. When I was introduced to the mayor, he was in his late sixties and had mellowed somewhat from his infamous days of rants and tyranny in the corridors of city hall, but he still had quite a temper. He was gentler in style but was still the super-tough boss on the fifth floor, not to be messed with. I remember once at a press conference with the mayor, a reporter questioned him on why his son Michael was given the contract to provide insurance services for the city. The mayor replied, in a quiet voice, "Soon I will be meeting my maker. When that day comes, no one will say I didn't support my family. I hope this answer satisfies you, but if it doesn't, I also have some mistletoe that I can put behind me, and you know what you can kiss."

Soon after receiving my first contract with the mayor, he died. I think I was surprised at how saddened I was by his death. I did not always agree with the mayor or his policies. I believe many of his policies led to a very segregated Chicago in more ways than one, but I will always be grateful to him for motivating me to be an entrepreneur and facilitating my acceptance with Chicago power brokers, both in government and the larger Chicago business community. In Chicago, you are either in, or you are out. If you are in, you are connected, and you have access to power in this big city that often operates more like a small, closely integrated town.

At times, I had some very enlightening experiences, which were also very uncomfortable. One I will never forget was the time I was the only black in a room of thousands at the annual Irish Fellowship Dinner. I was invited to the dinner by a couple of dear friends, who some fifty years later are still friends today, and they happened to be Irish. Viewing over a thousand Irishmen in one room enjoying life and doing deals had a tremendous impact on me. There was limited dancing, no cries of how poorly the world was treating the Irish or how they were being held down. Instead, a thousand Irishmen spent that time solidifying their power, developing mutual beneficial plans, and focusing on creating wealth for themselves, their families, and other Irishmen. I never went to another Irish Fellowship Dinner, but the image of this event stayed with me for years.

When I started my company in 1975, there were very few Republicans in Chicago. There were many national Republicans, but in Chicago, there were very few. This has not changed in forty-one years. As a result, Chicago is a city that tends to work well for those with clout, irrespective of national party affiliation. Unfortunately for the nonplayers, Chicago can be a very tough place to live. Although my sponsor had died, I had established relationships with many who were part of the inner circle. For me, the most important and supportive were four men who made up the core of Chicago's black leadership and who had been the mayor's trusted advisors. They were state Senator Cecil Partee, who had been elected to the House of Representatives in 1966; the extremely smooth Alderman Wilson Frost, who had begun his political career in Chicago in 1967 after he became the alderman of the Twenty-First Ward; city comptroller Clark Burrus, who later went on to serve as the board chair of the Chicago Transit Authority and C-suite executive at First National Bank; and ward committeeman Earl Neal, an attorney and founder of the prominent, Chicago-based law firm Earl L. Neal and Associates. These men were very powerful and caring leaders who, with diplomatic skills and moral conviction, maintained their power with the fifth floor, while at the same time fighting for the minority community. For Peter and me, that meant successfully competing for city consulting contracts. They each played a significant role in our success. For example, as the city comptroller, Clark Burrus always ensured our invoices were paid rapidly, so we never had to go into debt. I often asked why we received this quality support from them. We had been working in Chicago for only a short period, and we were not ward politicians. Before Earl Neal died, he gave me the answer. For them, we were the next generation. We demonstrated that we cared for the community, and we did excellent work.

Young Jim (age 3) and
brother, Bill (age 7) in
Woodlawn (1942)

Enjoying Jackson Park with
mother, Camille (1947)

Grinnell College basketball team (1960)

Sargent Shriver and I in Puerto Rico during my
time working at Outward Bound (1963)

Senator Robert F. Kennedy was an inspiration and friend (1964)

Speaking to the residents of Bedford-Stuyvesant in my
early days as a community organizer at the Bedford
Stuyvesant Restoration Corporation (1966)

My elegant mother attended many events with me over the years (1971)

Nettie holding our beautiful daughter Camille (1972)

My daughter Camille Aisha (age 5) and my motivation for success (1976)

Meeting at the Department of Commerce with Dan Henson, Congressman Parren Mitchell and Eddie Williams (1979)

At the Urban League Dinner with Jesse Jackson (1980)

Cindy Pritzker has been a true friend and confidante for many years (1982)

Joe Anderson (1983)

Peter Stroh and Roger
Friedholm (1986)

BCG President Carl
Stern (2000)

Backstage with John Legend (2005)

My daughter Camille
accompanied me to the ELC
Recognition Gala (2017)

Matt Krentz honoring me at my
retirement party from, Boston
Consulting Group (2010)

Receiving the Alvaro L. Martins Award at the Executive
Leadership Council 2017 Recognition Gala, with John
Legend, and BCG partners Joe Davis and Justin Dean

CHAPTER 10

JHLA GROWTH THROUGH GOVERNMENT CONTRACTS

To date, Chicago had been the focus of our business. But that all changed one day when a young West Point graduate by the name of Joe Anderson[41] came into our office. Joe had been an infantry officer in the Eighty-Second Airborne Division of the US Army and was a White House Fellow assigned to the Department of Commerce working under Juanita Kreps, then secretary of commerce. Evidently, for over a year within the department, they had multiple task forces address the issue of how to grow minority business enterprises. Despite the many hours invested, there had been very little produced and no final report. At the urging of then White House aide Larry Bailey, Joe Anderson reached out to me. Joe was very direct and told me that within thirty days, Secretary Kreps was going to visit Chicago as a guest of the Chicago business community and wanted to have a forum to discuss minority business enterprise development. He asked me to organize a group of minority leaders to attend and prepare a slide presentation on the topic for Secretary Kreps.

---

[41] Joe Anderson currently serves as the chairman of the board and CEO of TAG Holdings, LLC. Prior to beginning a career in business, Anderson served two tours in the Vietnam War. He received a BS from the United States Military Academy.

Before I replied, I remembered the advice one of my McKinsey associates and partner, Leo Mullin, once said to me, "Jim, you only get ten major opportunities in your professional career, but 10 percent of the people are not smart enough to realize what they are. And of the 10 percent who do, only 10 percent can exploit the opportunity." I realized this was one of those opportunities for me, and I intended to be in that 10 percent to exploit it.

I took all my savings and produced a quality, fact-based slide presentation. Next, I reached out to friends and allies to convene a breakfast meeting at the First National Bank of Chicago. Obviously, the presentation impressed Secretary Kreps, because she invited me to Washington, DC, to meet with her senior policy advisor, Assistant Secretary Jerry Jasinowski, to outline how JHLA could assist the Department of Commerce in developing the federal government's strategy for minority business enterprise development. After an hour, he asked me to prepare a formal proposal.

When I presented my initial proposal to Assistant Secretary Jasinowski, he said he was disappointed. He said he had heard great things about me from Joe Anderson and Secretary Kreps but thought my proposal lacked substance. It was at this point I knew I had made a major mistake. I had spent hours making it look like a McKinsey document, but I did not address the issues. The criticism may have bruised my ego, but reading my proposal, I had to accept he was right. I asked him for another opportunity and that if he would accept a handwritten draft (I could not type and time was critical), I would resubmit a new proposal within twenty-four hours. That night from my hotel room, I produced a new proposal where I outlined the issues, developed my hypothesis, and presented him with a course of action with projected benefits for his department and the nation. When he read the new proposal, he told me that this was what he was expecting, and said, "I'll give you $90,000, including fees and expenses, and you have three months to produce the report."

Accepting Leo Mullin's sage advice, for the next three months I dedicated my life to preparing the first major federal government strategy for minority business enterprise development. This is not to say that previous administrations had not done a lot in this space. Under the dynamic leadership of President Nixon's special assistant Bob Brown, a native of North Carolina, the Nixon administration had created many organizations and had passed numerous laws focusing on the growth of minority business enterprise, but there was never a written and comprehensive federal strategy.

I had to work fast to develop the plan of action. The first thing I did was organize a team that would be based primarily in Washington. Obviously, Peter was going to be the team leader. I also asked my nephew Glen Loury[42] to join us. Glen, with his PhD from MIT, had just been given an endowed chair at Harvard University in the Economics Department. Although he was a distinguished economist, he had a keen interest in community development. I also recruited Paul Pride, a true black Washington insider with expertise in international finance. To complete the team, Peter recruited Liz Harris-Dugger and George Price, two Harvard Business School alums. We didn't have much of a budget, but we did have the support of the secretary of commerce, and so, with rocks in our jaws, my team and I set out to make history.

While I depended on Peter's writing skills to assist me, he still had to run the Chicago office, a responsibility he energetically accepted because he had just started dating a gorgeous Playboy Bunny who was studying to be a lawyer in Chicago. So, with my core team in DC, we conducted our research, interviewing more than a hundred business and civic leaders. Every night, I would

---

[42] Glen's father, Everett Lowry, legally changed his name from Lowry to Loury in his twenties.

retreat to my room at the Cosmos Club,[43] and with my interview notes and notepad, I would draft the report. While conducting my research, I was fortunate to work with brilliant minds like Professor Dick America, graduate of and professor at Harvard University; Professor Al Osborne, the former senior associate dean at UCLA Anderson School of Management; Dan Henson, who was the head of the Office of Minority Business Enterprise (OMBE); and Major Clark, who was the assistant general counsel for procurement policy for the SBA. However, the person who had the greatest impact on my thinking was Congressman Parren Mitchell.

Parren Mitchell was a strong advocate of minority business enterprise development, sponsoring much of the legislation that accelerated the growth in that industry, thus changing our society. Growing up black and poor in Maryland, his father a waiter, Parren was just eleven years old when he and his older brother Clarence witnessed a black person lynched. Parren made a promise he would devote his life to fighting for the rights of African Americans. He was an outstanding black leader and a credit to our country. Many of the laws and policies affecting minority business enterprise development were authored by Congressman Parren Mitchell.

During this period, I was introduced to Washington political and civic business leadership by my old friend Ron Brown from Bedford-Stuyvesant. Ron was the deputy executive director for programs and governmental affairs of the National Urban League in DC, and in the late seventies, a top officer working with the Urban League's then president Vernon Jordan. The two of them had elevated the Urban League to new heights of national prominence and economic prosperity. With Ron running the

---

[43] The Cosmos Club is a legendary private social club located in Washington, DC. Notable members include John Hope Franklin, Theodore Roosevelt, and Woodrow Wilson.

DC office, the Urban League was able to influence policy holders in very effective ways and safeguard the interests of black communities. However, it was Vernon Jordan who made the Urban League a national organization, carrying considerable clout with major foundations and large corporations. They were both world-class pioneers, utilizing charm, smarts, and style to increase the Urban League's outreach and budget. The Urban League under Vernon Jordan was a favorite of the Ford Foundation, and it was said the Urban League had a line item in the Ford Foundation's annual budget. With its annual contribution from the Ford Foundation, the League was able to distance itself from other civil rights organizations.

I have often wondered why Ron and Vernon were so successful at the Urban League and then later in their respective careers, Ron as head of the Democratic Party and Vernon a highly successful lawyer, investment banker, corporate board member, and advisor to presidents. I know there were many reasons, but I feel one of the most important was they were both trailblazers at small liberal arts colleges, Ron at Middlebury College and Vernon at DePauw University. Both were college leaders, and they were among the few blacks on campus. Neither was intimidated by working with, and diplomatically confronting, whites. They got it out of their systems early while in college. Both Ron and Vernon had the gift of being able to light up a room when they entered, work the crowd, and quickly discern the powerful from the powerless. Still, when they met people, they made everyone feel they were important. Ron later became the secretary of commerce. He died tragically in a plane crash in 1996 while on an official trade mission to Croatia.

In addition to our limited budget, we had a very tight deadline, so we leveraged every available minute we had. I knew our findings and recommendations had to be tight and persuasive to protect the firm from potential political attacks. Utilizing an approach that I learned at McKinsey, called the Minto Pyramid Principle,[44] I crafted a report that was clear, logical, fact based, and in a format that could be easily followed by a Harvard Business School professor, as well as the beautician who did my mother's hair.

We established early in the report that racial discrimination might be a factor, but there were other challenges that prevented minorities from achieving economic progress. We concluded that to achieve this goal of economic parity by the year 2000, it was necessary to address the fact that historically, minority businesses had been unable to gain access to (i) the nation's markets, (ii) capital, and (iii) managerial skills. Once again, utilizing my McKinsey training, I decided I would devote 30 percent of the report to defining the problem and 70 percent to the recommendations on how to effect change." I have used the same approach my entire career, accepting that most people can define the problem, but few have the talent, skill, and motivation to solve the problem.

It became clear pretty quickly that the budget was too small to retain my team for the full three months, so for the last month of the project, I was forced to complete the document by myself with the help of an ex-McKinsey editor, Jane Pogeler. This partnership was highlighted in the book *Business Communication Today*, published by Random House in a chapter titled "Gathering, Organizing and Interpreting Information." When the final report was completed, titled, *A New Strategy for Minority Business Enterprise Development*,[45]

---

[44] The Minto Pyramid Principle, created by Harvard MBA grad Barbara Minto, "refers to a process for organizing your thinking so that it jumps easily off the page to lodge in a reader's mind. It notes that people ideally work out their thinking by creating pyramids of ideas (i) grouping together low-level facts they see as similar; (ii) drawing an insight from having seen the similarity; and (iii) forming a new grouping of related insights, etc."
[45] James H. Lowry & Associates, *A New Strategy for Minority Business Enterprise Development*. United States Department of Commerce report (1978).

it was positively received by Jerry Jasinowski, Secretary Juanita Kreps, and Under Secretary Sidney Harmon. They completely embraced the report and asked Joe Anderson to bring in Hispanic and black leaders from all over the country, including my old friend Earl Graves, so we could present our findings. Joe did an outstanding job of organizing the event, and my presentation was well received by the majority of the attendees. With the support of the group, the Department of Commerce developed and carried out a national public relations strategy.

The first order of business was changing the name of the agency. Immediately the OMBE was now the Minority Business Development Agency (MBDA). The Department of Commerce implemented most of the report's major recommendations:

- *Produce a solid base of minority entrepreneurs and managers.* Unless there is a solid core of capable entrepreneurs/ managers, MBED cannot occur. The managers develop the deals, insights, and innovative approaches that start the development process.
- *Maximize the leverage of limited government funds.* Because of past inequities, nearly all minority businesses need some type of government assistance. However, the federal government has a limited amount of human and financial resources to allocate to MBED. As such, these funds must be allocated in a manner that obtains the highest return and provides the greatest potential for attracting private sector support.
- *Increase private investment in minority-owned and operated firms.* Although the federal government is taking the leadership role in MBED, the greatest source of manpower and capital is the private sector. The extent to which private sector becomes committed to MBED will be the measure of its success.

- *Increase the number of medium- and large-sized MBEs.* It is not enough to increase the number of MBEs. Quality is just as important as quantity, if not more so, in terms of effecting change. Economies of scale, mass advertising, material distribution, and heavy research and development are competitive advantages that only accrue to firms of substantial size. To be competitive, MBEs must adopt the profiles of their competitors.
- *Gain greater access for MBEs to the largest markets in the world.* The keys to growth are profits, asset base, and return on investment. As long as MBEs continue to market their products to limited markets, they will experience limited growth and success. MBEs must not be limited to the markets where they are located. They must penetrate the majority, international, and government markets where there is real purchasing power.

One of the additional key recommendations was to utilize majority consulting and financial services firms to provide technical assistance to MBEs. This was somewhat controversial because, in essence, a large part of MBDA's new budget would go to large consulting firms instead of community organizations who had previously received such funding. This was painful for me, but our research told us the community organizations were not effectively providing the necessary advisory support to MBEs.

During this period, the Carter Administration demonstrated its commitment to minority business by increasing the budget of the new MBDA to $80 million, with increased dollar allocations to regional offices, allowing for the creation of many new programs. It has saddened me to observe how this budget has been reduced from $80 million to $40 million over a thirty-seven-year period under both Republican and Democratic administrations. A $40 million budget[46] severely limits the capacity of the MBDA to provide the needed resources to accelerate the growth of MBE development.

Our report for the Department of Commerce, with its aggressive public relations campaign, officially put JHLA on the map. Before the report, we were a well-respected, small, local, struggling business. But with the report's national press coverage, our firm grew from five to fifty-five overnight, with offices in Chicago, DC, and Oakland. I have to share one funny incident that occurred after the report was published. Secretary Kreps received a letter from Dr. Edward Irons,[47] dean of the business school at Clark-Atlanta University. Dr. Irons's career was rife with stories of discrimination and roadblocks. After attending Attucks High School, Irons was drafted into the navy, and while recovering from rheumatic fever in a VA hospital, he and several other patients organized a sit-in to protest segregation in the hospital. He earned a PhD from Harvard, where he studied the banking industry. In 1964, he and his partners opened Riverside National Bank in Houston, Texas, the first bank given a charter to African Americans in forty years.

In the letter to Kreps, he wrote asking her how she could have contracted a white firm to prepare this important document on MBED. In response to his letter, I had to explain that JHLA was indeed a black-owned firm and I owned 100 percent of the stock. Also, I proudly informed him the firm was comprised of five members, three with Harvard Business School degrees, one with a doctorate from MIT who had an endowed chair at Harvard, and they were all black. Later, I became a friend of Dr. Irons, a

---

[46] The current administration has proposed a FY2020 budget for MBDA of $10,000,000.00.

[47] Dr. Edward Irons also worked for USAID and served as the founding dean of Howard University's business school. After leaving Howard, he worked as a consultant to dozens of organizations around the globe.

person I highly admired because of his brilliant academic record, his research, and commitment to educating his students on the importance of economics in our community.

Between 1978 and 1980, we conducted various studies for the SBA, the Department of Labor, Toyota Motor Engineering & Manufacturing North America, Inc. (TEMA), and the Department of Commerce. In 1979, we were asked by the Department of Commerce to expand our original study and to go into greater detail and specificity on various growth industries. To do a truly comprehensive analysis, they increased our budget from $90,000 to $500,000. This contract was a seal of approval and expression of trust from the decision makers in the department. As one would imagine, I also greatly appreciated the increase in our budget, because I realized the magnitude of the task and the need to increase the size of the team. We were told to start working immediately because they wanted a final draft by the fall of 1980.

Once again, I recruited a top-flight team. One of the new members was a young professor from Howard University, Dr. Barron Harvey. Barron was the first black to obtain a PhD in business from the University of Nebraska at Lincoln. He later became the dean of Howard University's Business School and founded Harvey & Co., one of the first minority consulting firms to have international clients. Others who joined the team were Claudio Barriga, Peter Morris, Walter Ross, Charles Stevenson, Michael Meyer, Toye Lee Lewis, James Lancaster, Kenneth Tatum, and of course, Peter Bynoe.

Unfortunately, although the team was working extremely fast, we could not meet our early fall deadline. Around this same time, Jimmy Carter lost the presidential election to Ronald Reagan. Since my only focus was to produce an excellent document, the Carter loss did not bother me. I thought to myself, if President Nixon and Bob Brown had put in place many of the MBE programs thus far, then these leaders of the Reagan administration would likewise embrace and support the study. I would later learn I was wrong and naïve on both accounts. We continued our work in DC, but now my CFO and Chicago team were tasked with working with the Department of Commerce to document how we utilized funds on both these studies. I had never heard of or been exposed to a "pre-award audit." Up to this point, we had just been granted extensions to our existing contracts. After their initial review, the auditor informed us that they would not approve our $500,000 contract. When I met with the chief auditor, I remember clearly what he said, "Mr. Lowry, our audit has shown that there was no mismanagement or misuse of funds. We just do not like the way your firm collected the data." I saw my life and my company being destroyed because I had already paid my team $180,000 out of my own pocket. This was a lot of money at the time (and still is today, especially for a small, growing business). The interesting thing for me was I had used the same expense sheets and data collection process as McKinsey. I thought, if these were good enough for McKinsey, it would be good enough for the federal auditors.

I was at a critical juncture and knew I had to be a problem solver or else I was going to lose my contract and my firm. Since Juanita Kreps had retired and returned to her home in North Carolina, the first thing I did was go to the new secretary of commerce, Phillip Klutznick, a brilliant entrepreneur from Chicago who was the former commissioner of the Federal Public Housing Authority. I had previously met Secretary Klutznick through the Pritzkers. He was cordial but straight to the point when he said, "Jim, you should not have started the work without a signed contract." I told him it was the top decision makers at the Department of Commerce who asked me to start the work. He candidly replied, "Jim, I'm sorry, but you learned an invaluable lesson in business. Do not start any work without a signed contract."

Facing the loss of the contract, my recently recruited staff, and my $180,000, I persisted in seeking an answer to my critical problem. One day I got a call from the secretary saying there might be a way for me to save my contract. His suggestion was to have Dan Henson present my case to the Republican transition team for the Department of Commerce. I learned again that it was sometimes better to be lucky than smart. Dan Henson was very direct and, I'm told, gave a very persuasive and compelling argument. His plea was not initially well received, and this is where the luck came in. The head of the team, Cal Collier, asked whether this was the same James H. Lowry that attended Grinnell College. It turns out that Cal was the 1964 first baseman for Grinnell's men's baseball team. Dan responded that he believed so. Cal then told Dan that Jim Lowry was one of the most outstanding athletes in the history of Grinnell and that we had both played baseball there together. And just like that, I had a meeting with Cal, during which he presented a compromise solution. He asked me to hire a top-flight accounting firm to redesign my accounting system and accept a new budget of $250,000. Considering I had no other option, I did not hesitate to accept his recommendation.

Facing a tough late-fall deadline with only $70,000 left in the budget, I had no choice but to return to the Cosmos Club and write the report myself. This time, Peter disengaged himself from work in Chicago long enough to contribute his truly exceptional writing skills, and with his help, we completed the contract on time. We crafted the new report with a backdrop of the new administration and recommendations, and we titled it *Minority Business Enterprise Development in the 1980s*.[48] We had hoped that we would get the same type of public recognition from the Department of Commerce that we received when we wrote the initial report. Unfortunately, this was not the case. In fact, it

---

[48] James H. Lowry & Associates, *Minority Business Enterprise Development in the 1980s* report (1980).

was just the opposite. One day, I received in a plain envelope a copy of a memorandum from a secretary in the Department of Commerce. It was authored by the number two person in the MBDA, advising his directors to "bury the Lowry report." I could not believe it. With respect to depth of analysis and quality of writing, this second report was far better than the first. It is telling that a few years ago, JHLA alumna Judy Mathews pointed out to me, "It's 2015, and the things you said in the 1978 and 1980 reports are just as valid today as they were then; we just never implemented your recommendations."

JHLA grew dramatically between 1978 and 1982 as a result of our work with the federal government, our 8(a) status, and an SBA loan. We were often rated *the* consulting firm of choice and *the* place to work. I believe the major reason for our success was the quality of our work and the outstanding commitment of the JHLA professional staff. With respect to the latter, I invested a lot of time and money to recruit the most qualified professionals I could find. We took great pride in our work, our analysis was thorough, and every report looked more professional than the next. Our work was McKinsey quality, with storylines that either persuaded or dissuaded our client to action. We sought and achieved repeat business with every client during this period. Even under a Republican Administration, we were able to do a lot of work with the various federal agencies.

As we became better known in the DC area, we were assisted in our recruiting efforts by Peter Bynoe's network of friends, Ron Brown, Pat Jacobs, and JoAnn Price.[49] Pat and JoAnn were constantly sending us the best and the brightest with the mantra,

---

[49] With Pat Jacobs (president) and JoAnn Price (deputy director) at the helm of the American Association of MESBICS (Minority Enterprise Small Business Investment Companies), we began a campaign of advocacy and support for its members with the Small Business Administration (which then issued SBIC licenses and regulated most of the investment companies).

"Train and treat our young, gifted professionals well." Price went on to cofound the notable investment management company, Fairview Capital. Under her leadership, Fairview Capital is one of the nation's largest minority investment firms, with $2.4 billion invested.

My life at that time was one of constant travel between our offices in DC, San Francisco, and Chicago. Our number one priority was to design state-of-the-art models to effect change; we were not merely focused on making money or increasing sales. Our growing reputation as a first-class consulting firm was enhanced by the size of our contracts and the tough issues we were forced to address during the fast-moving times of the seventies. For example, in 1979, we were asked to assist the Department of Labor determine the viability of intermediate nonprofit corporations for youth programs. The decision makers realized it was beyond the capacity of that department's resources to continue to provide such programming and much-needed training to youths in need. They asked us to design a strategy to increase the participation and support by private sector and nonprofit corporations. The Department of Commerce was dealing with major problems facing small and minority business—namely, lack of capital and credit. We helped them design an experimental credit model to enhance credit opportunities for minority business owners.

A couple of the most rewarding contracts we received were awarded by the Peace Corps. The first one in 1980 assisted the leaders of the Peace Corps in redesigning a program to improve how information was collected, executed, and disseminated around the world. In carrying out this work, I had the pleasure of again returning to Africa, this time visiting Sierra Leone, Ivory Coast, and Liberia. Later that year, we won a contract to conduct an in-country training project in Santiago, Chile. The work took place seven years after the 1973 coup d'état. We won the contract mainly through the hard work of ex-Peace Corps volunteer Ed

Howard.[50] Ed Howard was very helpful in aggressively obtaining and managing the Peace Corps study. He was a solid performer, but unfortunately, he had a drinking problem, which forced me to fire him. After JHLA, he got a job with the State Department and later the CIA. In 1983, he was forced to resign from the CIA after failing a polygraph test about petty theft and drug use. Howard was reported to have sold information to Soviet agents in Austria in 1984. He turned up in Moscow in 1985 and was granted political asylum on August 7, 1986. A number of American diplomats were expelled from the Soviet Union as a result of information he provided. Author David Wise wrote about it in 1988 in his book *The Spy Who Got Away*, mentioning that he had worked for JHLA. I will never stop asking myself, "Why didn't the State Department or CIA ever contact me for a reference check on Ed Howard?" I would have told them he was an alcoholic, and although a hard worker, he had low self-esteem and would be a risk to hire. Maybe if they had reached out to me, I might have saved global embarrassment to them and the American lives he exposed. Ed Howard died on July 12, 2002, at the age of fifty-one under mysterious circumstances with a broken neck from a fall in his Russian home.

Despite all his problems, Ed did initially help me tremendously. It was challenging having to travel to South America every other month while still managing my team in Chicago. This time it was not a language problem; it was a cultural problem. By law, I was required to hire Chileans, and Ed warned me that these Chileans did not like the idea they would have to report to an African American. When I got off the plane, I was met with a certain degree of coldness, to put it mildly. But I accepted this

[50] Ed Howard served as a Peace Corps volunteer in Bucaramanga, Colombia. In 1995, Howard published his book, *Safe House: The Compelling Story of the Only CIA Operative to Seek Asylum in Russia,* where he discusses his time with the CIA and his innocence.

challenge like any other, and I am proud to say when I left, I received many gifts of goodwill and was given a gracious and quite grand farewell party by my Chilean staff.

During the same year, the Department of Education asked us to conduct a two-year survey of the magnet school experiment.[51] The report, *Survey of Magnet Schools: Analyzing a Model for Quality Integrated Education*, responded to the Department of Education's request for a comprehensive, national survey of the effectiveness of magnet schools in improving public education quality and assisting school desegregation. JHLA found that there was an importance of principal leadership in the design of magnet schools and selection of staff. We concluded that in those districts with very effective programs, central district curriculum staff were involved in school design and staff selection, but the programs also had strong leadership from principals and gave teachers the opportunity to contribute in shaping the program.

In 1981, the SBA engaged us to conduct a comprehensive analysis of potential procurement opportunities for minority businesses. I had recently hired an extremely smart technical consultant to design a computer model to gather data. We were able to obtain a complete record of total federal government procurement, something that had never been done before with such specificity. We segmented information into categories: (1) Defense- repeat spend, (2) Defense- non-repeat spend, (3) Non-Defense- repeat spend, and (4) Non-Defense- non-repeat spend. We then used SIC codes[52] to calculate opportunities for

---

[51] James H. Lowry & Associates, *Survey of Magnet Schools: Analyzing a Model for Quality Integrated Education*, report (1983).

[52] Standard Industrial Classification (SIC) Codes are a standard series of four-digit codes created by the US government in 1937 for categorizing business activities. In 1997, the use of SIC codes was replaced in most (but not all) capacities by a six-digit code called the North American Industry Classification System (NAICS).

existing MBEs. There were thousands of budget items minorities had never taken advantage of, and many were billion-dollar opportunities. The largest opportunity was armament products. We carried out those studies, projects, and surveys at the highest level of quality.

Historical Background 1981–1990

Harold Washington became the first black mayor of Chicago in 1983, and Vanessa Williams became the first African American to win the title of Miss America in 1984.

This was also a time when there was the biggest surge in the use of crack cocaine. In 1985, the number of people who admitted using cocaine on a routine basis increased from 4.2 million to 5.8 million. The motto "Just Say No" was the tool to combat the growing use of drugs in the US, but it was obvious to the man on the street mere slogans were not going to be the answer to growing and complex problems of drug addiction.

- Bobby Rush, former Black Panther, was elected to the Chicago City Council.
- 1981: Ronald Reagan became president.
- 1982: Congressman Parren Mitchell worked to amend the $71 billion Surface Transportation Assistance Act to include a 10 percent set-aside for minority contractors.
- 1983: President Reagan signed the Executive Order 12432,[53] which required all federal agencies to develop specific goal-oriented plans for expanding procurement opportunities to minority businesses.
- 1985: US Congressman Parren Mitchell introduced H.R. 1961, which established criminal penalties for front companies that had taken advantage of minority programs, such as receiving an 8(a) contract, a small business set-aside, a subcontract awarded under the Section 8(d) subcontracting plan, or a contract awarded under the 10 percent set-aside of the Surface Transportation Assistance Act of 1982.

---

[53] Exec. Order No. 12432 (1983), 48 FR 33227.

- America celebrated Martin Luther King Day as a national holiday for the first time in 1986.
- 1986: President Reagan signed the Anti-Drug Abuse Act,[54] which was a "War on Drugs" bill that raised mandatory minimum sentences and disproportionally affected African Americans.
- 1986: In the case of *Wygant v. Jackson Board of Education*,[55] the Supreme Court ruled against a school board policy that protected minority employees by laying off nonminority teachers first, even though the nonminority employees had seniority. The high court reasoned, "Though hiring goals may burdensome innocent individuals, they simply do not impose the same kind of injury that layoffs impose. Denial of a future employment opportunity is not as intrusive as loss of an existing job."
- 1988: George H.W. Bush is elected president.
- 1989: Ron Brown became the first African American chairman of the Democratic National Committee.
- 1990: Douglas Wilder was elected governor of Virginia, making him the first black to win the popular vote for governorship.

---

[54] H.R. 5484 (99th), Pub.L. 99-570 (1986).

[55] *Wygant v. Jackson Board of Education*, 476 U.S. 267 (1986).

CHAPTER 11

A BETTER CHANCE AND TRANSITIONING TO THE PRIVATE SECTOR

Admittedly, I was a very tough taskmaster, perhaps too tough. I wish I had been wiser in my interactions with Peter and others, but deep down I believed I pushed them because I wanted them to be the best consultants and professionals they could be. I did not care how many Ivy League degrees my staff member had if their work did not meet the standards I demanded, and too often, I let that show. I let them know in no uncertain terms when I was not satisfied. In hindsight, I was probably too insensitive to the unique strengths of each staff member. I just did not accept excuses. I do not accept them now. I have always felt that excuses are for losers. Still, I should have been more sensitive and forgiving in my management style. I also did not recognize that I was under a tremendous amount of personal stress, and too often I was releasing my stress on the staff.

My rapid rise to fame was taking a toll on me physically and psychologically. I was constantly on planes, selling work, and managing many of the projects I sold. I had zero balance in my life. Not surprisingly, this took a toll on my marriage to Nettie, and unfortunately, divorce soon followed. No divorce is pleasant, but we both went out of our way to ensure it was amicable for the sake of our daughter, which is a testament to Nettie's character. Nettie chose to move to the Bay Area in California, so without hesitation, I opened up an office in Oakland, California, to be near my daughter, Camille. I made a personal vow to always be a loving friend to both of them and a supportive father for the rest of our lives. With respect to my married life, I have many regrets, yet I am proud of the fact Nettie and I worked together to raise our daughter, Camille, as best we could.

I was enjoying the success of JHLA, but I realized it came at the price of being irritable, extremely insensitive, and shortsighted. This was particularly true with Peter, who at that time was like my younger brother and number one mentee. Peter was smart, had his own style, and was highly effective with people. After he left JHLA, he went on to have a brilliant legal and business career and serve on numerous boards. He founded his own consulting firm; was formerly the only African American equity partner at DLA Piper; and in 1989, Bynoe, with his partner and friend Bertram Lee, purchased a stake in the Denver Nuggets, becoming the first African Americans to own an NBA franchise, opening the door for other minorities in sports management and development. Despite mistakes I may have made with him, he still greets me warmly whenever our paths cross.

I am extremely proud of my team for the work they produced, for the fun we enjoyed, and most importantly, for the success they achieved after leaving JHLA. Over the years, I often run into them at civic or political events, and in one way or another, they say, "Lowry, you were a tough SOB, but you helped me grow as a professional." Hearing them say this always brings a smile to my face and at the same time gives me a true sense of achievement. Making money, while rewarding, was never my number one priority. Effecting change and mentoring others were the goals that motivated me throughout my career.

In late 1981, I received a call from William Boyd II. At the time, William was the president of an organization called A Better Chance. A Better Chance was founded at Dartmouth College in 1963. In response to the turbulent times of the sixties, the headmasters at sixteen elite schools designed and started a program to identify and educate talented minority students. The first class of A Better Chance students consisted of fifty-five boys, and the vast majority were black.

For the first time, these prep schools allowed very smart and highly motivated young black students from the inner city to attend the same historic and prestigious secondary schools alongside kids from the country's richest and most powerful families—schools that educated students with last names like Roosevelt, Kennedy, Rockefeller, and Bush. The program was lauded for its vision, boldness, and in some cases for its courage. With respect to the latter, there were wealthy parents and donors who did not appreciate the schools opening their doors for the inner-city blacks and Latinos; the seats in the classroom were too few and too valuable to be given away to kids from the projects.

Initially, the program got off to a strong start, with only a few minor challenges. The program was praised in educational circles and became the source of recruitment for Ivy and little Ivy League schools on the East Coast. But after twenty years of existence, the program began to have some serious problems. It was at this time that JHLA received a call from Boyd, asking if we would be willing to conduct a short diagnostic study of the organization and make some recommendations to the board of trustees. Working with Dr. Sharon Collins, a sociology professor from the University of Illinois at Chicago, we interviewed more than twenty staff members and board members. We presented our findings and recommendations in a thirty-one-page report titled *Improving the Overall Effectiveness of A Better Chance in a Changing Environment*. We ended the report by saying, "Unless radical changes are made, A Better Chance, as an institution, will suffer irreparable damage." The powerful impact of our report was highlighted in the book titled *Black and White Elite, Will the Progress Continue?*[56] The board accepted our specific recommendations, and soon after, Boyd left to become a vice president at the World Institute for Computer Training. He later taught at City University of New York before serving as the first chief executive officer of the Educational Policy Center.

After completing our study, the board asked me to conduct an executive search for Boyd's successor. By this time, I had become a strong advocate of A Better Chance, and I truly admired the leadership of the program and the board for handpicking very smart black students from low-income communities to travel to New England to attend these elite schools. Obviously, from my personal experience, I could appreciate the value of attending an elite school. I admired those young students. Unlike me, they were asked to leave their families and communities to live for four years in isolated New England towns; but like me, they suddenly found themselves in classrooms competing with students who had been reading Shakespeare, Hemingway, and Chaucer since middle school.

Working again with Dr. Sharon Collins, we conducted a nationwide search for the next president of A Better Chance. One of the candidates I identified was Dr. Judith Berry Griffin, an old friend from Chicago and the University of Chicago Lab School. Judith's father was a distinguished Chicago physician, and I had known her quite well since the eighth grade and from Jack and Jill Clubs. After interviewing her, I knew she was the right person for the job. She had degrees from the University of Chicago and Columbia University, and she had just left the Carter administration, where she served as an executive assistant to the assistant secretary for elementary and secondary education. I told the headmaster she

---

[56] Richard L. Zweigenhaft and G. William Domhoff, *Black and White Elite, Will the Progress Continue?* (Roman & Littlefield, 2003).

was a strong person and would be an outstanding leader. She took
A Better Chance to new heights and was given a million-dollar
donation from Oprah Winfrey. After seven years, she left to start
Pathway to College to provide critically needed coaching from the
application through the financial aid process for students attending
targeted public schools and their families.

I will always consider the work we did for A Better Chance
as one of my favorite engagements for the quality of our work
and the lasting impact we made on generations to come. I take
great pride when I talk about the organization, reflecting on the
impact it has had on our society for the past fifty-three years.
Since it started in 1963, A Better Chance has grown to include
three hundred charter member schools and has educated more
than fourteen thousand students. Among their notable alumni
are Deval Patrick, ex-Massachusetts governor and partner at Bain
Capital; Steve Rogers, who was an esteemed professor at Harvard
Business School and Northwestern University's Kellogg School of
Management; singer/songwriter Tracy Chapman; Ford Foundation
President Luis Antonio *Ubiñas; Newsweek* national correspondent
Sylvester Monroe; and Bill Lewis, cochair of Investment Banking
at Lazard Freres & Co. And while not an alum of A Better Chance,
Raymond J. McGuire, cohead of Global Investment Banking at
Citigroup, had attended one of the charter member schools.

Over the years, I have gotten to know Deval Patrick and
witness the impact he had on the state of Massachusetts. He was
an early advisor and motivator for President Barack Obama and
up-and-coming elected officials such as Cory Booker. For twenty
years, I watched the brilliance of Professor Steve Rogers in the
classroom at Kellogg, where he was voted one of the top professors
year after year. Bill Lewis and Raymond J. McGuire are two of
the most powerful and effective bankers on Wall Street, and they
continue to reach back to help young professionals of color, while
at the same time bringing millions, if not billions, to shareholders

of the companies they serve. A Better Chance helped open the doors for them and so many more, leaving the nation better off because of that institution's boldness and vison.

When *Black Enterprise* prepared a special issue of the most powerful blacks on Wall Street, most of the executives were A Better Chance alumni. For me, A Better Chance was an affirmative action program that achieved its objectives, provided opportunities for deserving and talented students, and created a cadre of leaders who continue to contribute to our free enterprise system, making America competitive and great. While some may dispute the need, rationale, or fairness of affirmative action, A Better Chance is one example that proves affirmative action works. It was because of affirmative action that great leaders such as these were discovered, and their impact on our society continues to be significant.

As I indicated previously, I have always accepted I benefited from affirmative action. In 1991, *Reader's Digest* did a lead article authored by Rachael Flick, titled "Does Affirmative Action Really Work?" In the article, the author stated, "Its intent was to ensure that every American would have an equal chance at education and jobs. But affirmative action has moved from 'color blind' hiring to the pointed consideration of race. Those passed over have responded with anger and bitterness. This dissatisfaction, however, goes beyond those who feel they have been deprived of a job, a promotion or admission to a university. While many minority Americans continue to support affirmative action, others are uneasy about it. Some doubt the policy's success; some even are convinced it does great long-term harm."

In this article, I shared how I benefitted from affirmative action in the eighth grade in 1952. I was quoted saying, "I still believe in affirmative action. Racism is not as bad as when I was coming up. One reason is that affirmative action helped blacks move into every job and profession. There will always be those who will attach a stigma to people hired under affirmative action, so be it. Take the opportunity and then, so you can look yourself in the mirror, do the best you can."

The mistake people made is they evaluated the value on a near-term individual basis instead of looking at the potential value to institutions and society. The graduates of A Better Chance are a prime example that I was right.

While assisting A Better Chance and continuing my work with government agencies at all levels as the president of JHLA, I was seeking to get more private sector contracts. I will always be indebted to Secretary Juanita Kreps and Jerry Jasinowski for jump-starting my firm in terms of size and prominence, but the close call with the auditors convinced me that while working for the government might have allowed me to start my business, the private sector might offer a better and less political environment in which to operate. I had experienced firsthand how quickly your business can be taken away for political reasons, despite quality of service. I also realized that working almost exclusively for the federal government meant lower profit margins, so it was harder to stay afloat.

Facing these realizations, I decided to leverage the power of the brand, my high-quality staff, and the expertise we had developed to make our move into the private sector. The strategy worked, because I was able to expand the number and quality of my team, which allowed us to develop new products. I was able to heavily rely on my McKinsey network, leading to more top-level contacts in potential clients. And while I was still traveling from coast to coast, with the added support and cushion of bigger budgets, I was able to maintain my health and positive mental attitude. As I reflected on it, it is easy to see that the lion's share of my stress in those early days were caused by lack of cash flow. This lesson has been critical to my continued success.

Now committed to working in both the public and private sectors, my professional plans received a critical and unanticipated assist from Reverend Jesse Jackson. While JHLA was operating in the public sector, Rev. Jackson had started a national campaign to encourage large corporations to increase their procurement spending to minorities. Although not a legally binding contract, the concept he used to solidify this moral agreement was the Operation PUSH Covenant Agreement. The first Fortune 500 company to sign the one such covenant was Coca-Cola in 1981. President of Coca-Cola, Donald Keogh, and Rev. Jackson outlined the following agreements in the covenant to support minorities:

- Coke will appoint 32 black-owned distributorships and commit to their success;
- Coke will seek a black person to join their board of directors within a year;
- Coke will fill 12.5% of its management positions with blacks within a year;
- Coke will commit to filling 100 of its blue collar openings with blacks within a year;
- Coke will pledge to increase its deposits and loans with black-owned banks;
- Coke will give a black-owned advertising agency the responsibility for a company brand with a budget of $8 million; and,
- Coke will commit to advertising in black magazines and newspapers and double its spending to $2 million.[57]

After his success with Coca-Cola, Rev. Jackson quickly signed another covenant with Seven-Up Bottling Company. Officials in his organization stated that he also wanted to consummate a similar arrangement with Pepsi.

At the time, Don Kendall was the CEO of Pepsi Holding Company, and Andy Pearson, former head at McKinsey Global

---

[57] "Accord Ends Coke Boycott," *NYT*, August 11, 1981.

Consumer Practice, was the president. I was informed by Naylor Fitzhugh and Harvey Russell, the latter Pepsi's first black VP, that Kendall had no intention of signing such a covenant with Push, but Pepsi did want to do the right thing with respect to minority business enterprise development. Naylor suggested that based on our record with the federal government and our national reputation, we should meet with Andy Pearson and offer our services. I visited Andy Pearson, and with extensive selling on my part, he awarded JHLA a contract to design Pepsi's first minority business enterprise program. He informed us we would be working with John Scully, then president of Pepsi.

On one of my visits to New York, I ran into Bob Holland. Bob had left McKinsey with the goal of buying an ongoing company and becoming an entrepreneur. I had tried to discourage him, as he was a highly successful consultant on his way to becoming a senior vice president. I told him that we had just received a contract with his old friend and ex-partner Andy Pearson. It was Andy Pearson who had sponsored Bob's employment and later partnership at McKinsey. After a few beers, Bob offered to assist me on the study. I accepted his kind offer but told him I could not pay him at the McKinsey rate, so we worked out a deal where I would pay him six figures for working the equivalent of two days' worth of work.

Since both Bob and Peter Bynoe would only be working part-time, I knew I had to expand the team, so I brought on two outstanding consultants, Carlton Guthrie and Richard Holland. Carlton had two Harvard degrees and was an ex-McKinsey consultant. Richard had three degrees: a bachelor's in engineering physics from Cornell University, a master of science in nuclear engineering from MIT, and an MBA in finance from Columbia University's business school. He was also an ex-consultant from Cresap, McCormick & Paget.

Before we finalized the contract, Bob Holland took me aside and said, "Jim, you are working in the private sector. It's time to increase your budget." So, with a much larger budget and a signed contract, we started our engagement. As a team, we were highly successful motivating, elevating, and supporting minority business enterprise as a Pepsi Cola priority. We assessed and supported the MBEs to help grow their businesses and advised key buyers on how to screen and support viable minority businesses, all by utilizing what we labeled the "pain/gain" matrix.

While some form of the pain/gain matrix, or similar design tool, may have been utilized by other major firms, we felt ours was unique because, for the first time, our formula was utilized by a Fortune 500 company to grow minority business. With the successful utilization of this approach, we were able to do the following:

- establish CEO trust, allowing us to analyze the procurement dollars for the company;
- analyze the data and determine high-potential opportunities for MBEs;
- work with and motivate key buyers to do the right thing with respect to minority business;
- identify qualified MBEs of all sizes to take advantage of the opportunities presented; and,
- support MBEs working with Pepsi and assist them to grow their business.

Probably the most important thing the team achieved was to become trusted advisors at all levels of the organization.

Based on our success at Pepsi, we were asked to replicate our study at Frito-Lay for its CEO, Wayne Calloway. I could not turn down this opportunity, so I was forced to split the team. I had Peter Bynoe return to Chicago to run the office, while I split my time between New York, with Bob Holland and Carlton Guthrie on Pepsi, and Dallas, with Richard Holland on Frito-Lay. Bob Holland was not only a tremendous asset on the study, bringing ten years of consulting experience from McKinsey, but he was also a first-rate coach and mentor to our younger professional team.

While we were designing our MBE program at Frito-Lay, we observed some competition within the C-suite level at Pepsi to succeed the CEO, Don Kendall. Pepsi was a great company with top executives moving between Frito-Lay, Pepsi, and Taco Bell. As a result of this internal competition, there was obvious division between the companies to outperform one another with respect to growth and profitability.

When I first met Wayne Calloway, he stated, "Let's make the Frito-Lay MBE program the best, not only within PepsiCo but in the nation." To face the challenge, he assigned one of his C-suite stars, Jim O'Neal, to assist us in reaching this goal. He could not have made a better choice not only for JHLA and for Frito-Lay but for the national MBE community. Jim O'Neal was a charming, no-nonsense type of guy from Compton, California. In our first meeting, he looked at Richard Holland and me and said, "I do not know a thing about minority business enterprise, but I do have the power to effect change within Frito-Lay. Now let's make history." Right away, Jim was attracted to the potential positive impact of MBE development, not only for Frito-Lay but for the nation. Over my forty years in consulting, I never had a better and more supportive client than Jim O'Neal.

Working with Jim O'Neal and Richard Holland was truly stimulating and entertaining. Richard was like a sponge, rapidly and effortlessly learning about the culture of Frito-Lay and minority business. On top of that, he was very, very smart. Within a short period, we designed the initial program with Frito-Lay; assisted Frito-Lay in creating a small business investment corporation (SBIC); and, working with its CEO, supported the creation of the publication MBN USA Magazine with founder and visionary Don McNeely. Not all our meetings were at the Frito-Lay headquarters. At O'Neal's suggestion, we often had meetings at the renowned Rosewood Mansion Restaurant, over too many glasses of wine.

While working at Frito-Lay, Wayne Calloway was elevated to CEO of Pepsi, replacing Don Kendall. His replacement at Frito-Lay was Michael Jordan, an ex-McKinsey partner who was also extremely supportive of our work, perhaps even more supportive than Calloway. As Jim O'Neal got more engaged in our project, he soon became both a national and international advocate for MBE development. First, he became the change agent within Frito-Lay. He extended his reach to the greater Dallas area, became a major spokesperson within the National Minority Supplier Development Council (NMSDC), and later, chair of the NMSDC Executive Committee. Utilizing our unique business relationship at the time, he was able to get McKinsey to do a pro-bono study for NMSDC. It was a strategic study estimated worth more than $600,000. Under his leadership, armed with the McKinsey study, NMSDC grew in stature and size. However, NMSDC truly took off when O'Neal reached into his own pocket and hired a firm to conduct a search for a new president. One day, he called me in to say the search committee had identified Harriet Michel to be the next president. He asked me if I knew her. I replied yes, I knew her, and in fact, she had been my client at the Department of Labor when she was working under Ernie Green, who, interestingly, was part of the Little Rock Nine. He later went to Michigan State University, was assistant secretary of labor under the Carter administration, and became a managing partner at Lehman Brothers.

I was sincere when I said I loved the selection of Harriet Michel, and I assured him that she would shake things up. Under Harriet's leadership, working with O'Neal and the NMSDC board, the NMSDC grew even stronger and more financially viable. I am proud to say JHLA also played a part during this growth period, preparing various studies and presentations at national conventions.

In retrospect, I will have to give credit to Richard Holland for educating, motivating, and guiding Jim O'Neal on his MBE journey. Richard was so good that Jim O'Neal later stole him to head up Frito-Lay's MBE program. As to be expected, Richard did an excellent job, and Frito-Lay was named NMSDC Corporation of the Year in 2004.

With Frito-Lay and Pepsi as models, JHLA was in great demand by other companies. One of the most challenging engagements was Burger King. It was not challenging from a design perspective but from a political perspective. Like Frito-Lay and Pepsi, we quickly identified major MBE opportunities, the biggest one being in advertising. Within the first six months of our engagement, Burger King awarded a major contract to UniWorld Group Inc., an advertising company based in Brooklyn, New York, and headed by Byron Lewis. Based on the quality of their work, UniWorld has retained that contract for thirty-four years.

From a business standpoint, things couldn't have been better. Politically, however, was another story; specifically, the story was Rev. Jackson and Operation PUSH. It had gotten back to us that Rev. Jackson did not like us taking a leadership position in the field, and he was going to try to stop our work at Burger King. This really hurt because I had always respected and supported him. When I approached the CEO of Burger King, Jeff Campbell,[58] he assured us that the rumors had no merit and that we should

---

[58] Jeffrey Campbell earned a bachelor's from Fairfield University, an MBA from Columbia University, and an MA from the University of Miami. Currently, he is ex-chairman of the Pillsbury Restaurant Group, which included—at the time of his tenure—Burger King, Steak and Ale, Bennigan's, and Godfather's Pizza restaurant chains, totaling some six thousand units worldwide. He has also held the posts of senior vice president Brand Development for Pepsi-Cola and the Brinker Executive in Residence at the L. Robert Payne School of Hospitality & Tourism Management at San Diego State University.

continue our work. However, Rev. Jackson had a trick up his sleeve. Not to be outdone, he invited Jeff Campbell to his national convention and at the dinner sat him next to Hollywood actress Jayne Kennedy. When Jeff Campbell returned from Chicago, he informed us we would be sharing our work with PUSH. Obviously, the quality of our work was no match for the skillful tactics of Rev. Jackson and his beautiful ally, Jayne Kennedy.

Initially, I was very upset by the change of events. At the time, Pillsbury owned Burger King, and I knew someone on the board of Pillsbury. I wrote him a personal letter, the gist of which was that I was hurt and disappointed that the quality of our work was not being respected. I remember also stating I thought there should not be a double standard. If another firm or organization was better than we were, so be it. But we should not be eliminated because of political or social reasons. My friend took the matter up with Jeff Campbell, and they decided there should be two contracts. On principle, I rejected the compromise solution. I withdrew my team and left Burger King to Rev. Jackson and Operation PUSH. Burger King over the years designed a solid program, but unlike Pepsi and Frito-Lay, they never received the company of the year award from NMSDC.

Soon after departing from Burger King, we started work with Stroh's Brewery, a strong regional beer company. We were asked to assist the company in expanding its MBE procurement program and identify a possible minority entrepreneur to buy one of its distribution centers. The president was another ex-McKinsey consultant, Roger Friedholm. Our engagement was unique in many ways. First, in addition to working with Roger Friedholm, a personal friend, we were also working with the Stroh family and its owner, Peter Stroh. Peter Stroh, CEO of the family company, was an outstanding Detroit civic leader and community change agent. When he decided to move Stroh's headquarters to downtown Detroit, he asked us to ensure that there would be 30 percent MBE participation. We achieved this goal in 1982. He also asked me to form what I believe to be the first diversity advisory council in the nation. I was delighted with this request and reached out to my close friends and allies. The first council was comprised of Joe Anderson, Maynard Jackson,[59] Ann Jordan (formerly known as Ann Cook),[60] Jewel Lafontant[61] (mother of John Rogers Jr.), and Walter Douglas.[62] This council was featured in the August 1989 edition of *Black Enterprise*, where the article discussed the council's purpose: to give advice; help formulate direction; and review all aspects of our minority programs within the corporation, the marketplace, and the community.[63] Our work was well received, and at one of our monthly meetings with top management, I got the shock of my life when I was informed that Bob Holland was in talks to buy the Stroh's franchise in Detroit. I was glad Bob got the opportunity, because I knew he wanted to run his own shop, but I did not appreciate the manner in which I received the news. At around the same time, my other consultant, Carlton Guthrie,

---

[59] Maynard Jackson was the first black mayor of Atlanta, Georgia. Jackson served three terms as mayor, which makes him the longest-serving mayor in Atlanta history. Jackson is a graduate of Morehouse College and later received his JD from North Carolina Central University.

[60] Ann Jordan is the vice chairman and secretary of WETA-TV. In 2005, Jordan became one of the first five members of the board of directors of the Clinton Foundation.

[61] Jewel Lafontant-Mankarious was the first female deputy solicitor general of the United States. She received her bachelor's from Oberlin College. In 1946, Lafontant was the first black woman to earn a law degree from the University of Chicago Law School. Lafontant lost her battle with cancer in 1997 at the age of seventy-five.

[62] Walter Douglas is a chairman at Avis Food, Inc. From 1979 until 2001, Douglas served as the president and CEO of DHT Transportation. He holds a BS and MBA from North Carolina Central University and an honorary doctorate degree from Wayne State University.

[63] Stroh, *Black Enterprise* (August 1989): 1–168.

put together a package to buy an existing automotive supplier. I was losing two of my best, and their pending departure hurt even more since as a firm we were growing very rapidly. I did not stay mad long because Bob was one of my best friends, and I knew both Bob and Carlton would be outstanding entrepreneurs and create jobs and wealth for our communities.

While my staff was being depleted in Detroit, I was approached by Ford Motor Company to design a state-of-the-art MBE program to surpass the existing programs at General Motors and Chrysler. With Bob and Carlton preparing to leave, I had to make a tough choice. Should I accept or decline Ford's request for the proposal? I knew I and my small team would be challenged if we took on the Ford project, but I thought I could deliver a quality product because I still had Richard Holland and had recently recruited Smith College graduate Olivet Ames, who I knew would be outstanding. But how could I turn the request down? Ford was a leader in the automotive industry, one of the largest industries in the world. We had never done work in the automotive sector, and they were going to pay us big bucks. I guess all of the above factors entered into the equation, and we soon began our engagement for Ford.

When we started at Ford, our direct client was Gary White. It was a pleasure to work with Gary. He and his wife had a personal relationship with Ford's CEO, Henry Ford. We did not work together long, however, as Gary soon left Ford to start his own trucking company. He was replaced by Dr. Ray Jensen. Ray had an English degree from Howard University and had previously served in the US Air Force. He was one of the first two African Americans to earn master's degrees in aerospace engineering from the US Air Force Academy. He worked on the Minuteman missile crew at Malmstrom Air Force Base in Montana. As a combat crew commander, he participated in the first successful launch of a dual-mode intercontinental ballistic missile from Vandenberg

Air Force Base. He retired as an officer and was honored as one of the Military Makers. Ray was a proud, highly intelligent man who carried himself with a stiff military posture, which to some bordered on arrogant.

Initially, I thought this was not going to be an easy partnership. But one day I confronted him and, taking a lesson out of Jim O'Neal's playbook, said, "Ray, you do not know a thing about minority business, and I do not know a thing about Ford. Let's work together and make history." We did exactly that, and Ford became the first company to purchase over $1 billion from minorities. Under his leadership, MBE procurement spending increased to $3.7 billion. Ray was highly effective working with growth-oriented MBEs, developing a unique partnership with existing Tier One[64] suppliers, and supporting the key buyers in their efforts to identify and leverage the growth of strong firms.

One of the first key decisions Ford made to reach the $1 billion goal was to establish increased revenue, rather than number of MBEs, as their most important metric. I convinced Ray the latter metric would force him to invest a disproportionate important amount of time helping MBEs who would never be able to serve Ford. We initiated the same pain/gain metric we utilized at Pepsi, and the rest was history. In many ways, the Ford project was far more challenging than Pepsi, Frito-Lay, or Stroh's because it was so much larger and procurement decisions were decentralized. There were many buyers, and each buyer had tremendous power. It wasn't easy to end relationships between existing nonminority buyer/supplier relationships, some of which began more than ten to twenty years prior, cemented by legacies or started over a round of golf in Detroit country clubs. Unlike at consumer goods companies, many of Ford's major opportunities demanded manufacturing experience.

---

[64] A Tier One supplier is a company that is large enough and financially secure enough to be a direct supplier to major corporations.

Through the combined efforts of many people, Ford became highly successful. Most notable in our crusade were Rev. Jackson and Dr. Clifford Wharton. Where I might have considered Jackson's tactics questionable if he was challenging me, when he was on your side, he was exactly the man you wanted in your corner. Rev. Jackson applied constant pressure by always meeting with the CEO, arguing the MBE case with Ray Jensen in the room. Dr. Wharton, who at the time was the president of Michigan State University and also a Ford board member, was invaluable in asking the question at every quarterly board meeting, "What is Ford's MBE spend?"

For me, Ford will always be the model for change and expansion within the field of minority business enterprise development. At Ford, there was outstanding MBE advocate Rev. Jessie Jackson, armed with powerful research on the size and nature of Ford's procurement program; they had two high-level and respected black executives leading the effort; and there was a prominent black board member asking the critical questions to keep the pressure on the CEO. JHLA was able to play a significant role by designing the strategy and pulling all the players together. Ray Jensen and I remained friends for many years; he was even one of my groomsmen at my wedding to Dr. Sharon Collins. Equally important, in 2005, we were both inducted into the inaugural class of the Minority Business Hall of Fame, along with Harriet Michel, Earl Graves, and Parren Mitchell. And with the Burger King episode behind us, Reverend Jackson and I became close friends.

One of my models of the societal benefits of minority business enterprise development is Dr. William Pickard from LaGrange, Georgia. He received an associate degree from Flint Mott College, a bachelor's from Western Michigan University, and a master of social work from the University of Michigan. After receiving a PhD from Ohio State University, he sought a career as a change agent heading up the Cleveland Chapter of the Urban

League. When approached by McDonald's to identify potential minority franchise owners, he and his friends purchased the first minority-owned McDonald's in Cleveland. Not satisfied with one franchise, he expanded to Detroit and purchased more.

Soon thereafter, utilizing the profits from his McDonald's franchises, he bought and expanded an automotive manufacturing company in Detroit. Acknowledging the risk in the Detroit-based automotive industry, he moved part of his operation to new manufacturing centers in the South and formed strategic partnerships with large companies and non-American auto manufacturers. He became a civic leader in Montgomery, Alabama, and other southern cities. Known for his civic leadership, philanthropy, and mentoring of young professionals, Dr. Pickard has been awarded countless recognitions. Affirmative action helped Dr. William Pickard become a multimillionaire,[65] and in the process, communities and black youth have benefitted from his contributions. He has been a close friend for many years and to this day gives me credit for encouraging him to diversify his holdings in automotive and to other markets.

---

[65] In 2017, Pickard released his book titled *Millionaire Moves, Seven Proven Principles of Entrepreneurship*, Real Times Media (2017).

CHAPTER 12

THE HAROLD WASHINGTON YEARS

JHLA's reputation and workload continued to grow. From a one-city shop in Chicago, tackling the DC circuit with our federal government practice, our list of cities continued to grow. One of the last studies we did for McKinsey was to design the organization of Mayor Maynard Jackson's office in Atlanta, an experience I enjoyed so much that over the years I maintained contact with the mayor and members of his executive staff. My time there ensured that the city of Atlanta would always hold a special place in my heart. Under the outstanding leadership of Maynard Jackson, and later Mayor Andrew Young, Atlanta became the model for the nation in my eyes. Atlanta set the standard for bringing people of all ethnic backgrounds together and fostering economic development for all citizens. Hence, I was extremely pleased when Mayor Young and the chair of the city council, Marvin Arrington, invited JHLA to design Atlanta's first MBED program.

I did not know Mayor Young well personally, although I had a great respect for him and his courageous leadership during the civil rights movement. I did, however, know one of his chief advisors, Walter Huntley. When I first met Walter Huntley, he was one of the brilliant young interns serving in Mayor Jackson's administration. He was a graduate of Trinity University in San

Antonio and an All-American football player. Walter was smart, hardworking, and ambitious. When we did work for Maynard Jackson, I introduced him to McKinsey, and he in turn introduced me to the city of Atlanta, its culture, and its black leadership.

We maintained communication after I left McKinsey, and between the time of 1974 and 1985, Walter had become a true insider and leader in Atlanta. So I was thrilled to be asked to do the study and grateful to Walter because he obviously had a role in steering the contract to us. The one problem was, because of the demands of our other clients, I personally could not free myself to conduct the study. So as a favor to me, Peter Bynoe accepted the responsibility. He did an outstanding job and, in the process, built some invaluable connections in Atlanta. His work provided JHLA a blueprint for future assignments with other major cities interested in designing a state-of-the-art MBED program.

For me, Maynard Jackson will always stand out over all the other mayors for his vision, boldness, political sagacity, and devotion to MBED. Because of Maynard Jackson's leadership, blacks in Atlanta benefitted immensely. Through competitive bids, they were awarded lucrative concessions at the airports, recruited by major Atlanta corporations, and received major contracts from the city and country. Many of those who benefited from his leadership are now pillars of the community and visionaries for the next generation.

Soon after completing our Atlanta engagement, Congressman Harold Washington of Chicago decided he would once again try to make history by becoming Chicago's first black mayor. Although I was running a national company with offices in New York, Chicago, and Oakland, I still made the effort to maintain my Chicago presence, serving on the boards of Northwestern Hospital, Michael Reese Hospital, Chicago United, and the Chicago Public Library.

When I was named cochairman of Chicago United,[66] only the top Chicago CEOs (minority and nonminority) were accepted to membership. We met every month to discuss the major problems confronting the city. Working with my cochair, Barry Sullivan, president and CEO of First National Bank, I tried to elevate the topic of MBED to be a high priority. Unfortunately, we did not get the majority of the CEOs to support us. I did not know Harold Washington well, but I had past allegiances with the other two leading candidates. Chicago Mayor Jane Byrne had appointed me to the library board at the recommendation of the board chair, my old friend Sally Berger, and it was Richard M. Daley's father who encouraged me to launch JHLA in the first place. I felt the prudent thing to do was take a neutral position in the campaign when Harold Washington challenged Byrne and Daley. Washington ran an excellent campaign with extensive focus on grassroots, garnering Hispanic and black support. With Byrne and Daley splitting the White vote, Harold won the primary.

Harold's victory brought joy and hope to thousands of those who felt they had been left out of the loop. However, it also brought fear to the hearts of Chicago insiders and the local business leadership. As a proud African American, I too felt joy and hope at this juncture. It didn't occur to me to concern myself with the possible negative impact on my business. In Chicago, politicians have long memories as to whose team you were affiliated. As I said, my company was started with the support of former Mayor Richard J. Daley, but we had received contracts over the past ten years from his successors, Michael Bilandic and Jane Byrne. Yet I couldn't help but be so very proud of Harold Washington's victory; if I was not accepted in his new administration because of

---

[66] Chicago United was created after the riots in Chicago. The mission of this organization was to advocate to achieve parity in economic opportunity for people of color by advancing multiracial leadership in corporate governance, executive level management, and business diversity.

my past allegiances, then so be it. Harold Washington becoming Chicago's first black mayor was bigger than JHLA.

Soon after the general election, I started getting calls, not from my friends but leaders from the business community. It was almost humorous, as in unison they were saying, "Jim, save us!" I tried to tell them there was nothing to fear, and contrary to what they might believe, I was not close to Harold Washington. I was equally candid in stating I was not involved in the campaign and probably had some enemies within his inner circle of grassroots followers. Notwithstanding my neutral stance or that I may not have been the most popular with certain groups, it wasn't long before I received a last-minute invite from my friend Tom Burrell, president of Burrell Communications Group,[67] to join a small group of minority business leaders that was meeting with the new mayor and the white corporate leaders in a secret, behind-closed-doors meeting at the University Club.

The meeting at the University Club was plagued with a lot of nervous dialogue between Harold Washington's team, the minority business leaders, and the corporate CEOs. It was also plagued with very little action. When it was over, we were met by a plethora of cameras and newscasters. One of the newscasters, Andy Shaw, asked what I thought of the meeting. Thinking I was back in Brooklyn in front of the cameras again, as if on cue, I jumped right into my role as TV show host, and I proceeded to embellish and expand on what was otherwise an uneventful and bland meeting. Basically, I tried to allay the growing fears of the local business community and give Harold some flexibility.

---

[67] Tom Burrell coined the phrase "black people are not dark-skinned white people." Recognizing that there existed inherent cultural differences, and the fact that these differences drove patterns of consumption, became a driving force and inspiration for future ad campaigns at Burrell. With that focus, he helped create a more than $128 million multicultural advertising with clients like McDonald's, Toyota, and Allstate.

Evidently it worked, because I was soon getting positive calls from both sides on my comments. One such call was from my dear friend Cindy Pritzker, who saw the interview and teased me because the TV station identified me as a lawyer, not a consultant.

Soon after that first University Club meeting, I received a call from Bill Ware, the mayor's chief of staff and a University of Chicago–educated lawyer, asking me to come and meet with the mayor. Mayor Washington asked me to be part of his transition team. The role he envisioned for me was that of vetting agent, confidentially screening all potential candidates he was considering in his administration. I did not have the time to handle this responsibility, but I could not say no to the newly elected mayor. So, for the next thirty days at the University Club, I quietly screened candidates. It felt very clandestine to me at the time because the meetings were invite-only and held in private. I thought it was ironic that we were meeting in the University Club, a club I helped integrate only ten years earlier.

In my interviews, I tried to be fair and sensitive to those who were early participants and loyal supporters throughout the campaign. But I also did not want to burden the mayor with unqualified managers or key advisors, regardless of loyalty. A few notable individuals who served in the cabinet were Ernest Barefield (chief of staff), Maxine Leftwich (advisor), Sharon Gist Gilliam (deputy budget director), James Montgomery (corporation counsel), Kari Moe (deputy economic development), and Doug Guthrie (deputy housing commissioner).

At the end of the process, I felt good about what we accomplished over a short period of time. My assignment complete, I thought I would have my last meeting with the mayor and return to running JHLA full-time. I was shocked when the mayor asked me to assume the responsibility of the chairman of the Chicago Public Library Board. I knew this would be a challenge since historically the Chicago Public Library had been very political and had been rife with administrative problems.

Initially, I rejected the offer; I truly did not want to accept the responsibility because I knew it would be time-consuming, politically risky, and maybe a challenge to my health. But Mayor Washington was very persistent and even more persuasive. Finally, I told him I would accept his offer on two conditions: (1) that he name Cindy Pritzker to the board, and (2) that he allow JHLA to prepare a MBED study for the city of Chicago. The former was an easy ask because Cindy had just had her sixtieth birthday, and she was looking for something different to do. She was an outstanding civic leader, and more importantly, she would be a nonpolitical and objective trusted advisor; she wouldn't pull any punches.

Being the chair of the Chicago Public Library Board proved to be a much more challenging role than I anticipated. It was extremely time-consuming with a seemingly endless number of meetings, many of which were in an open and public forum with exposure to media coverage. In addition, there were numerous problems of varying degrees throughout several of the libraries in the system. Initially, I had to work with a reluctant incumbent commissioner and two board members who challenged my almost every move to address the deficiencies in the library system. In addition, Chicago was greatly in need of a new central library. The old central library had exceeded its capacity. The big public debate was whether the city should renovate the old Goldblatt's Building on State Street or build a brand-new building. With much time invested and the unfortunate resulting lost revenues for JHLA, together with the strong support of board members Lerone Bennett Jr.,[68] Cindy Pritzker, and Chanute Russell, we turned the situation around. After I left as chair, Cindy Pritzker became the chair, and under her leadership, the new library was completed.

---

[68] *Ebony* magazine's executive editor, Emeritus Lerone Bennett Jr.

JHLA had successfully made the transition from a public sector firm to a predominately private sector focus. As a firm, we were now accepted as one of the most preeminent companies in the nation in the field of supplier and human resource diversity with top-name national clients. We were doing well and also doing good; we were making money while also making a difference. I was running a very successful company, and I was respected in the community for the work I was doing. I certainly did not need to create additional stress in my life. But that's exactly what I did when I started designing the city of Chicago's first MBED program. After my success with the library, I thought I could easily take on this next challenge. I knew I had to prepare a deep, highly analytical, strong, and fact-based report similar to the one we had just completed for the city of Atlanta. I was realistic in assuming it would be challenged in a court of law or hotly contested in the city council, a place the mayor lacked majority votes. Even without the votes in the city council, the mayor wanted to make MBED the cornerstone of his administration, and he would strongly support my recommendations. Naïvely, however, I did not accurately gauge how vicious the atmosphere would be and the toll it would take on me personally or the impact it would have on my business.

I organized a JHLA team with Carlton Guthrie as the engagement manager to conduct the necessary research to determine the weaknesses in the city's procurement system and outline how the city could do a better job of including women and minorities in the procurement process. After completing the first phase of fact gathering, I prepared a ten-page detailed outline of the final report. Carlton and his team did an excellent job of filling in the gaps and producing the final report. The report, titled *Study of Minority and Women-Owned Business Enterprise*

(M/WBE) Procurement Program for the City of Chicago,[69] was well received by the mayor, along with our recommendations that the city adopt procurement "goals," not quotas of 25 percent for ethnic minorities and 5 percent for women. I wish I could confess that the numbers we used as goals were the result of an exhaustive analytical study, but I can't because they were not. It was just my gut feeling that the numbers were fair and achievable. When Mayor Washington asked me if we could achieve the goals, I remember saying, "Mr. Mayor, they will be achieved, but the real challenge will be to ensure the M/WBEs will be legitimate and not fronts."

With what would come to be called "the Lowry report" in hand, Mayor Washington felt armed to make minority business enterprise development his administration's top priority. He asked me to present the findings and recommendations to the various communities across the city before releasing it to the press. Around the same time, I was approached by a young but impressive reporter on staff of the *Chicago Tribune* by the name of Dean Baquet.[70] Dean was a friend but not a close friend, so when he asked for a copy of the report, I refused. I did not want the *Tribune* to have an exclusive copy. Instead, I suggested he accompany me to the first community meeting, just hang out in the back of the room, and take notes. Dean took copious notes and wrote a superb piece on the study with Douglas Frantz on April 24, 1985. Later, Dean wrote a very positive and complimentary article in the *Tribune* about me, titled, "Lowry a Model for a Minority Contract Plan," with my picture in print for all to see.

---

[69] James H. Lowry & Associates, *Study of Minority and Women-Owned Business Enterprise (M/WBE) Procurement Program for the City of Chicago Report* (1985).

[70] Dean Baquet is the first black American to serve as executive editor, the highest-ranking position in the *New York Times* newsroom. In 1988, Baquet won the Pulitzer Prize for leading a team of reporters at the *Chicago Tribune* who exposed corruption on the Chicago City Council.

Coming out of one of those town hall meetings, Earl Neal took me aside and said he was proud of me but that I better be careful about who and what I criticize in the previous administration. He reminded me about those famously long politicians' memories. It was good advice then, and it is good advice today.

I always knew politics were tough, but by working for Mayor Harold Washington and Andrew Young, I was forced to accept this reality on a personal level. When I started working for Senator Bobby Kennedy, the goal was to create wealth to minimize poverty in our community.

If there were strong minority businesses within our communities, jobs could be created and wealth accumulated. But I was not so naïve to think that the concept of sharing wealth with people of color was going to be easily accepted. In the case of the city of Chicago, shifting city procurement dollars to minorities and women was going to be a new approach and would be challenged.

CHAPTER 13

MR. CONTRACT

With my very public role as the chair of Chicago's library system, coupled with the highly controversial Lowry Report, I was no longer flying under the radar. I was now a local celebrity with many admirers and even more critics. But I have to admit I was having fun. For four years in a row, we had won the City Labor Market Training contract, a very popular summer program from the Mayor's Office of Employment. This program gave me great pride because not only were we providing invaluable skills training for inner city youth, I was able to hire some highly skilled certified teachers in the summer, who also happened to be my friends.

It was around this time that the Chicagoland Sports Foundation asked me to sponsor a team in its summer basketball league. The summer league was unique because it included players from five different categories: graduating high school seniors, collegiate players, pros from European leagues, the CBA, and the NBA. In 1985, some of the big-name pros in the summer league were Chicago Bulls' Wes Matthews, Utah Jazz' Rickey Green, Philadelphia 76ers' Maurice Cheeks, the New York Knicks' Patrick Ewing, and Mark McGuire from the Dallas Mavericks. There was also a European pro named Craig Robinson, who is now well known as the brother-in-law of President Barack Obama. The star on my team was Rod Strickland, who played for the Knicks. The team that won that year was stacked with the likes of Milwaukee Bucks' Terry Cummings, Chicago Bulls players Reggie Theus and Orlando Woolridge, and a young player by the name of Michael Jordan. Michael Jordan's contract stated he would be allowed to play anywhere he so desired. He would amaze me and countless others as he played with the same drive and passion in our summer league that he exhibited over his fourteen-year career with the Bulls and two years with the Washington Wizards. With the boys from the neighborhood, he was fearless in taking on anyone who challenged him. I was a Bulls fan before seeing Michael Jordan, but after that summer, I became a loyal fan. I have been a season ticket holder for the last forty-four years and have enjoyed countless games with friends and family. During the height of Jordan's Bulls years, those seats were an excellent way to court new clients. In 1985, I was honored by the Chicagoland Sports Foundation for my time sponsoring leagues. On that same day, they also honored Ben Wilson. Ben Wilson was voted the top high school basketball player in the country and the first player from Chicago to receive this honor. Sadly, his award was posthumous; he was shot and killed the year before.

In that same year, I was approached by Don Jackson, owner of Inner City Marketing Company, to assist him in producing a TV show to highlight the success of MBED. The show was named *The Minority Business Report*, and he asked me to be the associate producer and host of the program. The program was sold to WGN TV superstation and transmitted across the nation, the Caribbean, and Mexico. Here I was running a successful business, active in the community as a civic leader, and now I was a TV personality talking about a subject dear to my heart. I was happy and feeling as though life was good.

For me, running a national firm with three offices and constantly marketing the firm was extremely demanding but also very satisfying. I was utilizing all my McKinsey skills and contacts to build a quality, highly intelligent, and successful enterprise. Equally important, I was training, mentoring, and motivating young professionals. This meant more to me than my newly earned wealth. Looking back, the employees I enjoyed training the most were my three special assistants, my nephew William A. Lowry,[71] David Rone,[72] and Hershel Tolson.[73]

My nephew Bill was the son I never had. Over the years, he might say he took the diplomacy and charm from his father and the business acumen from me. Obviously, his mother and marvelous wife also played a part in his success, but he has done extremely well since his teenage years as an intern with me. Bill Lowry and David both attended Francis W. Parker, and Hershel was Bill's classmate from grade school. All three later became highly successful professionals and over the years have given me credit for not only providing summer employment but also for being a business mentor and model they could emulate and aspire to surpass.

Every day, I got up with a smile on my face, enjoying my journey, and when I looked in the mirror, I knew I had accomplished this honestly, through hard work and dedication. I

---

[71] William A. Lowry is a president and managing shareholder at Nyhan, Bambrick, Kinzie & Lowry, P.C. He earned his bachelor's from Lake Forest College and his JD from Loyola University.

[72] David Rone was the president of Time Warner Cable Networks and Time Warner Sports. In 2004, Rone was named one of the "101 Most Influential Minorities in Sports" by *Sports Illustrated*, and later in 2005, he was named one of the "50 Most Powerful African-Americans in Sports" by *Black Enterprise*. Rone holds a bachelor's from Tufts University and a JD from Northwestern University.

[73] Hershel Tolson serves as president and CEO of Premier Learning Academy (PLA). Prior to his work with PLA, Tolson served as deputy director of contract compliance for Cook County Government and Cook County Health and Hospitals Systems. He holds a BS from Xavier University.

accepted there were a lot of crabs in the barrel, and my mission in life was to try to separate them from the good and lift as many positive blacks and young professionals as I could. I was having a fulfilling personal and professional life, but it would soon change dramatically.

Leaving my condo one morning, I walked by the newsstand and caught a glimpse of my face on the front page of the *Chicago Sun-Times* newspaper. In large print, with my image larger than life, read the caption "Mr. Contract, Mr. James H. Lowry." Evidently, the *Sun-Times* did not appreciate me facilitating the scoop for Dean Baquet at their competitor, the *Tribune.* It was also obvious the anti–Harold Washington group did not appreciate my recommendation that the billion-dollar procurement pie be cut up and shared with women and minorities.

In this scathing article and the many that followed, the *Sun-Times'* lead reporter characterized me as an unsavory insider, unfairly being awarded contracts under the new percentage goals that I had developed. Neither points were accurate, and most of my contracts were either competitive bids or were subcontracts under contracts given to Fortune 500 companies. I soon learned that during those days of the city council wars, the truth was never the issue. Instead, the real issue was whose team you were on. Either you were on Mayor Washington's side or the anti-Washington side, which also happened to hold a majority in the city council. I later learned that many thought I was uppity and disloyal. It was also felt that since my firm was created by a nod from former Mayor Richard J. Daley, my place should have been with the anti-Washington faction.

Throughout my career, and this instance was no exception, I never sided with a party because they were white or black. I sided with the party I liked or respected, irrespective of race, gender, or religion. I took pride in Mayor Washington for being Chicago's first mayor of color; this I would not deny. When he asked for my help, I supported him and his decision to expand opportunities for all groups. In one of those articles, the *Sun-Times* published a list of all my city contracts with amounts and dates, provided to them by the anti–Harold Washington city council establishment. When all the dollars were added up, the revenues were significant, especially for a person of color. I was asked by the local CBS news station to appear on a TV show hosted by top-rated news anchor Walter Jacobson. Appearing on the program with Walter Jacobson was a top-flight investigator/reporter named Pam Zekman. They wanted to question me about my report, the fees, and my city contracts. Without hesitation, I accepted the offer because I had nothing to hide.

When I appeared on the program, I put our report next to ten other contracts and boldly stated, "I will compare our report on a cost basis with one or all of those ten contracts!" Simply looking at the reports stacked next to mine, there was a vast difference. My one report was the size of all of the others combined. When you actually compared the quality, it was obvious our report was superior, and both Zekman and Jacobson thanked me for not only the quality of the report but also for my professionalism and candor.

After the show, a print reporter asked me to identify contracts that had provided low-quality work to the city. I said nothing because not only did I not want to embarrass my establishment friends that had some of those big contracts, I also did not want to shine light on the fact that some firms had taken advantage of the city. While the TV show put an end to most of the negative publicity I had been receiving, behind the scenes, there were still many who wanted to destroy me and JHLA, and they were doing an effective job. Because of the spotlight on me, many companies were reluctant to do business with us. What hurt the most was jealous minority consulting firms that started working with the enemies to bring us down. They would claim they could provide the same professional support for a third of the money. Of course, they couldn't, but we found out that for some of the companies who hired them, it didn't matter because they were not seeking quality consulting work. Rather, what they needed was protection from Jesse Jackson and Operation PUSH.

It was an especially hard blow when the local Urban League chapter, led by a close friend, started a MBED office to conduct studies and certify companies. Many of the companies they certified were later discovered to be fronts. In the business world, it was common for such front companies or corporations to be used to shield the parent company from legal exposure. Even if the Urban League had good intentions, I knew they could not get the job done because their teams were weak and lacked the analytical skills to conduct high-level research.

Had I relied only on Chicago for revenue, my firm might have gone under, because after that "Mr. Contract" article, we lost a lot of local work. The one local client we did not lose was the First National Bank of Chicago. We had a very strong relationship with the bank. My direct client was Executive Vice President A.D. Frazier. Frazier started his career as a lawyer at C&S Bank in Atlanta. When asked by Mayor Maynard Jackson what I thought about him as a potential candidate for heading Atlanta's Olympic bid, I strongly supported him. Frazier became chief operating officer for the Atlanta committee for the Olympic Games. He went on to manage the 1977 inauguration of President Jimmy Carter and headed the team reorganizing the White House and Executive Office of the president, also under President Carter. After the 1996 Summer Olympics in Atlanta, Frazier went on to be president and CEO of INVESCO, a global investment management group. During his career, Frazier has also served as the chairman and CEO of the Chicago Stock Exchange. Working under Frazier was Shirley Franklin, one of Maynard Jackson's superstars, who later became the mayor of Atlanta for two terms.

I still credit the bank's loyalty and continued support of their CEO, Barry Sullivan. I will always have a special place in my heart for Barry. When I was at my lowest, he supported me as a client and as my friend. He also supported me to be cochairman of Chicago United.

I had not understood how much I had angered certain people in Chicago. It wasn't until years later when my nephew Bill and I were departing Ruth's Chris Steak House restaurant one night. We ran into a gentleman we all know as "Project," and with him was golf icon Calvin Peete. Project introduced us by saying, "Calvin, this is Jim Lowry. He is a friend of Clark Burrus, he was the first black member at Medinah Country Club, and he's the author of Harold Washington's MBE procurement policy, and they had a contract out on him." I had to focus for a minute because I wasn't sure I had heard him right. With his last statement, the effects of too many martinis quickly disappeared as my nephew and I suddenly sobered up. I knew a lot of people would be upset with the new procurement program, but a contract on my life? I never thought their hatred would go that far. That's when I truly realized there is often a price for being a change agent.

One night in a popular restaurant on the far southeast side of Chicago, I accepted a dinner invitation with one of the leaders of the anti-Washington faction in the city council. He said, "I might like you, and I am not bothered that you are working with Harold, just do not mess with our money!" Personally, I never tried to because I did not have the power or desire to do so. I guess that is why I am still around.

I will always remember with mixed emotions my involvement with Mayor Harold Washington and the days of Mr. Contract. I reflect on what we changed, how public dollars were allocated, and how many minority- and women-owned businesses were created, and that progress remains in place after thirty-four years. Because of the executive order we drafted, Chicago's 25/5 goal setting became the model for the nation. When I traveled to different cities, it always put a smile on my face when I would inquire about their M/WBE programs, and in describing their programs, they would mention they had goals of 25 percent minorities and 5 percent for women, numbers we came up with in Harold Washington's living room.

Those days were also demanding and eye-opening, removing any of my earlier naiveté. I was forced to accept we lived in a cruel world where friends turned against me out of jealousy and envy. A world where corporations used other minorities for protection, and the very concept of MBED as something many never wanted to see modified and expanded. Now, many different groups qualify as minorities, including military veterans. I strongly believe veterans should be rewarded and supported for service to our great country, but I have a problem with them being labeled a minority and grouped with others. I have witnessed how major executives in corporations utilized their relationship with their country club golf friends who happen to be a minority to fill the minority slot. This was never the intention of the program. The original goal as articulated by Senator Robert Kennedy and Congressman Parren Mitchell was to create economic development and reduce poverty in communities that needed help. If veterans from the country club could demonstrate their commitment to those goals, I say let them in.

Cecil Partee over dinner once shared with me that after the smoke clears, it's all about money. He said that my long-term vision was morally correct, but on Monday morning, individuals, communities, and even corporations will try to block, discourage, or destroy you if you try to take away dollars that historically they feel belonged to them. He said, "Your Mr. Contract episode taught you a good lesson. Don't change your principles, but next time do a better job of arming yourself for battle."

Historical Background 1990–1999

- 1990: *Metro Broadcasting, Inc. v. FCC*,[74] the US Supreme Court upheld a race-based preference in granting broadcast licenses. According to the majority, while racial preferences created by state law must meet the test of strict scrutiny, benign race-based preferences that are enacted by Congress need not satisfy strict scrutiny but must simply be substantially related to the achievement of important governmental objectives.
- 1992: Officers who beat Rodney King were acquitted from any charges, resulting in riots in LA shortly after the announcement.[75]
- 1992: Carol Moseley Braun (D-IL) became the first African American woman elected to the US Senate.[76]
- 1993: Bill Clinton became president of the United States.
- 1995: After hearing *Adarand Constructors, Inc. v. Pena*,[77] the US Supreme Court once again called for "strict scrutiny" in determining whether discrimination existed before implementing a federal affirmative action programs have a "compelling government interest," and be "narrowly tailored" to fit the situation. In the 5–4 decision, the majority opinion asserted that "the unhappy persistence of both the practice and the lingering effects of racial discrimination against minority groups in this country" justified the use of race-based remedial measures in certain circumstances. In responding to this ruling,

---

[74] Metro Broadcasting, Inc. v. FCC, 497 U.S. 547 (1990).

[75] https://web.archive.org/web/20091203041211/http://jurist.law.pitt.edu/trials24.htm.

[76] https://history.house.gov/People/Listing/M/MOSELEY-BRAUN,-Carol-(M001025).

[77] *Adarand Constructors, Inc. v. Pena*, 515 U.S. 200 (1995).

President Clinton outlined the White House's guidelines on affirmative action, calling for the elimination of any program that "(a) creates a quota; (b) creates preferences for unqualified individuals; (c) creates reverse discrimination; or (d) continues even after its equal opportunity purposes have been achieved."

- 1997: Spearheaded by a member of the University of California Board of Regents, the state of California passed Proposition 209,[78] a state ban on all forms of affirmative action. The proposition stated that, "The state shall not discriminate against, or grant preferential treatment to, any individual or group on the basis of race, sex, color, ethnicity or national origin in the operation of public employment, public education, or public contracting." The controversial ban was delayed in the courts for almost a year before it went into effect.

- 1998: The state of Washington approved Initiative 200,[79] making it the second state to abolish state affirmative action measures.

- 1999: President Clinton signed Public Law 106-50,[80] the Veterans Entrepreneurship and Small Business Development Act, which among other requirements, established additional procurement assistance for veterans, including a 3 percent government-contracting goal for service-disabled veteran-owned small businesses. It required the head of each federal agency to take the necessary steps to establish the 3 percent goal in that agency's prime contract and subcontract awards.

---

[78] https://ballotpedia.org/California_Affirmative_Action,_Proposition_209_(1996).

[79] https://www.washingtonpolicy.org/publications/detail/a-citizens-guide-to-initiative-200-the-washington-state-civil-rights-initiative.

[80] Public Law 106-50 (1998).

CHAPTER 14

TRANSITIONING FROM AFFIRMATIVE ACTION TO DIVERSITY AND INCLUSION

The nation was still in a battle between the pro and con affirmative action forces, but over a ten-year period, there had been a major shift from affirmative action to diversity and inclusion (D&I). A lot of credit goes to the authors of the 1980 US Department of Labor report titled *Opportunity 2000*, which created the report, *Affirmative Action Strategies for a Changing Workforce*.[81] The research was done by the Hudson Institute. In the report, the authors produced an in-depth analysis of the American labor market's emerging challenges. They listed eight major trends that would revolutionize the future US workforce:

1. The number of workers will fall
2. The average age of workers will rise
3. More women will be on the job
4. One-third of new workers will be minorities
5. There will be more immigrants than any time since WWI
6. Most new jobs will be in services and information

---

[81] Hudson Institute, United States, Employment Standards Administration, *Opportunity 2000: creative affirmative action strategies for a changing workforce* (Washington, DC: The Administration, 1988).

7. The new jobs will require higher skills
8. The challenges for business will be immense

They concluded that those who accepted and addressed the challenges would have a competitive advantage. Major corporations now recognized affirmative action as a business imperative, and for the first time, the definition of diversity included women, immigrants, and other classes of people. As a result of increasing the different groups under the tent, a new industry called Diversity and Inclusion was created.

I quickly saw this was a growth industry, one I felt we could attack while maintaining our national reputation as a preeminent firm in the field of minority business enterprise development. Many Fortune 500 companies were aggressive in their strategies to increase the number of women, Latinos, blacks, immigrants, and, later, gays and lesbians. But few were successful.

McKinsey & Company

One of my first major diversity studies was for my old firm McKinsey & Company. In 1987, I read a very laudatory article about McKinsey, describing how fast they were growing around the world, the power of their alumni network, and the number of ex-McKinsey partners who were now CEOs of major Fortune 500 companies. At the bottom of the article, almost the last paragraph, the author stated there were only four blacks in the firm and no female partners. Upon seeing this, I immediately sent off a letter to my old mentor, Ron Daniel, who was the new president of McKinsey, saying how disappointed I was with the lack of progress. I pointed out that when I was at the firm, I personally recruited nineteen blacks to McKinsey. Ron quickly responded and asked if I would discuss the matter in his New York office. Evidently, he had gotten a similar letter from a senior partner who also was not proud of McKinsey's lack of progress in diversity. When I arrived in New York, he introduced me to that senior partner, Tom Woodard. He told us to work together and solve the problem. Tom had just returned from six years in the UK office, but prior to leaving the NY office, he had been mentored and motivated by Bob Holland on his path to partnership.

Tom and I hit it off immediately, and together we vowed we would solve the problem and provide the model not only for McKinsey but for all professional services firms in America. Fortunately, we immediately concluded there was no institutional bias against blacks and not a hint of racism; there was no ill will to foster change. Tom took the initiative and reached out to the head of North American recruiting, every partner with recruiting responsibility for each key business school. Together we would hold meetings with the North American office manager. Tom also decided he would be the behind-the-scenes mentor for the two most senior black consultants, Pamela Thomas and Roger Ferguson.

We were aware of the fact because there were no black partners at McKinsey and most high-potential blacks at our targeted schools had limited interest to interview for positions. To counteract this reality, Tom and I went to as many black student organization events on campus as we could. We communicated a simple message, "McKinsey is serious about recruiting black MBA candidates." We repeated the same message at Wharton, Harvard, and Stanford, and I would whisper in the ears of high potential blacks, "You see that white baldheaded guy over there? Do you know how much money he is making? He is here because he is committed. Trust me, trust him. We want you at McKinsey."

Because of our internal and external strategy, the number of blacks interviewing and joining McKinsey increased dramatically from four to 106 within two years. Once they joined the firm, we supported each of them, and like Tom used to say, "We treat as scarce resources." Tom was tough on the individuals we recruited, and he was even tougher on the white partners who he felt were not involved in our mission and who could help us solve the problem.

With Tom's support, Pamela Thomas became the first black female partner at McKinsey and Roger Ferguson the third black partner. They eventually left McKinsey and have had outside corporate careers. There were other superstars who were part of that initial growth, such as Tony Miller, Robert Taylor, Dwight Hutchins, Jerry Johnson, Vivian Hunt, Dale LeFebvre, Jim Shelton, Susan Rice, Byron Auguste, Samme Thompson, and Bernard Loyd.

Working with the McKinsey leadership, we assisted the black community via the Black Client Service Staff (BCSS). The BCSS is still in existence today to support black consultants. Tom and his wife have remained close personal friends for more than thirty years. We write constantly, trying to solve the problems of the world. We don't always agree, but the bond remains strong. I once asked Tom why he thought we were so successful. He responded, "We were successful because we were a motivated team, we gained both the BCSS and partners' confidence, and we were committed." He then added, "If you pit personalized versus institutional, personalized will win every time."

American Express

Although the city of Chicago contracts had all but dried up as a result of my *Mr. Contract* notoriety, JHLA continued to grow outside the city. In 1986, Lou Gerstner asked me to return to American Express to expand their Human Resource Diversity Initiative. During this engagement, Lou confronted me with the question, "Jim, we are recruiting a large number of minorities, but few are making it to the top. Why?"

Returning to Chicago, I reflected on his question. I also considered Lou's outstanding career at McKinsey, as well as his rapid growth to the top. It was from this thinking that I developed what I labeled *The Rules of the Game.* I then followed an old consulting adage that a well-designed chart or diagram can be more impactful than a thousand words, so I got to work and produced what became known as the *Rules of the Game: Corporate Success Pyramid:*

Rules of the Game: Corporate Success Pyramid

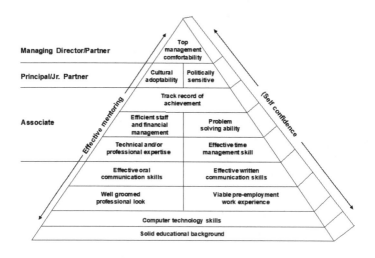

With this simple diagram, I created a training module to illustrate the skills and experience one might need to obtain a job at a company like American Express and how those skills had to be enhanced and broadened with every rung of the corporate ladder. If one did not enhance and expand this set of skills, they were destined to fail or remain as a middle manager, never to rise to a key decision maker or revenue producer. I also tried to illustrate that with every success step, the professional should gain more self-confidence. The key factor for success was the ability to identify and maintain a relationship with strong mentors to assist the professional manager or consultant along the way. The other factors, broken down into greater detail, are as follows:

1. **Self-Confidence.** You can't fake it. Either you have it, or you don't, but with each success, your self-confidence should be strengthened. What does self-confidence look like?
   - making your point in succinct and logical statements that add value
   - making recommendations before being told what to do
   - always walking and talking with positive and energetic composure
   - selling yourself in a nonarrogant way
   - if need be, being a pest to those who can help you win at any given situation

2. **Mentoring.** You can't make it in your organization or corporation without strong and positive coaches and mentors.
   - Although race might be a positive factor, the most important factor will be the ability, commitment, and effectiveness of the mentor, irrespective of race, gender, or sexual orientation.
   - The onus will be on you to ensure mentoring is mutually beneficial for the mentee as well as the mentor.
   - The mentor is critical in translating and transferring political information and the corporate rules of the game.

How do you choose a mentor?
- Identify who are the key decision makers and who are the most sought after by other decision makers.
- Of that group, determine with whom you have synergy.
- Gather the resources that will allow you to give your mentor(s) what they find is value added.
- Accept that you might sometimes outgrow your mentor. So change mentors when necessary without destroying the relationship.

3. **A solid educational background.** It is assumed that you have a solid educational background and you are well mannered.
   - You have to leverage your educational training as well as the contacts and associations of the school you attended.
   - Accept the fact that a degree from a prestigious college or university will help you get in the door, but your day-to-day performance will get you up the corporate ladder.
   - Accept that top firms in most industries only look for candidates with high grade point averages; they will not look at low B-grade candidates, however well-rounded.

4. **Computer technology.** You must be efficient in the use of technology and basic computer skills. The key to success will be taking your basic knowledge to a higher level. We live in a highly technical global economy, and every day new technological advances are disrupting how we conduct business.

5. **Well-groomed professional appearance.** The key is to always remain well-groomed and dress in a way consistent with your clients and peers. While acceptable business attire has changed over the years, most companies have basic requirements for proper dress, especially when in front of clients.

6. **Viable preemployment work experience.** As with a basic education, your previous work experience should be leveraged as well as the contacts and previous associations for:
   - marketing
   - recruiting
   - key information gathering for a case
   - business and social networking

   If your current affiliations don't do this for you, then add some that do or recommend such inclusions in your existing ones.

7. **Effective oral communication.** You must be a good listener. In the majority of cases, if you are a good listener, the client will tell you his or her priority, problem, or what he or she considers the major opportunities.
   - Master the art of speaking logically, sequentially, and effectively.
   - Be proficient in dissecting long, complicated concepts and problems into three to five points.
   - Learn to catch yourself when talking aimlessly and watch your audience to see if you're persuading or dissuading them.

8. **Effective written communication.** Whether you are preparing a 1-page memo or a 15-page deck you have to write an effective storyline, with structure, logic and clarity. To assist you I recommend:
   - Request examples of winning documents from clients and supervisors.
   - Use charts/diagrams to tell the story.
   - Use dot/dashes in formatting memos, correspondence, and letters.
   - Read Barbara Minto's book, *The Pyramid Principle*.

9. **Technical and professional expertise.** As soon as possible, develop skills and expertise that make you indispensable.
   - Always think to add value to a memo, report, and/ or product.
   - Accept the fact that your client and your supervisor, not you, will define the value you offer.
   - A few good questions to ask yourself at the end of *every day* are:
   - Did I deliver what is expected and what I promised?
   - Did I deliver products that made a significant difference, and do the right influencers know about it? If the answer is no, then you know what to do in the morning but preferably before you go to bed.

10. **Effective time management.** In the field of consulting, the key to success is to be able to plan and leverage your time.
    - The more quality products you produce on or before the deadline, the more valuable you will be to your team.

- Do not procrastinate to achieve the unattainable perfection. You will be better served presenting an 80 percent completed document on time and completing the "10 percent" later.
- You can negotiate a deadline before you start but never after you have missed it.
- Establish realistic deadlines and develop a plan to ensure you hit your target.

11. **Efficient staff and financial management.** If you want to reach the highest rung of the corporate ladder, you must demonstrate that you can effectively and efficiently manage people and budgets. Toward this end, you'll need to force yourself to:
    - accept constructive upward feedback
    - form and manage teams with unique and valuable skills
    - develop effective and lasting client relationships

12. **Problem–Solving.** The world is full of people who are able to define problems, but few are able to solve them.
    - The quicker you learn to solve problems, the more valuable you are.
    - Quickly, and with fact-based analysis, reach hypotheses and either prove or disprove them.

13. **Track record.** With a solid track record, you should be able to crash the glass ceiling, provided you can:
    - adapt to and adopt the culture of the company
    - feel comfortable with members of top management on both a social and professional level

14. **Cultural adaptability.** Corporate cultures will not change overnight. Thus, you must be able to adapt to the unique culture of the firm and the office in which you are working.
    - For many young professionals, corporate cultures can be very demanding both professionally and socially.
    - Determine the elements of your organization or corporation's culture.
    - Identify the cultural strengths that make your company preeminent in its field.

15. **Political sensitivity.** It is often essential that you know which team to be on, which team leader to follow, and, when necessary, which team to abandon. To determine if you are politically sensitive, ask yourself:
    - How much can you tell me about the managers, partners, and clients with whom you are working?
    - Are you politically sensitive to who are the top current, former, and rising stars?
    - Who are the most important political players at work, and why they are politically effective?

16. **Top management comfortability.** In the end, you have to be acceptable to top management. That comfort might be based on school ties, track record, or political party affiliation. Consider a quote of a CEO who said to me:
    - "The only people that I want in my corporate suite are those individuals I would be comfortable spending two weeks alone hunting ducks in my personal duck blind."

    When I heard this, I knew that individuals like myself would never be accepted in this man's executive suite.

When I presented my *Success Pyramid* to Lou on my next trip, his first response was, "Jim, doesn't everyone already know this?" I quickly answered him, "No, Lou, and that is why you are the president and they are not." He'd learned it at an early juncture in his career and performed at a high level with the support of strong mentors and sponsors, becoming the youngest director at McKinsey at the time. Wanting to get the last word in, as was his style, Lou proudly professed that he indeed had a very talented young black professional named Ken Chenault, who not only "got it" but whom he planned to mentor and sponsor. And later, after Lou's departure to RJR Nabisco, his successor and fellow ex-McKinsey alum, Harvey Golub, continued to mentor and sponsor Chenault.

History would prove Lou's strong conviction right, because in 1997, when Golub departed, Ken Chenault would become president of American Express, only the third black to become president of a Fortune 500 company. By 2001, Chenault not only became the CEO, a position he would hold more than twenty years, but he was also voted one of the top CEOs in the country. Throughout his tenure, Chenault has not only been an outstanding CEO for American Express, he has been honored as one of the most respected and honored business and civic leaders in the country. In 1995, *Ebony* listed him as one of fifty "living pioneers" in the African American community. He has also been a generous philanthropist and supporter of many individuals and community industries. On November 15, 2010, the Old North Foundation recognized Chenault with its Third Lantern Award for individual commitment and dedication to public service. In the wake of 9/11, among the many causes to which he devotes his time is the National September 11 Memorial & Museum at the World Trade Center Foundation.

Ken Chenault was a superstar not only at American Express but for the nation, a role he continues to fulfill to this day. In February 2018, Ken Chenault retired as the CEO and chairman of the board of American Express. He continues to serve the New

York business community and recently went on the boards of Facebook and Airbnb. He also announced recently that he will be chairman and managing director of General Catalyst Partners.

Lou Gerstner and Ken Chenault will always be my models for corporate leadership, but it was Chenault who became my model for how black executives should conduct themselves if they hoped to reach the top. To this day, I have never told him that I used him as the model for a speech I gave at the African American Retreat for the Harvard Business School, titled "The Timing of the Smile." In this speech, like the many others I gave at Stanford, Kellogg, Wharton, and Booth, I endeavored to leave the audience with advice they might use on their journey. The key message I try to convey is that contrary to what most nonminorities want to believe, when blacks walk into a room or work within teams, they are perceived differently. Often, blacks are judged, and opinions are quickly formed about them that may have no basis. Thus, I urge the listeners, "It is important to handle yourselves in a manner that advances your agenda, as opposed to one that might have a negative impact on you." The key, I noted, was to handle the initial communication in a way that allows both parties to feel comfortable and equal.

In many early careers, I observed too often that black executives and leaders went over the top with giant smiles on their faces and laughter that was a little too loud in an effort to make the nonminority in the room feel more comfortable. That was the safe approach. Yet I noticed the result was that the minority was never accepted as an equal. The opposite of this behavior was no better. When the minority remained stoic, he was perceived as hostile, resulting in the nonminority feeling uncomfortable or even threatened. When this occurred, communication was minimal or phony. With Chenault, and others like Ron Brown, Barry Rand, Vernon Jordan, and Franklin Thomas, they seldom laughed, and when it was appropriate, they merely smiled. With this one well-placed smile, both parties felt comfortable and equal.

To the African American alumni audience, I summarized my talk by saying, "If you laugh and smile too much, you will not be taken seriously as a peer. The same is true if you act like a leader of the Black Panthers, wearing a stern face and exuding hostility. The key is to time your smile like those of other highly successful blacks. Do as the Ken Chenaults of the world would do."

Ken and others have done a tremendous job mentoring and developing young minority talent. In present high-level executive ranks, there are some truly outstanding professionals such as Anré Williams,[82] Ursula M. Burns,[83] and Ronald Williams.[84] Because of Ken Chenault and his executive cadre, American Express is developing minority talent that will increase revenues and market share for its shareholders.

Morgan Stanley

The year 1987 was a good year for me personally and for JHLA.[85] While we were doing work with American Express, we were also

---

[82] Anré Williams currently serves as the president of Global Merchant Services and Loyalty at American Express. Williams received a bachelor's from Stanford University and an MBA from the Wharton School of the University of Pennsylvania. In 2016, Williams became a director of the USA Track & Field Foundation Board.

[83] Ursula M. Burns is a member of the American Express board of directors and was the CEO and chairman of Xerox Corporation. Burns holds a BS from New York University Tandon School of Engineering and an MS from Columbia University. In 2009, Burns became the first black American woman CEO of a Fortune 500 company.

[84] Ronald A. Williams served as the CEO and chairman of Aetna, Inc. and is a member of the American Express board of directors. Williams received a bachelor's from Roosevelt University and an MBA from the MIT Sloan School of Management. In 2011, he was appointed to President Barack Obama's management advisory board.

[85] In 1987, JHLA was voted by *Kennedy* publication as one of the top consulting firms in America.

supporting a major hotel chain. I was contacted by the hotel's CEO, who informed me that his hotel had been negatively portrayed on a popular talk show for firing a female employee for wearing her hair in "cornrows." While this style may be much more common today, it was not the case in the mideighties. I agreed to mediate the situation to help the hotel chain avoid a costly legal battle. I met with the young woman suing the hotel and agreed with her that she had every right to wear her hair any way she wanted. But she should also be willing to accept the consequences of her actions. This is the advice I often give to young professionals, as well as myself. As we all travel up the road, we must make some difficult decisions. Not only should we think hard about these decisions, but we also must think of the possible implications in the short term along with potentially damaging consequences in the future.

In 1988, thanks to the support of a young in-house lawyer at Monsanto, we were awarded a contract to conduct a diagnostic study of Monsanto's Affirmative Action Initiative. That young lawyer was Clarence Thomas. Soon after our engagement, Clarence Thomas started his career in government as the assistant secretary for civil rights at the Department of Education (DOE). Apparently, Thomas recommended us to Monsanto because he had heard our concept of the "Rules of the Game" and believed in its principles. After serving only one year as assistant secretary at DOE, he was appointed chairman of the Equal Employment Opportunity Commission (EEOC), a role he maintained from 1982 to 1990, making him the longest-serving chair of that agency. While at the EEOC, he asked us once again to assist him, this time to help the EEOC prepare hearings on the participation and upward mobility of minorities and women in corporations. Although I did not always agree with his opinions, we got along well and were always able to communicate openly. The few times we spoke, I recall him having a great sense of humor.

Fast-forward a few years later as millions were glued to television sets to witness Clarence Thomas's confirmation hearings to be the second black US Supreme Court justice in history. I remember being in the office of then city comptroller Carol Moseley Braun when the final votes were cast. One of the key votes from the democratic side was Senator Alan Dixon. Senator Dixon had never lost an election in the state of Illinois in his more than forty-two years in office. When the roll call came to him, Carol said, "If he votes for Clarence Thomas, I am going to challenge him for his seat." Sure enough, Senator Dixon cast his vote for the confirmation, and Carol victoriously shouted, "I am running!" Watching this critical moment on television at the same time was a federal judge who quickly arranged a meeting with Braun to talk her out of running. Carol asked me to leave the office for the private meeting with the judge. After a very brief meeting, Carol asked me to return to her office, where she shared with me that the judge told her she would never win because she was black. Knowing Carol like I do, I knew that was the added incentive she needed, sealing her conviction to run for Senator Dixon's seat.

With the support of women voters in Illinois, along with many other factors, Carol Moseley Braun became the first black woman to be elected to the Senate on November 3, 1992. In addition, she was the first woman to be elected by Illinois and the first black person to be elected as a democrat.[86] Knowing historically that the city of Chicago and the state of Illinois have not always been the most hospitable for blacks, I often wondered how this happened. I came to believe that within its population segmentation throughout the city and the state, there were leaders always willing to cut a

---

[86] The first black person elected to the United States Senate from the state of Illinois was Hiram Revels in 1870 during Reconstruction. In 2005, Barack Obama, also an attorney, would become the second black senator from the state of Illinois, followed by Roland Burris in 2009. In the history of the United States, there have only been three black senators who have come from Illinois.

deal to ensure all sides win. Too bad the same cannot be said of Washington, DC. Carol did a good job as a US senator, and I was sorry to see her lose her next election, because she would have been an outstanding senator for many years to come.

In early 1992, we received a request to bid on a contract to assist Morgan Stanley to design a comprehensive diversity and inclusion strategy. We would be competing against four other consulting firms. The evaluation committee was headed by managing partner, Bill Lewis, and was comprised of the top minority and women principals and managing directors of the firm. When we initially received the invitation to bid, I was on my annual vacation in Puerto Vallarta, Mexico. Fortunately for me, I had just hired the truly exceptional Marilyn Booker, who would turn out to be one of the smartest people I ever had the opportunity to work with. Marilyn, who finished second in her class at Spelman College, was extremely intelligent, witty, quality driven, a great writer, and highly persuasive. Although a new hire, Marilyn did not hesitate to tell me in no uncertain terms, "Jim, get off your butt and get to work. You need to prepare a well-thought-out deck and get on the next flight to New York."

I took her advice, and with deck in hand, I made my presentation to the committee and immediately returned to Mexico, not knowing whether we had prevailed. I did get a little support when one of the evaluators, Pamela Carlton,[87] thanked me and said I had done a great job. She also added that while I had never met her personally, I had actually once brought a gift back from Peru for her husband, Charles, because, coincidentally at the time, I was dating his sister. *What a small world*, I thought

---

[87] Pamela Carlton serves as the president of Springboard, a leadership and organizational consulting firm. She is also the cofounder of The Everest Project Research Initiative. Carlton earned a bachelor's from Williams College, a JD from Yale University, and an MBA from the Yale School of Management.

as I reflected on that trip to Peru, fondly remembering Charles's lovely sister, Pam, his very smart brother, Ron, and his father who was the head of Pittsburgh's Urban League during the period I attended the University of Pittsburgh. I recalled that her husband had also been a classmate of Peter Bynoe at Harvard College and Law School. Once again, the notion of the Talented Tenth[88] "network" was alive and working.

We received the committee's vote soon after, and I informed the JHLA team that this contract could be the largest and one of the most important contracts in the history of the firm. Personally, I felt the same way when we were asked to assist McKinsey. With that contract, we proved we could have a major impact on a major institution. The key to our success at McKinsey was accepting the culture, while at the same time tweaking the internal processes and working with key decision makers. We aspired to do the same with Morgan Stanley, one of the largest and most respected firms on Wall Street.

Although we were selected by the task force, we still needed to obtain the final approval of the three big partners who were leading Morgan Stanley at the time. Barton Biggs was the chairman of the diversity task force, Dick Fisher was a Wall Street icon, and John Mack was rumored to be the future head of Morgan Stanley. My first two interviews with Dick Fisher and Barton Biggs went smoothly. John Mack, on the other hand, was a different story. He had been a tough football player at Duke University and a marine, and needless to say, he carried that toughness into our interview. I'll never forget the first question he asked, "Has your firm ever done any diversity work on Wall Street?" I proudly answered him, "Yes, we had a two-year engagement with Dean Witter." He sternly

---

[88] Talented Tenth by W.E.B. Du Bois, refers to the notion that within the black community, if provided the right education, one out of ten blacks had the capacity for intellectual excellence and could become leaders in the community.

responded, "Dean Witter is not Wall Street." I will never forget that response because five years later in 1997, when Dean Witter merged with Morgan Stanley, to the surprise of many on the street, it was my old McKinsey boss Phil Purcell, the CEO of Dean Witter, who was selected by the board to head the merged company, not John Mack. Ultimately, John Mack became the president, and Phil Purcell took an exit package worth an estimated $113.7 million. Phil gave $12.5 million to Notre Dame, his undergraduate alma mater, and $4.25 million to the University of Chicago Business School, $3.75 million of which was in the form of a challenge grant.[89]

Joining JHLA at this juncture was my lifetime idol and brother Bill Lowry. My brother had a very distinguished career at Inland Steel. He was an expert in the human resource field, had his own TV show, and for more than thirty years had been a leader in the community. Although he was well liked at Inland, after many years with the firm, he felt he should have been promoted to vice president. I always felt he deserved the promotion, but at the same time, I was happy I could offer him a position at JHLA. I thought we could have fun working together, make money, and retire in a grand flash. When he finally accepted that he was not going to get the VP position at Inland, I jumped at the opportunity to have him join the team. So, on that first day at Morgan Stanley, we met Bill Lewis with our core JHLA team of Marilyn Booker, my brother Bill, and me.

Bill Lewis was a product of Phillips Academy as A Better Chance scholarship recruit. He was also a graduate of Harvard College and Harvard Business School and had risen through the ranks of Morgan Stanley to be their first black managing director. For me, then and still today, Bill represented the model professional and behind-the-scenes corporate leader, especially considering the social change that was occurring in the nineties.

---

[89] Challenge grants are typically made to nonprofit entities and educational institutions, with the grant maker being corporations, government agencies, foundations, or trusts.

Once he got to Morgan Stanley, he learned the trade, expanded his core skills, and operated effectively within the culture. Morgan Stanley gave him a well-deserved promotion, but he never forgot where he came from. After becoming a managing director, and while working as a minority leader in his field and continuing to be a revenue generator for Morgan Stanley, he used his unique position in the firm and shifted his attention to effecting change within the company for people of color. He formed a task force with other like-minded minority and women leaders: Pamela Carlton, Derrick Penn,[90] Carla Harris,[91] and Eugene Flood.[92]

When we started our work with Morgan Stanley, we interviewed more than thirty top executives. Initially, we got pushback from the white female managing directors who questioned why such an initiative was even necessary. These sentiments were echoed by the same nonminority women on the task force, but when we met with them one-on-one and discussed the unique challenges they faced, their attitudes changed. What the women soon began to articulate was that the issues women faced in terms of diversity were different from racial diversity

---

[90] Derrick Penn is the head of equity sales and trading with the capital markets division for the BNY Mellon Markets Group. Prior to a career in business, Penn played in the NFL. He received a bachelor's and MBA from Duke University.

[91] Carla Harris currently serves as a vice chairman, managing director, wealth management and senior client advisor at Morgan Stanley. In 2011, Harris was named to *Fortune* magazine's list of "The 50 Most Powerful Black Executives in Corporate America." In addition to a successful business career, Harris also is an author and singer. She holds an AB and MBA from Harvard University. She presently sits on the boards of Sponsors for Educational Opportunity, A Better Chance, and St. Vincent's Hospital.

[92] Eugene Flood is the managing director of Next Sector Capital, former managing partner of A Cappella Partners, and former CEO of asset management firm Smith Breeden Associated. He earned his bachelor's from Harvard University and PhD from MIT.

issues and therefore should be addressed differently. As a result, two diversity task forces were established. The newly formed women's task force had their own consultant, Katie Herzog, who was a true professional. Katie and I worked well together for the next two years, sharing best practices and making much progress for the different groups.

Accepting that Wall Street's battle for talent was very fierce, we once again had to think outside the box to move Morgan Stanley ahead of the competition. Marilyn knew there were many talented students among the HBCU ranks because she herself was a graduate of Spelman College, one of the most well-known HBCUs. At Marilyn's recommendation, Morgan Stanley established a scholarship fund, and Dick Fisher, albeit reluctantly, added his name to it. I am proud to say that Morgan Stanley still supports the fund, and as a result, hundreds of minority students have attended colleges and universities such as Morehouse College, Spelman College, Howard University, and Florida A&M University.

Getting talented students into a company is one thing; getting them to the level of vice president and higher up the corporate ladder is another. To assist Morgan Stanley with this challenge, we designed our own model mentoring program. Within the program, we outlined the key factors of success, including the necessity of not only being a good mentor but how to be a good mentee as well. We also devoted a significant amount of time in our training course on the differences between having an effective coach, a strong mentor, and a powerful sponsor. When we shared the design with recruiting partners, one very senior partner said, "Jim, we all need to be exposed to this course, not just women and minorities." His remark meant a lot to me and the team. We knew we had done our job well.

We were effecting change within the leadership, all the way up to the C-suite decision makers, not only by providing funding for students at four outstanding universities and colleges but also the culture of Morgan Stanley itself. Prophesizing that Morgan Stanley was not going to fund JHLA for the next five years, we designed and recommended an internal diversity organization. They accepted our recommendation, and it was at this point I realized we'd perhaps done our job too well. I was somewhat taken aback when Bill Lewis asked me if I would be upset if Morgan Stanley recruited Marilyn Booker to run it. Without hesitation, I said Marilyn would be an excellent choice to head the new office because she was the total package. Still, I felt a great deal of pain; I was losing my close friend, an ally, my number one consultant, and the visionary on our team. If I am honest, I was also hurt they offered the position to my mentee and not me. But as a friend, I knew it was time for her to leave JHLA and start her own career—and what better place than Morgan Stanley and New York City. I also knew she would be outstanding and had the smarts and the drive to separate Morgan Stanley from the competition.

Over the next twenty-five years under Marilyn Booker, Morgan Stanley had one of the best, if not the best, diversity initiatives in the country. With the support of the partnership and Bill Lewis, Marilyn expanded Morgan Stanley's diversity efforts to include minority business enterprise development, government relationships, and human resource development. At Morgan Stanley, Marilyn Booker established a close relationship with every CEO at the firm during her tenure. Because she was successful, Morgan Stanley became successful and a model for the country.

Although I never left the field of minority business enterprise development, I shifted the focus of my firm to diversity and inclusion. It was clear for multiple reasons that corporate America was beginning to place more importance on identifying, training, and promoting diverse populations. With the increase of minorities, immigrants, and women in the workplace, corporate America would invest in internal and external experts to address the problem of low representation of all these groups, especially at the C-suite level.

As a firm, we were highly successful working for many industry leaders, mainly because of my staff, the uniqueness of our product offerings, and my ability to be a trusted advisor to CEOs. Working with AT&T, Morgan Stanley, Xerox, and Frito-Lay over the years, I observed that when the company's CEO got involved, change occurred. Our findings and recommendations were more readily accepted when CEOs gave us their full support. Without CEO support, few things can be accomplished within major corporations. This is especially true with respect to D&I, with all its complexity and internal critics. Tragically, so few of the many solid D&I consulting firms are able to achieve a close working relationship with the CEOs. As a result, many of their recommendations and programs go unsupported.

Eventually, Marilyn stepped down from her position as head of diversity and inclusion and now leads Morgan Stanley's Urban Marketing Group. Over the years, I have taken great pride in observing Marilyn's success as a highly productive professional. However, I have taken greater pride in her role as a mother of three beautiful children and a courageous mentor in and outside of Morgan Stanley.

About the time Marilyn was assuming her new responsibilities at Morgan Stanley, my brother, Bill, had been tapped to be the new vice president for administration at the MacArthur Foundation. As in the case of Marilyn, I was sad to see him go, but I knew my brother would be outstanding and a true asset to the foundation under the new president, Adele S. Simmons.

With the departures of Marilyn and my brother, Bill, a divorce from my soul mate of more than twenty years, Sharon Collins, and rapidly approaching sixty years of age, I was probably at my lowest point psychologically. It was around this time I was seriously thinking about getting out of the consulting business altogether. I had enough money in the bank and enough work, and even with just a skeleton staff of five to ten people, I could live the life I was accustomed to without dipping into the trust I had set up for my daughter. My firm had designed state-of-the-art diversity programs with Pepsi, Frito-Lay, Ford Motor Company, McKinsey, and Morgan Stanley. In addition, we played a significant role in the turnaround of A Better Chance, one of the most significant educational programs for minorities in the nation. I was proud of our accomplishments, but I was still not a happy person. When Grinnell College named me a life trustee after twenty years of service, I knew I was beginning my elder stage of life. I had to accept that life changes were around the corner, but deep down, I did not want to retire. There were too many problems to be solved, too many young professionals to be mentored, and we had not achieved economic parity.

McDonald's

In the spring of 1995, I received a call from a high-ranking black executive from McDonald's by the name of Bob Beavers. Bob Beavers was a legend in the black business community because not only was he the first black vice president at McDonald's, he was also the first black board member. To get to this elevated position at McDonald's, he had worked his way from a store manager in Washington, DC, to the C-suite in Oakbrook, Illinois. Utilizing his clout on the board and his close friendship with McDonald's founder, Ray Kroc, Bob Beavers assisted McDonald's in developing model programs in the areas of diversity and inclusion, minority business enterprise development, and black franchise ownership. Because of Bob Beavers and McDonald's' leaders, hundreds of blacks became McDonald's franchise owners and multimillionaires. McDonald's diversity program was the model for the nation, ensuring black executive leadership at all levels of the organization and creating jobs in our communities across the nation. Another outstanding example of a black executive coming up in the organization and reaching the top was Don Thompson, who was named president and CEO of McDonald's in 2012.

Knowing Bob's background, I had no idea why he was reaching out to me. I was hoping he was calling to offer me a consulting contract, but much to my surprise, he was calling me to see if I wanted to be the first black member at Medinah Country Club, a private club just outside of Chicago. Medinah had asked Bob if he wanted to apply, but since he was not a golfer, he thought I was a better candidate. He also was aware that as the president of Chicago United, I had been urged by many of my corporate friends to open membership in elite country clubs to minorities, women, and Jews.

Over the years, I had played the course at Medinah as a guest of my JHLA CFO, but I was never asked to join. The offer provided by Bob was a tempting one because Medinah was rated the top golf club in Illinois and one of the best in the nation. I was an avid golfer and was also aware that Medinah was trying to get the PGA golf tournament, and the PGA was not going to award the tournament to clubs who did not have minority members. Thus, while I did want the honor of being the first black member at Medinah, I had my concerns. I wondered how I would be accepted by the club members, and considering how much an annual membership cost, would my golf game really improve?

I shared my concerns with Bill Daley, who at this time was the regional chair of JPMorgan Chase, and it was his advice that motivated me to present myself to the selection committee. Bill said, "Jim, you have to join, be the model not only for other blacks but also for the many Medinah members who do not know quality people like you exist." So motivated, my wife, Sharon, and I met with the selection committee. To my surprise, the chairman was an old Lab School classmate of my brother, Bill. He shared with other members that he had known me for thirty years. We were quickly approved seven months later. Many months later, we were elated to be standing at the eighteenth hole watching Tiger Woods as he raised the PGA trophy over his head after his first PGA tournament win.

I have retained my membership at Medinah. It is a great club, and I proudly bring guests to play every summer. I entertain my BCG partners and families, clients and potential clients, and my boys from Woodlawn who were avid golfers but never had the opportunity to play at an exclusive suburban country club. I will never forget an incident where one of my closest A. O. Sexton friends, named Freddie, accompanied me to Medinah. For more than thirty years, he had been playing golf at the South Side public course. I suggested we grab a bite in the club before hitting the course. To my surprise, Freddie said, "If we go to eat, who is going to watch our clubs?" Holding back a smile, I let him know that the cost of my monthly fees would be all the security we'd need. We ate, we golfed, and Freddie had the time of his life.

Many years after joining Medinah, I got to know Bob Beavers on a more personal basis. One day over lunch, I asked him why he recommended me to become a member. He told me that he had been hearing stories about me for years from fellow McDonald's board member David Wallerstein. I told him how David Wallerstein helped me get into Francis W. Parker and how much I loved him and his wife, Carolyn. It warmed my heart when Bob responded by saying, "Jim, did you know how much they loved you?"

After living in a very comfortable bachelor apartment for five years after my divorce, I decided to buy a large condo in the neighborhood near Francis W. Parker. I had always desired to live in one of those large condos like David and Caroline Wallerstein had. After an exhaustive search, I found the penthouse condo that met my childhood dreams. It was a block away from

Lake Michigan, had an outdoor patio and indoor solarium, four bedrooms, maid's room off the kitchen, and a twenty-four-hour doorman. As George Jefferson used to say, "I was moving on up." In my mind, I had finally arrived. This fact was anchored when I was told that the original occupant of my penthouse was Joseph L. Block, chairman of the board and CEO of Inland Steel. Block was the uncle of one of my former Francis W. Parker classmates and former chairman of the board of Francis W. Parker. When I graduated from Parker, I had career and financial goals. When I moved into my condo the first day, I said to myself, "Jim, you haven't achieved all your career and financial goals, but now there is a light at the end of the tunnel." I also had to admit that I had done all right for a black boy who was previously turned down for admittance into the seventh grade at Francis W. Parker because he did not do well on a standardized test. From that rejection, my early teachers, my mother, and others motivated me, as did the dream of living in a beautiful penthouse that I now owned.

When I was asked by the principal of Francis W. Parker to host my class's fiftieth reunion, I did not hesitate to say yes. At my long dining room table, over drinks and catered dinner, I toasted each and thanked every one of my classmates for the support they offered me and Jim Simmons during our time at Francis W. Parker. They too had played a significant role in my life, and I would always be grateful.

I was proud of the fact I finally was able to purchase my dream condo. But then fifteen years later, I was reminded that I was still black. One day while I was parked and idling in the front of my building, waiting for my wife to come down so we could head to church, the back door to my black 460 Lexus suddenly opened. To my surprise, one of the building tenants had the doorman throw his bag into my car as the man angrily stated, "Because you are late, I will miss my flight at O'Hare!" In not so subtle terms, I told him he had better get out of my car immediately. I turned to my doorman of ten years and said, "You are as dumb as he is. No Christmas bonus for you this year!" My episode, along with numerous other examples by notable African Americans, was later detailed in a book titled *The Presumption of Guilt: The Arrest of Henry Louis Gates, Jr. and Race, Class and Crime in America,* by Harvard law professor Charles Ogletree.[93]

---

[93] Charles Ogletree, *The Presumption of Guilt: The Arrest of Henry Louis Gates, Jr. and Race, Class and Crime in America* (St. Martin's Press, 2012).

Historical Background 2001–2009

Probably one the most important and impactful events in our nation's history was the election of Barack H. Obama in 2008 as the first African American president of the United States. He came into office with a message of change. On his inauguration, Washington, DC, had more than a million visitors covering the National Mall, in a way reminiscent of the civil rights march of Martin Luther King forty-six years earlier.

- 2003: In *Grutter v. Bollinger*,[94] the most important affirmative action decision since the 1978 *Bakke* case, the US Supreme Court (5–4) upheld the University of Michigan Law School's policy, ruling that race can be one of many factors considered by colleges when selecting their students because it furthers a "compelling interest in obtaining the educational benefits that flow from a diverse student body."
- 2005: Civil rights leader Rosa Park died.
- 2006: In *Parents v. Seattle and Meredith v. Jefferson*,[95] affirmative action suffered a setback when a bitterly divided court ruled, 5–4, that programs in Seattle, Washington, and Louisville, Kentucky, which tried to maintain diversity in schools by considering race when assigning students to schools, were unconstitutional.
- 2009: *Ricci v. DeStefano*,[96] in a lawsuit brought against the city of New Haven, eighteen plaintiffs—seventeen white and one Hispanic—argued that results of the 2003 lieutenant and captain exams were thrown out when it

---

[94] *Grutter v. Bollinger*, 539 U.S. 306 (2003).
[95] *Parents Involved in Community Schools v. Seattle School District No. 1*, 551 U.S. 701 (2007).
[96] *Ricci v. DeStefano*, 557 U.S. 557 (2009).

was determined that few minority firefighters qualified for advancement. The city claimed they threw out the results because they feared liability under a disparate-impact statute for issuing tests that discriminated against minority firefighters. The plaintiffs claimed that they were victims of reverse discrimination under the Title VII of the Civil Rights Act of 1964. The Supreme Court ruled (5–4) in favor of the firefighters, saying New Haven's "action in discarding the test was a violation of Title VII."

CHAPTER 15

BCG PARTNERSHIP, AN OPPORTUNITY TO MENTOR THE NEXT GENERATION

About to hit my sixtieth birthday and entering a new century, I was still not ready to retire. I was looking for something different to do. I also wanted another chance at becoming a venture capitalist. On an earlier yet unsuccessful attempt, I had been approached by ex-McKinsey consultant Bob Cummings to form a venture fund with two of his friends. We set a target of raising $200 million. While we received some initial funding from the state of Wisconsin, we eventually closed the fund down when we realized we were not going to achieve our target. I confess I did not invest enough time making presentations to the various public and private pension funds, and looking back, I can admit that I did not really appreciate the rejections from very young fund managers right out of business school. But over that six-month period, I learned a lot about the industry, its key players, and the competition. Later, I became a consultant to the National Association of Investment Companies (NAIC) along with my good friend Robert Greene. My experience at attempting to raise a fund helped me to be a better advocate and trusted advisor for my client.

I had another learning experience as a court-appointed trustee for Sengstacke Enterprises. At one time, Sengstacke Enterprises was one of the largest, most profitable black businesses in the country. As a holding company, it owned the *Michigan Chronicle, Memphis Tri-City Defender,* the *Pittsburgh Courier,* and the *Chicago Defender.* Before and during the height of the civil rights movement, these four newspapers were the most respected and history-laden journals written for black communities around the country. Pullman porters used to distribute the *Chicago Defender* and the *Pittsburgh Courier* on the Illinois Central Railroad. As a child, I remember the paperboy yelling, "Come and get your *Chicago Defender, Chicago Defender!*" In these historical and iconic newspapers, we followed our great entertainers, the Negro Baseball League, and its stars Josh Gibson and Satchel Paige. Most importantly, we learned of all the social injustices perpetuated against blacks both in the North and the South.

Unfortunately, when I was appointed trustee by the court, all four newspapers had lost their power and ability to be the voices of the black community. Their positions of power had been taken over by the publications of Johnson Publishing Company, large newspapers in major cities, and television. Of the four newspapers, only one, the *Michigan Chronicle,* remained profitable. It was the hope of the court and the board that I could facilitate the sale of the properties and pass the proceeds to John Sengstacke's grandchildren in Chicago. When I accepted this responsibility, I thought it was going to be an easy and quick transaction. Unfortunately, this was not the case for multiple reasons; the two biggest: we could not find buyers for these properties, and the grandchildren and their legal counsel overvalued the four newspapers. After many months and countless hours invested, we finally sold the properties to a group out of Detroit. The new owner was a company founded specifically to purchase the four newspapers and was called Real Times Inc. As a result, we were able to liquidate the assets for the sake of the grandchildren and keep these iconic institutions in the hands of black owners.

At this point in my life, I felt that maybe I was finally ready to retire or at least assume the role of trusted advisor with another diversity consulting firm or a larger minority professional services firm. I had recently been part of a joint venture with Kaleidoscope Consulting Firm, conducting a twelve-month diversity study for Deloitte & Touche. By the end of the study, Deloitte's partners offered me an opportunity to be a strategic partner. I thought Deloitte would be a good place to hang my hat. Just prior to finalizing a contract with Deloitte, however, I received another call that would change my life and put an end to my semiretirement plans. The call was from Larry Shulman, senior vice president at the Boston Consulting Group (BCG). I had heard great things about Larry Shulman, but I had never met him. I had gotten to know and respect John Clarkson, the former president of BCG, when we both served on the Harvard Business School Visiting Committee. Larry Shulman had been given the assignment to increase the number of minorities at BCG. Evidently, BCG was having a difficult time recruiting minorities from the top schools, repeatedly losing talent to McKinsey. According to Larry, the most critical factor for McKinsey's success at the top schools was the 104 blacks we had helped recruit as consultants, many of whom remained at McKinsey, and even the ones who had left were very effective as on-campus recruiters for the firm.

I cannot say I was surprised by this turn of events. Shortly after my successful two-year engagement at McKinsey, I approached the head of the Chicago office at BCG, Carl Stern, to offer exactly these services to BCG. I boldly told Carl that, working together, we could do the same thing for BCG that I had done for McKinsey with respect to identifying, recruiting, and developing minorities. Back then, Carl diplomatically rejected my offer saying, "Jim, I do not think we need any help. BCG is a meritocracy, and we are skilled in identifying and recruiting top talent." With a knowing smile, I informed Carl that I had heard statements like that from many CEOs of other global companies and that "too often, meritocracy is in the eyes of the beholder." I strongly believed the metrics used by major companies often define success too narrowly and lacked the ability to effectively judge candidates that are slightly different, irrespective of color or gender.

When I started my career as a diversity consultant, I would explain that a black or Hispanic résumé looked different. Minority résumés often had to avoid creating red flags and somehow not direct attention to the fact that during the summer they had to accept whatever job paid the most money, clearly not having the luxury of making a choice based on what looked best for their résumé. Many minorities had to work to pay for school and even provide family support. For me and others, the fact that they were committed to both goals, showing dedication and discipline, meant more to us than a 3.4 versus a 3.7 grade point average. Over the years, I have observed many of my clients' unwillingness to conduct deep-dive studies on the success rates of the 3.5 grade point average candidates and above recruiting model. They assume the 3.7 is a more accurate prediction of success, without doing the research to prove such a hypothesis. Now ten years later, after having my services rejected by Carl Stern, I was being invited back to the table, and it felt good.

Larry had done his homework on me and JHLA. He knew what we had achieved at McKinsey, and he wanted me to achieve the same dramatic success at BCG. Initially, although I was honored by the request, I had finally come to terms with the notion of retirement, in some form anyway. I had reduced my staff significantly, and at this point in my career, I was only accepting personal contracts. Upon reflection, I thought this would be a great opportunity for a grand exit, with me effecting change for minorities for the top two consulting firms in the world, McKinsey and BCG.

I got back to Larry and told him I would be willing to accept a six-month assignment, provided I was able to work directly with him and Carl Stern and that he would provide strong internal support. Further, I made it clear they had to accept that in order to be successful, as was the case at McKinsey, they had to be willing to think outside the box if necessary and be willing to accept that within the BCG culture, there would be slight change.

Agreeing to my conditions, Larry assigned Reggie Gilyard[97] and Cecilia Edwards,[98] two strong black consultants, to support me and assist in leading the project. Reggie was a very bright young principal, a graduate of the Air Force Academy and Harvard Business School. He was highly recruited and had done well his first few years at BCG. He was well trained, extremely loyal, and on track to become the first black partner in the Los Angeles office. He accepted the diversity assignment, but it was not his passion. In fact, at the time, Larry was a more passionate change agent at BCG, even to the point he upset many partners with his style and commitment. Cecilia also served in the US Airforce and had received her MBA from the University of California at Berkeley. She, like Reggie, was on track to become partner, and because she had a real passion for diversity, she was excited to be on the project. We kicked off the project with a diversity retreat in New Orleans, and for this initial retreat, we decided to have only the eleven black consultants in the firm attend.

---

[97] Reginald (Reggie) Gilyard was a partner and managing director at BCG's Los Angeles office. He serves as the dean of Chapman University's Argyros School of Business and Economics. He also received a master's from the Air Force Institute of Technology.

[98] Edwards held various leadership positions and served as a manager at BCG for more than five years. Currently, Edwards is a partner with global consulting firm Everest Group. She has a BA from Smith College.

BCG PARTNERSHIP, AN OPPORTUNITY TO MENTOR THE NEXT GENERATION

The retreat was my first exposure to BCG culture and its partners. Both Larry and Carl remained for the full three days and not only participated but also listened to the special concerns and issues articulated by the black consultants. Basically, they were the same concerns and issues that were presented by similar groups at McKinsey and Morgan Stanley that focused on how blacks were recruited, assigned, mentored, evaluated, and supported. The sessions were long and lively but with a spirit of cooperation and a focus on how to solve the problem. It was not all work; in the evenings, we ventured to New Orleans' finest restaurants and clubs. Often during our breaks, we would approach the piano and listen to a young BCG associate with a bachelor's from the University of Pennsylvania who would play beautifully. His name was John Stephens,[99] and at the time, he was attempting to have a dual career as a BCG consultant in the New York office during the week and as a musician on the weekends.

Like so many others, I was immediately attracted to young John Stephens. Not only was he very bright, he was always very humble, hardworking, committed, and deeply spiritual. After New Orleans, whenever I would visit the New York office, I would try to mentor John, along with his good friend, Kweli Washington,[100] a Rhodes Scholar from Harvard University. Rounding out my

---

[99] Singer, songwriter, musician, actor, director and producer, John Legend, has won ten Grammy Awards, two Billboard and BET Awards, one American Music Choice, an African American Film Critics Award, a Golden Globe, a Critics' Choice Award, a Tony Award, and an Academy Award. He received a BA from the University of Pennsylvania.

[100] Kweli Washington serves as the chief operations officer at Piano, a subsidiary of the SaaS company that specializes in advanced media business processes and online commerce optimization software. Washington graduated from Harvard University phi beta kappa magna cum laude and went on to be a Rhodes Scholar at Oxford.

favorite trio was Alexander Ulanov,[101] a brilliant, very intense, and very proud Puerto Rican Princeton graduate with a PhD from Yale. To me, these three diverse young professionals represented the diversity within the minority communities: John Stephens, a child prodigy raised in a deeply religious family, son of an auto factory worker from Springfield, Ohio; Kweli Washington of mixed race, raised by a single mother from Berkeley, California; and Alex Ulanov, son of a Russian father who was a jazz icon and a Puerto Rican mother raised in Spanish Harlem. I recall Alex put huge speakers in his BCG office to play the latest reggaeton hits, proudly displaying his Hispanic heritage. This small group of brilliant young men were my favorites in the firm; they were my posse, and I was their mentor and confidant. Of the three, only Alex Ulanov became a BCG partner. I will always be indebted to them for their support during my early years with the firm and the many dinners we enjoyed as friends, bonding to make history both in and outside of BCG.

When I accepted the original diversity engagement, I had envisioned effecting the same type of change that we achieved at McKinsey, allowing me to ride off into the sunset of retirement. That was my plan anyway. One day Larry Schulman and I were having lunch and comparing notes on our various Fortune 500 clients. I do not believe my list overwhelmed Larry, but when I mentioned that over my forty-year career, my firm was able to get repeat business with 96 percent of our clients, this figure got Larry's attention. He quickly said, "Jim, I believe that if I talk to Carl and others, I can provide you with three options: one, stay on as a consultant under a new contract; two, become a senior advisor, nonpartner expert; or three, become a BCG partner." I

---

[101] Alex Ulanov rose from principal to partner and managing director (industrial goods and operations practice area lead) and is currently a partner at McKinsey & Company. He was a Fulbright Foreign Scholar at Princeton University and received a PhD from Yale University.

had not achieved partner status at McKinsey, so I thought this could be an excellent opportunity to leave the consulting field on a high note. I told Larry I would prefer option three, and I promised I would only stay in this position a short period and then I would retire.

Larry quickly went to work, and that is when I witnessed the cultural difference between BCG and McKinsey. Overnight he arranged personal interviews with five partners. The first was Michael Silverstein, then head of BCG's Global Consumer Practice. Next was Ron Nichols, head of BCG North America based in Dallas. Third was Matt Krentz, a newly minted consumer goods partner based in Chicago. Finally, there was Barbara Hewitt, another recently elected partner who was very close to Michael Silverstein and Neil Fiske, head of the Chicago office. Fortunately for me, they all supported my selection to become a partner, and at the next worldwide official meeting, I was officially made a BCG partner.

As much as I truly admired the McKinsey culture and partnership, there was no way I would have made partner at that firm with five interviews. I remembered back in 1968, it took nine interviews to be selected as a consultant. Similarly, at age fifty-nine and knowing the culture as I do, I would not have been allowed in the club. I also knew, with my 3.5 grade point average and a degree from the University of Pittsburgh, I would not have gotten one interview with BCG starting as a candidate off campus. BCG's hiring guidelines were different in the sixties. They looked only for candidates with a minimum of a 3.7 grade point average and mostly from Ivy League schools. Times had changed slightly, and I was going to be a partner at BCG in the year 2000. I will be forever grateful to those five BCG leaders who approved of my candidacy. I was committed to be a valued partner, a change agent, and, at sixty years old, a respected leader and a credit to my race.

I was given a wonderful opportunity by BCG, and I was prepared to take advantage of it. I did not bargain hard in negotiating my contract; financially, this contract was favorable. In hindsight, I made a mistake in agreeing to split my time between running the diversity practice both internally and externally. In any professional services firm, one's expertise is often valued. In the end, however, the ones who move quickly up the ladder are the ones who have the biggest clients, manage the largest teams, and generate the greatest revenues. I was in charge of the diversity practice, so I had to feed the people in my group and still lead the internal diversity initiative. The most important difference between the diversity practice and other BCG practices was there were limited possibilities of obtaining and sustaining multimillion-dollar clients. In my first months at BCG, we won a major diversity study at AOL-Time Warner that demanded 90 percent of my time, leaving me little time to market or invest the appropriate amount to BCG's internal diversity efforts.

The study was challenging because it was during the time of the merger. Top management was in flux, and I had only been at BCG for a very short time. However, it was satisfying because I was returning to Time Warner after fifteen years. Previously, I conducted a diversity inclusion report for a young, talented black professional named Toni Fay. She was one of the early bright superstars in corporate America who truly cared for the community and influenced decision makers to make the necessary investments and policy decisions. She and other early trailblazers like George Lewis at Philip Morris, Tom Shropshire at Miller Brewing Company, and Darwin Davis at Equitable Life Insurance opened big doors for minorities, and my own company benefited greatly from their leadership.

For this new project, we were to report to Dick Parsons, a key leader from the Time Warner Company. Dick later became the CEO but at that time had the title of president. I admired

Dick Parsons for the way he operated in a very difficult position during some nasty, competitive bargaining between AOL and Time Warner forces. I appreciated the fact he asked me and BCG to design the first holistic, fully integrated diversity initiative I had ever witnessed. First, he organized a high-level task force comprised of division presidents. He was very clear he wanted divisions within each profit center to focus on diversity as a high priority throughout the company. Diversity of people, diversity within the supply chain, diversity in foundation giving, diversity in images on TV and in movies, and even diversity in the allocation of capital from the fund they had established.

When I formed my BCG team, I was supported by a young partner, Kevin Waddell, who provided me invaluable insights on how to format decks, organize the team, and attack problems in the BCG way. I arranged my team with two of my young geniuses, John Stephens and Alex Ulanov, with Alex being the project leader. One day we were organizing a client presentation for the person representing all the AOL-Time Warner music labels. Both Alex and I saw this as an opportunity to seek a record contract for John Stephens. We presented John's case as best we could, but the label executive was not buying. I read her body language and decided this bird was not going to fly, but in true Alex style, he remained relentless until the executive said, "Alex, when I need BCG to judge talent for me, I will get out of the f—king business." In this case, she should have listened to her consultant's advice because soon after, John Stephens left BCG and got a record deal with Sony. John Stephens changed his name to John Legend, and the rest is history.

John Legend seemed to blow up relatively quickly, but I remember the early days when he was performing at Harvard Business School or appearing at weekend functions or clubs with an audience of fewer than fifty people. Whenever he would come to Chicago, I would take him to dinner. After his first record came out, I started taking John and his bodyguard, Hassan Smith, to dinner. I watched his fame grow, greatly supported by Oprah Winfrey, Stevie Wonder, Quincy Jones, and others. His singing and composing skills elevated him to world-class status. But through it all he has remained humble, positive, and committed to making life better for those less fortunate. The only advice I ever gave him was when he got his first contract. I told him, "Your music will make you famous, but it is your brand and how you present yourself that will gain you respect." I am proud of John for winning ten Grammys, earning a number one hit in the world, being a great husband, and being the commencement speaker at his alma mater, the University of Pennsylvania. I am proud of John for being the second youngest and first black EGOT winner, having won an Emmy, Grammy, an Oscar, and a Tony. I am proud of John for being a loving and devoted family man as husband to his beautiful and talented wife, Chrissy, and father to his precious children, Luna and Miles. I am also proud of him for being loyal to Hassan Smith, who is now his road manager. But my greatest source of pride is seeing he is still committed to being a change agent for the world. In 2017, he was named one of the top one hundred influential persons in the United States; by this evaluation, obviously others have the same high opinion of John that I do.

In the many speeches I have given over the past twenty years, I speak fondly about my professional relationships with McKinsey and BCG. McKinsey gave me my training as a young consultant and my skill set that allowed me to effect change. The firm also provided a network of friends and allies that assisted me to become a highly successful entrepreneur, and to be honest, McKinsey gave me a title that has followed me for fifty years, the first black consultant.

While McKinsey gave me the skill set, a global network, and a title, it was BCG that changed my life. Approaching my sixties,

I could say I had accomplished a lot for my family. I was a civic leader and a leader in the field of minority business enterprise development. But deep down, I felt I had so much more to give and to accomplish. BCG gave me the opportunity to do this and the financial security to approach life with confidence and certitude. Being a partner in this world-class consulting firm gave me a true sense of security as a person and the tranquility I had been seeking and needed all my life. Before that, I was angry, ambitious, and not quite as together as the facade I portrayed. It helped that I joined BCG with my own brand, a reputation as a national leader, and my own accumulated wealth. To the partnership and to many in the firm, I was respected as a national networker supreme, a title most partners did not aspire to. Every day was fun, enriching, and enlightening in some way or another. The most important thing that attracted me and kept me at BCG years beyond what I had originally envisioned was the unbelievably bright and motivated young consultants. Often, I would have groups of them join me at my condo for pizza and beer to discuss consulting and how to achieve success in a tough environment such as BCG. With my advice and the support of many others, some made partner. I continued mentoring even with those who did not make partner, as I wanted to motivate them to be successful even after their BCG experience. I still maintain contact with them, like I did previously with Alex Ulanov, Kweli Washington, and John Legend. Collectively, they, along with my daughter, inspire me to continue to mentor and be a change agent.

The BCG partnership possibly does realize how appreciative I am for making me a partner and supporting me over the years. What started out as a two-year engagement has ended up being a twenty-year commitment. I was so fortunate to be accepted, valued, and supported in my seventies by a world-class firm. Not too many people can say that. Hopefully I can be a model for AARP's Life Reimagined. There are many Jim Lowrys out there who have maintained their health, lust for life, and desire to make a meaningful contribution to our communities and country. All they are asking for is an opportunity to serve and make a difference. I have tried to repay the firm by opening doors for company success, representing the firm within institutions, universities, and halls of power, and once again being a model of achievement for young professionals both in and outside of the firm. It is and has been a great ride and has added years to my life. I am grateful to BCG for all the support, combined wisdom, the opportunity to serve, and for encouraging me to continue my work on behalf of people less fortunate and supporting me in my passion in the field of minority business enterprise development. I learned the value of global partnerships where quality was never sacrificed. I got a better understanding of the uniqueness of each client and the strength of the partnership. BCG also supported me to the fullest in my effort to have social impact. They have helped me make a difference in lives of others both in and outside of the firm.

BCG is a great company, and that is why year after year it is rated one of the top five companies to work for by *Fortune* magazine. I am proud of BCG for the outstanding firm it is and the quality services we provide, for the total commitment to the clients we serve, the communities we support on a nonfee basis, and to the thousands of professionals we recruit. For those fortunate enough to be recruited by BCG, I hope they value and appreciate the comprehensive and excellent training they will receive—training that will be the foundation for the rest of their careers. Because of all of the above, I gladly and proudly recruit at colleges and universities across the nation to have top students join our firm. BCG, like many professional services firms, has made significant D&I progress with women and members of the LGBTQ community. And although we have increased our numbers with ethnic minorities, we have not cracked the code. I believe under the leadership of Joe Davis and our key leaders, such as Justin Dean, Robbin Mitchell, Adrian Mitchell, Ian Pancham, Dan Acosta, Raj Varadarajan, Alicia Pittman, Gabrielle Novacek, and Jennifer Comparoni, we stand a fighting chance.

Historical Background 2010–2019

- 2010: President Obama signed the Claims Resolution Act[102] that pays $4.6 billion to Indian tribes and black farmers for decades of government discrimination, particularly from the US Department of Agriculture.[103]
- 2010: President Obama signed the Fair Sentencing Act,[104] which reduces the disparity of sentencing for crack cocaine and powdered cocaine from 100:1 to 18:1. Blacks use crack cocaine at a disproportionally higher level than whites.[105]
- 2012: In the case *Shelby County v. Holder*,[106] the US Supreme Court overturned part of the Voting Rights Act of 1965 that required states to obtain federal permission to change any state voting laws or practices, ultimately making it easier for states to suppress votes.
- 2012: During the November 6, 2012, election ballot, a majority of Oklahoma voters voted yes to Oklahoma Affirmative Action Ban Amendment, which ended affirmative action in college admissions and employment.
- 2013: George Zimmerman was acquitted of the murder of Trayvon Martin. The country erupted in protest, and the Black Lives Matter[107] movement was born in response to the acquittal and police brutality against black Americans.

---

[102] The Claims Resolution Act of 2010 Pub.L. 111–291, H.R. 4783.

[103] https://www.telegraph.co.uk/news/worldnews/barackobama/8190469 /Barack-Obama-signs-law-for-Indian-tribes-and-black-farmers.html.

[104] The Fair Sentencing Act of 2010 Pub.L. 111–220.

[105] https://www.aclu.org/issues/criminal-law-reform/drug-law-reform/ fair-sentencing-act.

[106] *Shelby County v. Holder*, 570 U.S. 529 (2013).

[107] https://blacklivesmatter.com/about/herstory/.

- 2013: *Fisher v. University of Texas Austin.*[108] In 2012, Abigail Fisher challenged the University of Texas at Austin's consideration of race in the undergraduate admissions process after being denied by the university for the fall of 2008 term. Fisher argued that UT Austin's use of race in admissions decisions violated her right to equal protection under the Fourteenth Amendment. The US District Court ruled in favor of the university holding that race can be considered as a factor in admissions but must be able to prove that "available, workable race-neutral alternatives do not suffice." The Fifth Circuit also ruled in favor of the university, and the case was ultimately brought to the US Supreme Court. In a vote of 7–1, the Supreme Court ruled to send the case back down to the Fifth Circuit for further review under the *strict scrutiny* standard, which is the highest standard of judicial review. On July 15, 2014, the Fifth Circuit voted 2–1 to again uphold UT Austin's consideration of race in admissions.
- 2015: Nine African Americans were shot and killed at the Emanuel African Methodist Episcopal Church in Charleston, South Carolina, by white supremacist Dylan Roof.[109]

---

[108] *Fisher v. University of Texas Austin,* 579 U.S. ____(2016).
[109] https://www.npr.org/tags/415878235/charleston-shooting.

CHAPTER 16

CONTRIBUTING ON CORPORATE AND NONPROFIT BOARDS

For most of my professional life, I have been an active participant on many boards. Early on in my career, I probably joined too many boards. When I returned to Chicago in the seventies as a consultant, I quickly joined the Chicago Youth Center Board, the Michael Reese Hospital Board, and the Northwestern Memorial HealthCare Board. I briefly served on the Francis W. Parker Board, but after two meetings lasting more than five hours, I realized participating on this board was too time-consuming and probably expensive. Thus, I diplomatically resigned but over the years maintained contact with the school and made annual contributions to the scholarship fund.

In any city, serving on boards is a very effective way to be introduced to the corporate power structure. This is especially true in Chicago, where many of the civic, academic, and hospital boards are interlinked with the same people. Unfortunately, the same power structure will often only identify five to ten black executives or entrepreneurs and members they feel comfortable with to invite on their boards. In the seventies and eighties, I was one of those persons. I accepted the invitation to serve because I wanted to gain the access, but equally important, I wanted to know how the CEOs thought, what their business priorities were, and possibly how I might secure contracts for McKinsey and later JHLA.

Because of these corporate relationships and my reputation, Mayor Jane Byrne put me on the Chicago Public Library Board. Later, when Harold Washington was elected, he asked me to serve as the chairman of the same board. Government boards, unlike civic, university, and hospital boards, can be very time-consuming, politically charged, and open to public scrutiny. I served on the Chicago Public Library Board for eleven years, but if I had to do it again, I would not have joined. I was running a small but growing business with offices in three cities, and I just did not have the time or patience for the political infighting. I did not have positive memories serving on the library board for those years, but we did make positive change. However, I have nothing but fond memories for the three academic boards I served on.

Kellogg School of Management

At the request of Dean Don Jacobs, I joined this board in 1996, and I have been an active member of this board for twenty-three years. In addition to serving on the board, I was an adjunct professor teaching an academic course in diversity. I also served as academic director of Kellogg Corporate Governance, and minority and academic director for the Kellogg Advanced Management Education Program. This program, sponsored by the National Minority Supplier Development Council (NMSDC), was started when I received a call from NMSDC's iconic leader, Harriet Michel. Harriet requested my help to design a special program. Her then board chairman, Arthur Martinez, CEO of Sears, felt there were not enough MBEs with the capacity to be Tier 1 suppliers, and he asked Harriet to address the problem. In true Harriet fashion, she called me and said, "Jimmy, design the program and solve the problem." From our previous work with Pepsi and Ford, we knew this was a serious problem. Major corporations were consolidating their supply chain and forming multiple-year partnerships with suppliers who were capable and financially strong enough to be Tire 1 suppliers for multiple years.

Since Harriet was feeling the pressure from her board chair, I accepted the challenge with a sense of urgency and excitement. Over a weekend, assisted by Steve Sims of Harriet's staff, I designed the program. Although Dr. Len Greenhalgh had designed a state-of-the-art minority business training program at Dartmouth Amos Tuck School of Business, I wanted this program to be different. Thus, I designed a growth-oriented program to address what I considered to be the biggest shortcomings of MBEs: their inability to plan, attract, and manage capital. The other major shortcoming I identified was their inability to think *big*. Too often, they were satisfied with being what I call "leisure class" entrepreneurs. Translated, firms large enough, generating profits, and affluent enough to send their kids to college, to have two Lexus cars in the driveway and a large home in a nice neighborhood. To change this mind-set, for five days I remained on campus to motivate the participants to think *big*. I also reminded them to remember the brave souls who lost their lives to put them in their seats and accept that it is just as easy to manage a billion-dollar company as it is a million-dollar business.

We were able to start the program quickly at Northwestern's Kellogg School of Business because I was on the Kellogg board. Dean Don Jacobs was an instant supporter, as was Sears CEO, Arthur Martinez. All three of us were friends. Our first class started with twenty participants, but because of the popularity of the program, the numbers quickly doubled. We had MBEs coming to Evanston, Illinois, from across the country, representing many different industries as well as ethnic backgrounds. I learned as much from the participants in both the classroom and night cocktail sessions as they did from me.

Janice Howroyd will always be one of my favorite alumni of the program, sitting in the first row, asking question after question with a soft North Carolina accent. Like Don Richards at Francis W. Parker, she asked a lot of questions and was also an A student. She credits me for recommending that she should not sell her professional staff business to a major company. I told her to think big and have a goal of a billion dollars. Her company ACT-1 Group in 2018 had total revenues exceeding a billion dollars, and she currently has North American offices in both Torrance, California, and Las Vegas, Nevada, as well as other offices in Europe.

Not all our alums reached the billion-dollar goal, but many are highly successful and local civic leaders, such as Adam Walker, Beatriz Manetta, Anjali "Ann" Ramakumaran, Andrea Rush, Al Limaye, Randal Pinkett, Jimmy John Liautaud, Tom McLeary, Dan Arriola, Terri Quinton, and Susana Robledo. I often run into the AMEP alums in airports, and they thank me for the AMEP program and usually say, "I was very comfortable financially before the AMEP program at Kellogg. Now I am rich. Thank you, Professor Lowry."

The program has been judged one of the most effective short courses for training growth-oriented minority entrepreneurs in the nation. The program has been in existence for twenty-three years and has trained the top minority executives in the country.

Howard Business School

Around the turn of the century, I was beginning to reduce my workload. I received a call from another dean of a business school, this time from former JHLA consultant Dr. Barron H. Harvey. When Dean Harvey asked me to join the Howard Business

School Board, I jumped at the opportunity. As the dean of the business school, Barron was doing an outstanding job motivating and encouraging students to enter the field of business. Equally important, he was a very effective salesperson, advocating the uniqueness of Howard University and HBCUs in general to the leadership of corporate America. It was a perfect opportunity for me to support both Howard University and Dean Harvey, and I looked forward to meeting new friends and joining old friends who were on the board, people such as Carl Brooks, Shelley Stewart, Maurice Cox, Ron Parker, Carla Harris, JoAnn Price, and Terry Jones.

Like at Kellogg, serving on this board was a labor of love. I was supporting young, intelligent students at Howard to be corporate leaders or owners of black businesses. Soon after joining the board, the Kauffman Foundation asked me and Richard Holland to do a major study on minority business enterprise development. With the strong support of BCG, we undertook an extensive study, out of which came (i) *A New Agenda for Minority Business Enterprise Development for the Kauffman Foundation*, and (ii) *Realizing the New Agenda for Minority Business Development*. The reports were well received by the Kauffman Foundation, BCG, and the minority community. While conducting our analysis, we formed close relationships with Kauffman top executives. Over lunch one day, they mentioned that the Kauffman Foundation was going to provide grants to universities across the nation to establish entrepreneur centers. I quickly started selling the idea to Kauffman that Howard be a recipient of one of those grants. My marketing skills must have been successful because Howard received a grant of $3 million, and the Center for Entrepreneur and Business Excellence was established. I was asked to chair the center's advisory board. I quickly created a board of advisors with outstanding young and mature business leaders. My years affiliated with Howard hit a high note for me when I was asked by the business school to be the commencement speaker for the graduating class of 2019.

Grinnell College Board

I will always have a special place in my heart for Kellogg and Howard business schools, but my favorite board I had the honor to serve on was for Grinnell College. My Grinnell experience did not end upon graduation or at my year abroad on the Grinnell Fellowship to Tanzania. After joining McKinsey in 1968, Grinnell College's chairman of the board of trustees, Bob Noyce, invited me to join the board. I served as a trustee for more than forty-three years, most years visiting the campus twice a year. Initially, my trips were funded by distinguished lawyer Sam Rosenthal, a founding partner of Sonnenschein, Nath and Rosenthal. At the time, Bob Noyce, Sam Rosenthal, and distinguished lawyer and investor Joe Rosenfield were leaders of the board. Joe had developed a social and business relationship with another outstanding investor by the name of Warren Buffett, and he too joined the Grinnell College Board of Trustees.

Of this powerhouse board member group, only Joe and Bob had attended Grinnell. Joe Rosenfield dedicated his life to Grinnell College because of Grinnell's academic training and because, he said, the faculty and student body accepted him as a student, not a Jewish student. Rosenfield went on to start Youngers Department stores and later became the chairman of General Growth Properties. Bob Noyce felt indebted to Grinnell also. He was a brilliant student who graduated Phi Beta Kappa and continued his education at MIT, where he received a PhD in physics, and he credits much of his success and direction to his Grinnell physics professor, Grant Gale, who motivated him to excel and to apply to MIT. When I joined the board, Bob was a top executive at Fairchild Semiconductor. In 1968, he and

Gordon Moore, both members of top management, left Fairchild, along with Andrew Grove, and together they founded Intel.

Participating on Grinnell's board was enlightening, educational, and at times challenging. It was challenging because I wanted to accelerate Grinnell's recruitment of more blacks and Latinos. I was often very vocal, perhaps to my detriment, in pushing for increased enrollment of minority students and international students, but I was always supported by fellow black board member Randall Morgan, whose son attended Grinnell. But the third black who was serving on the board always seemed to provide contrary advice—in essence, telling the board to slow down. It was frustrating, but in the end, Randall and I did influence the board to increase the number of minority and international students. Thus, in my early thirties, I was on a prestigious college board, gaining business wisdom from industry giants, while learning how to be a management consultant at McKinsey.

While I was on the board's finance committee, at one meeting Warren Buffet announced to the board that Bob Noyce was going to start a new company. Buffet stated he would not expect Grinnell College to invest in Bob's company, but that if two trustees would agree to invest and commit to turn over the stock to Grinnell, then he would support the decision. Sam Rosenthal and Joe Rosenfield became the two trustees who invested $150,000 each in Bob's new company, and true to their commitment, they donated their stock to Grinnell College. That company was Intel, which has grown to a $59.38 billion company. This and other unique investments helped to increase Grinnell's endowment dramatically. I will never forget these two outstanding individuals for making these investments that elevated the status of Grinnell College to be one of the top small liberal arts colleges in the nation. I will also never forget what a mistake I made by not investing even one dollar in Intel after it went public. But I was a young, first-generation businessperson and had a mortgage. Still after saying all of this, I was stupid!

Over my forty-five years on the board, I had the privilege of serving with many other corporate and civic leaders, including Carolyn Bucksbaum, whose husband, Matthew Bucksbaum, was CEO of General Growth Properties; Mary Sue Coleman, president of the University of Michigan; Steve Jobs, CEO of Apple; and many other corporate and civic leaders. Unlike many other colleges, at Grinnell, trustees could serve unlimited terms, so I was graced to be with these leaders sometimes up to thirty years.

Of all the trustees I served with on the board, none had a greater impact on me than Cindy Pritzker. When I joined the board, I had no idea who she was or that her father was Judge James Friend, a former Olympic champion and the judge who presided over the White Sox betting scandal. Dubbed the Black Sox, the betting scandal was the basis for the movie *Eight Men Out*. I also didn't know that Cindy was the wife of Jay Pritzker, head of the Pritzker family empire. She was a fellow alumna who, like me, preferred to stay at the Grinnell Motel rather than the official residence or other motels closer to the college. Each morning, we would take turns getting the other coffee. Our friendship started at Grinnell College and has grown even stronger over the years.

When I tell people that I served on the board for more than forty-five years with Warren Buffett, Joe Rosenfield, Bob Noyce, Steve Jobs, and others at this small liberal arts college in the middle of Iowa, they are amazed. I watched Grinnell build an endowment of $26 million to $1.5 billion. The questions usually asked are what the experience was like and what I learned being around these great business leaders. My first response is always that it was fun, enlightening, and inspiring. Upon reflection, my biggest takeaways were as follows:

1. Establishing and implementing major goals was the key to institutional and corporate success.
    *   Joe Rosenfield envisioned elevating Grinnell College from a solid academic institution to one of the top nationally ranked colleges in the nation.
    *   Rosenfield and Buffett set a goal of having a multibillion-dollar endowment, which would allow Grinnell to offer scholarships to attract high-caliber, deserving US and international students.

2. A board could be both highly diversified and highly effective.
    *   During my tenure, Grinnell never had fewer than four women and four minorities on the board.
    *   Including life trustees, at one time Grinnell had eight black trustees on the board, including my cousin Ron Gault.
    *   During this period, Grinnell's academic standing remained at the highest levels, and the endowment steadily increased.

3. Individuals could be respected for the contributions they made even if they could not make large donations.
    *   During my initial years on the board, I could not afford to pay for my airplane ticket to attend board meetings, but my contributions were always respected. Later, I was able to make large annual donations.
    *   Once I was on a presidential search committee that voted against an internal candidate favored by Joe Rosenfield and Warren Buffett. My candidate was selected, and he gave us four years of solid leadership until he was replaced by Dr. George Drake, an

outstanding college professor who led Grinnell as its president for the next twelve years.

4. A college board leader can be effective without a lot of academic pomp and circumstance.
   - Dr. Drake would convene our two-day board meeting always focusing on existing problems and opportunities for improvements instead of shining light on himself or his team.
   - We received our materials weeks in advance to allow the board to analyze and solve problems.
   - I resigned from another college board because I got tired of going to meetings where the president would read verbatim and make long, boring presentations while the university was going bankrupt.

5. People are people.
   - I was initially intimidated by sitting next to multimillionaires and billionaires, but over time, I soon realized they were just people, good people with good hearts.
   - We were all tied together on one mission—to solidify and elevate Grinnell's image, financial stability, and high academic standing.

6. Having a purpose is the key to success.
   - Collectively, we all basically agreed on what kind of institution we wanted Grinnell College to be.
   - Randall Morgan and I had our own purpose. We wanted Grinnell to elevate itself to include people of color in all phases of Grinnell's growth.
   - I am confident that at times other members of the board grew tired of our articulated concerns and

hopes for minority students, but in most cases, they supported us.

- When I retired from the board, I was pleased to see that out of the total enrollment of 1,663: 5 percent were black, 6 percent were Latino, 7 percent were Asian, 22 percent were Pell Grant recipients, and the current president was black and gay.

7. I regretted not taking advantage of the true business genius around the table.
   - Although I was often in the homes of Bob Noyce and Joe Rosenfield, I never picked their brains to learn more about Bob's vision of Intel and the next twenty years of Silicon Valley growth or how Joe Rosenfield and Warren Buffet invested and made money.
   - Although he was on the board for two years, I never really got to know Steve Jobs or his vision for Apple and the technology revolution.
   - Unfortunately, all three have passed away, and I regret I had so many opportunities to learn so much from them but failed to leverage my time with them to the fullest.

Overall, my tenure on the board and my four years as a student at Grinnell were very special. I gave back to the school all I could offer, but I received so, so much more in return. I was elected to the inaugural Grinnell Athletic Hall of Fame, and in 2008, I was given an honorary doctorate, so I assume my small contributions were appreciated.

Toyota Diversity Advisory Board

Over the years, I served on and was heavily involved in many nonprofit boards. I was lauded for my commitment, problem-solving abilities, and overall support of the organizations on boards I served. Naturally, I expected I would have the opportunity to serve on one or more corporate Fortune 500 boards. Maybe I was too progressive or too opinionated and later in life too old, so I never was asked to serve. For this reason, I will be forever grateful to Toyota and my dear friend, former secretary of labor Alexis Herman, for asking me to serve on the Toyota Diversity Advisory Board (DAB). The DAB was originally established to assist Toyota in developing and implementing a state-of-the-art D&I initiative. Over the years, this board has had outstanding civic and corporate leaders as its members, such as Phyllis Campbell, Howard Buffett, Jyoti Chopra, Gil Casellas, Federico Peña, and Judge Nat Jones. Working closely with Toyota's North American leadership team, we functioned as high-level advisors. DAB has been highly successful, and I believe over the years I have made major contributions to the program and also to Toyota's top executives on matters outside of the scope of diversity and inclusion. Toyota's Japanese global company consolidated their North American operation in Plano, Texas. I am proud of Toyota as a global automotive company, for yearly purchasing more than $1 billion from MBEs and for elevating blacks to the highest level in the new leadership structure. Sandra Phillips Rogers was made group vice president, chief legal officer, and corporate secretary, in addition to her general counsel role and recently added title of chief diversity officer. From chief diversity officer and general counsel, Chris Reynolds was named deputy chief officer, general administration and human resources group for Toyota Motor North America. As chief administrative officer, he oversees manufacturing and corporate resources for all of North America and is responsible for functions of manufacturing, accounting and finance, HR, government affairs, corporate communications and strategy, social innovation, diversity and inclusion, and legal. Al Smith was named group vice president and chief social innovation officer, where he is responsible for the organization's shared impact, including philanthropy efforts, the Toyota USA Foundation, the corporate diversity and inclusion strategy, and the organization's environmental sustainability functions across North America. Alva Adams-Mason is director of African American Business Strategy (AABS), where she manages the national marketing and communication strategy to increase African American market share and raise this community's awareness of the Toyota brands. These outstanding African American individuals were elevated to positions of power, positions in corporate America that were earned and well deserved.

CHAPTER 17

TEN-POINT PLAN TO ACCELERATE BLACK ECONOMIC DEVELOPMENT

In business and life, I've always known there would be competitors attempting to take you down. The unfortunate thing in the area of MBED is that unless there was a committed CEO, many companies would hide behind weak consulting firms providing inferior services at much lower fees.

I always considered the importance of a strong MBED agenda outweighed whether JHLA was awarded contracts. MBED was about societal change and creating wealth in minority communities. Within minority communities, there is serious structural unemployment. Technology has changed the world, and our youths were not and are not positive contributors to it. Not only should jobs be created for youths but equally important— hope. Growth-oriented minority firms could provide both.

I have dedicated my life to the advancement of minority business enterprise development for multiple reasons:

- to create wealth in our urban and rural communities to ensure stability, job creation, and hope;
- to involve larger numbers of minorities to participate in the US free enterprise system in a meaningful way;

- to foster business and social relationships among minorities and nonminorities;
- to ensure better and deeper understanding with and mutual respect for businesses of all sizes;
- to increase wealth to support those less fortunate and reduce poverty in our communities;
- to increase the size of endowments to historically black colleges and universities; and,
- to be able to utilize the unique skills of young, highly innovative entrepreneurs.

Over the years, I have witnessed MBED progress, but I would be less than honest if I didn't tell you I expected greater advancement by this time, and greater acceptance of this concept both in and outside of government. There are many reasons why this is the case, the most important being:

- The mind-set of the MBE entrepreneur who cannot envision growing and managing a billion-dollar concept.
- MBED and MBEs do not appear to be a high priority of minority leaders in or outside of government.
- Minorities have avoided mergers and strategic partnerships with potential minority and nonminority partners.

Hopefully, these barriers will be analyzed in depth, and the new leaders and entrepreneurs of the millennial generation will embrace change and turn the ship around. As I stated in our original 1978 Department of Commerce study, all leaders, minority and nonminority, have to accept that Americans can't have a strong, growth-oriented economy if 30–40 percent of its population are not participants or leaders in the free enterprise system. The government can be the catalyst for change, but it is the private sector that leads it. Latinos and blacks can make major contributions to the free enterprise system, but they must be allowed to fully and meaningfully participate in it. The markets to support US growth will be populated by black and brown people. Our minorities can facilitate entrance and growth within these markets.

To change the tide for the less fortunate in the United States, we all must broaden our thinking and accept change is difficult. We also must accept we have to remove aging nonminority and minority elected and civic leaders if they are not affecting and impacting the problems facing us—issues that, if not addressed, will affect all Americans irrespective of race, religion, and gender. Limited economic growth in minority communities is a national problem and should be treated as such. Ernest Hemingway's novel *For Whom the Bell Tolls* made a significant impact on me. The story reminded me that we all suffer every time a family goes to bed hungry, a person loses a job, a youth loses hope, or a five-year-old dies as a victim of a drive-by shooting. These individual acts weaken the fabric of society as a whole.

The problems confronting America are complex and challenging. However, we must face the issues with commitment, strong leadership, and significant capital investments. Just like the growing deficit, if we do not start now to address these problems, our grandchildren and great-grandchildren will suffer, and America will be weaker globally. To that end, and to try to solve the problem rather than just identify it, I offer my simple ten-point plan to accelerate black economic development:

Ten-Point Plan to Accelerate Black Economic Development

1. Black leaders must accept that those who control capital control the country.

The majority of the problems that beset black America are symptomatic of the fact that we do not manage, control, or invest large sums of capital. Problems such as inferior education, slow growth of small- to medium-size businesses, high crime rates, and poor health will not be solved overnight, but greater and lasting positive change could be achieved if we controlled more capital.

Religious and ethnic groups have historically accepted this premise. Consider how in the United States, Jews, Greeks, Iranians, Cuban Americans, and other groups have united to foster economic wealth and capital accumulation to promote and protect their interests. Blacks did unite and build their own economic infrastructures in places like Tulsa, Oklahoma, and Rosewood, Florida, only to have whites tear them down, murdering hundreds in the process. This occurred in the thirties and forties. Since that time, blacks collectively represent over a trillion dollars in buying power, and there is no reason we can't use this buying power to build economic independence like other groups. However, research conducted by the Pew Research Center shows we are losing ground. Between 1983 and 2015:

- White household net worth increased 42 percent from $100,000 to $141,000.
- Hispanic household net worth increased 40 percent from $9,800 to $13,700.
- African American net worth decreased 16 percent from $13,000 to $11,000.

Increasing family income and net worth are two important measures of success, but if blacks are to gain greater control over our economic destiny and increase our capital base, we must change our mind-set. The major mind-set change must be letting go of the belief that the government can solve all of our problems. The government can be a catalyst for change, but ultimately it has to be the people who control this destiny within the US economy—a US economy that is more global, innovative, and ever changing. For blacks to be an integral part of this economy, we have to change our mind-set and work together.

Our educators and political, religious, and civil rights leaders must gain greater knowledge and understanding of our US economic system and the world's economy to create positive change. In our classrooms and in our homes, we must start educating our youth about our historic business icons like Madam C.J. Walker, A.G. Gaston, John Johnson, and others. We must show them that there were fortunes built by others who were not athletes or entertainers. We can highlight our sports heroes, but highlight only those who used the wealth they earned as athletes to invest and create large, viable enterprises like Michael Jordan, Magic Johnson, Alan Houston, Junior Bridgeman, Oscar Robertson, and LeBron James.

This mind-set change cannot occur overnight, but to save our children, we must start now and with vigilance if we want to make an impact in the inner cities of Chicago and across the nation.

2. Working collectively, we must create as many billion-dollar black businesses as possible.

We cannot accelerate economic growth on the backs of micro businesses. Billion-dollar businesses create many jobs, different models for change, and, most importantly, seats at the table of power. The majority of all businesses are sole proprietorships. In the black community, the percentage is high. According to the United States Census Bureau, there are more than two million businesses in the country that are owned by African Americans. More than 94 percent of these businesses are made up of sole proprietorships or partnerships that have no paid employees. Don't get me wrong. I believe in these small businesses; they are critical to the US economy. But if we hope to accelerate economic growth in our community, we must create large, billion- and multibillion-dollar companies.

My business models will always be Bob Johnson, founder of BET, and Oprah Winfrey. Both created their brands and grew their businesses to billion-dollar enterprise status. Equally as important, they diversified their investments, creating other viable businesses; hired and trained people of color; supported politicians of all races and genders who helped the black communities; supported worthy nonprofits and universities; and became the mentors of blacks who thought big and had vision. Bob Johnson even created a $250 million investment fund, Robert L. Johnson Equities, under the leadership of Rufus Rivers and Jerry Johnson to invest in minority and nonminority business. There are other black entrepreneurs operating below the surface like most successful businesspeople, such as Janice Bryant Howroyd, Dave Steward, Robert F. Smith, Tyra Banks, Joe Anderson, Bill Pickard, and John Rogers.

In the new US economy, one can create a billion-dollar enterprise with unique products, patents, and services. This has been demonstrated in Silicon Valley where individuals have become billionaires overnight in the field of technology.

Examples:

- Mark Zuckerberg of Facebook has a net worth of $74.2 billion. He founded Facebook in 2004 and later dropped out of Harvard to run the company full-time. Facebook boasts 1.86 billion users and $40.7 billion in revenue. The company has made numerous multibillion-dollar acquisitions, including the purchase of WhatsApp for $19 billion.
- Jan Koum of WhatsApp has a net worth of $9.5 billion. Born in Ukraine, Jan and his mother immigrated to California when he was sixteen and got an apartment

through government assistance. She babysat, and he swept floors to make ends meet. In 2009, Jan started WhatsApp, which is now the world's biggest mobile messaging service with 1.5 billion users.

- Travis Kalanick of Uber has a net worth of $5.9 billion. Kalanick dropped out of UCLA in 1998 to found Scour Inc., which filed for bankruptcy in 2000. In 2001, Travis founded Red Swoosh, which sold in 2007 for $19 million. In 2009, Travis and Garrett Camp founded Uber, a car service that competes with taxis in fifty-three countries and is valued at more than $48 billion.

Just imagine if those three successful entrepreneurs had been black. With the right mind-set, how many schools could have been supported or funded? How many strong and forward-thinking politicians supported and how many jobs created?

Unlike in previous generations, today's nation has educated thousands of very bright black investors, scientists, engineers, consultants, and entrepreneurs. Unfortunately, we seldom have examples of where they worked together, invested in one another, and supported one another to grow to billion-dollar enterprises.

3. We should support and select officials who work on our behalf.

Congressman Parren Mitchell of Baltimore, Maryland, authored many bills in Congress in the late seventies and early eighties, but there has been a limited number of high-impact bills positively fostering minority business growth since he left Congress more than twenty-five years ago. We should support and select officials who support economic development in our communities. We have many outstanding elected officials at the federal, state, and local levels. There are many who are hardworking and do the right thing. Most are very articulate and often emotional in defining the problem, but few have an economic agenda like Parren Mitchell. There are many reasons why this is the case, but the major one is most were not businesspeople when they entered office. Another reason is that most of their staff's previous experience was also not in business.

The black electorate is also a part of the problem. Blacks have historically been considered very emotional people. When we saw or felt injustices, we reacted in very emotional ways, like the successful demonstrations at universities in the sixties mainly in 1963 and 1968, and recent movements around Black Lives Matter. But after the demonstrations and marches, what economic laws were passed that would have a positive impact on millions of black people? How many elected officials were asked to prepare such legislations?

In the vast majority of cases, most elected black officials do not receive the majority of their contributions from blacks. We saw the difference it made in Chicago when black business icons such as Soft Sheen founders Edward and Bettiann Gardner wrote a check for $1 million to Harold Washington's campaign. For me, I could care less how long an elected official has been in office or how effective an orator he or she might be. For me, the key question is, what economic impact have they had on the communities they represented and how effective have they been in passing legislation that effected economic change?

4. Black leaders at the C–suite must leverage their clout to grow minority business enterprise programs.

Over the past fifty years, the theory has been that many blacks are ascending the corporate ladder to C–suite levels. While we do have CEOs and top executives in many of the Fortune 500 companies, I and many others argue it's not enough. Many benefitted from programs such as A Better Chance, Outward Bound, Management Leadership for Tomorrow (MLT), Jumpstart, COGME, the National Urban League, and other social organizations.[110] For nearly two decades, these member institutions supported the educational endeavors of almost two thousand African American and other nonwhite MBA students. They are a generation of blacks not relegated to positions in the four Ps, in which blacks were historically limited: positions in personnel, public affairs, public relations, and procurement. They have performed at high levels, enhancing shareholder values for the investors. In addition, there are many like Bill Lewis, Ray McGuire, John Utendahl, Frank Raines, and Dick Parsons, who

---

[110] Management Leadership for Tomorrow (https://ml4t.org), provides skills, coaching, and connections to African Americans, Latinos, and Native Americans needed to lead organizations and communities worldwide; A Better Chance (www.abetterchance.org) is a scholarship organization dedicated to giving students of color a better chance to attend college–prep private schools and public schools; Jumpstart (www.jstart.org) is a national early-education organization dedicated to preparing every child entering kindergarten with the skills to succeed; the Council for Opportunity in Graduate Management Education, COGME, (www.hbs.edu/svmp) was established in 1971 by Harvard Business School (HBS) and nine other leading graduate business programs.

look back to assist those coming up behind them to move up the corporate ladder. However, I wish more would use their clout to elevate their W/MBE programs. While working at Pepsi, AT&T, Toyota, Ford, and other large corporations, I observed how when nonprocurement executives get involved, corporate minority spend increases dramatically.

I have also observed that many of these same executives took early retirement, and some defer retirement to become successful entrepreneurs, like Jim Kaiser and Lloyd Trotter. So in a way, they might be supporting their own career and the success of many other qualified executives like themselves. I believe this should be the future trend. Black executives who retired from C-suite positions have the networks, experience, skill sets, and capital to be excellent partners and investors in growth-oriented companies. Too often, they decide to live off retirement savings when they should partner with others and create a billion-dollar business. Once again, there is need for mind-set change.

I saw an excellent example of this when three very highly paid General Electric officials left GE to start their own investment fund. Their first highly successful fund closed at $600 million. Their second fund was even larger. They are my models for mind-set change and bold thinking.

Despite their desire or drive, W/MBE executives cannot elevate these programs. The model programs at Pepsi, AT&T, P&G, Toyota, and Ford were designed, managed, and supported by CEOs and minority and nonminority executives and members of the boards at the highest levels.

5. High-income blacks must pool their capital to buy properties.

Although real estate is an industry that often fluctuates, it is still one of the largest industries in the US economy. In 2016, real estate transactions represented 8.9 percent of the GDP and $1.2 trillion in revenue. In the city of Detroit, we witnessed blocks of inner-city land being purchased by non-Detroit residents. The gentrification of major city blocks is occurring not only in Detroit but across the country, representing billions of dollars of potential revenues for minority businesses. The questions we must ask ourselves are: Are blacks meaningful players in this huge real estate play? Are we investing with one another to increase our net worth? Are we ensuring those being displaced have viable job opportunities and places to live? Are we investing in black companies, like Quinton Primo's Capri Capital,[111] to enhance their capital pool to allow him and others like him to play at a higher level, both domestically and internationally? Or will we miss even having a seat at the table like we did in the dot.com boom?

I am proud of the fact that the last two years, the Executive Leadership Council has started accepting entrepreneurs as members. Top black executives and entrepreneurs should work, plan, and invest with one another. My dream has always been that these black cadres would join forces and guide and create wealth. Hopefully, making the case more powerful, we could also entice athletes and entertainers to invest. I am proud of the musical millionaires who are investing and creating billion-dollar enterprises like Jessica Alba, Beyoncé, Jay-Z, P. Diddy, and 50 Cent, but there should be more.

6. We must increase the number of our members on corporate boards to effect change.

Over the years, many have advocated for the placement of people of color on corporate boards. Corporate boards are extremely

---

[111] Quinton Primo is cofounder of Capri Capital Partners, a Chicago-based real estate investment firm, and currently serves as Capri Investment Group chairman and CEO overseeing a diverse $3.7 billion portfolio.

powerful vehicles for positive change. This was demonstrated when the Reverend Leon Sullivan joined the General Motors Board and created the Sullivan Principles for General Motors and other Fortune 500 companies to justify continual investment in South Africa when it was under Afrikander rule. It was also demonstrated by the role played by Dr. Clifford Wharton on the Ford Board, assisting Ford in becoming the first company to reach a billion dollars in minority spending. I applaud other outstanding black board members like Vernon Jordan, Jim Cash, Steve Rogers, and Earl Graves who fostered positive change and effectively carried out their broader board responsibilities.

I have fought over the years to increase women, Hispanic, and black board representation. But I have been equally aggressive in stating that simply having a black on the board who is not effective or is unwilling or unable to articulate the business case for diversity is not helping anyone—not the company, not the shareholders, and not the race or gender they are representing.

I will never forget when I received a call from a very powerful white CEO who asked me for a reference on a black candidate for a board on which he was on. I did not want to deep-six the candidate, who was actually a friend, so I gave a solid but not strong recommendation. Six months later, the CEO called me back very angry and said, "Damn, Jim. I trusted your judgment, but I had a deeper understanding of black issues than your friend." We had to recruit another black person. Unfortunately, my friend was assigned to serve on three more boards, probably underperforming on each one of them, but they had a seat filled, and he was well compensated.

7. We must form strategic relationships with influential and global black leaders.

We must form relationships with influential and global leaders. The global economy is so much larger now. The Africa today is not the Africa I knew in the sixties and seventies. Many of the countries of Africa are blessed with rich natural resources, and elite Africans are leading large companies, generating billions of dollars and forming global, strategic business partnerships. In 2015, *Forbes* magazine published "Africa's Richest" index. This powerful group included some of the most sophisticated and globally connected business leaders and included ten Nigerians with a combined net worth of $27.3 billion. This year, in a per-country ranking, Egypt and South Africa are tied with five billionaires each, followed by Nigeria with four and Morocco with two. *Forbes* found one billionaire each from Algeria, Angola, Tanzania, and Zimbabwe.

I recently visited Nigeria for the first time, and I observed firsthand the many problems confronting the country, but I also saw a tremendous opportunity for US black business involvement. In the August 2016 issue of MBN USA Magazine, I highlighted the opportunities with respect to Nigeria. Nigeria is not the only country where there are major opportunities in Africa. But as my good friend Dorothy Davis has been telling me for years, the worldwide diaspora is real, be it in Africa, Latin America, the Caribbean, Europe, or the United States. What is missing is the leadership and the vision to tie all the potential business partners together.

8. Blacks must support well–managed nonprofits.

There are many nonprofit organizations and HBCUs in our communities. A significant number of them are well managed and have a positive impact on the targeted groups they serve. They should be supported. The others who do not perform at a high level on a consistent basis should be overlooked no matter how charismatic its leader. The goal of all nonprofits should be to have an impact on the individuals or communities they serve. To me, to be successful, they have to have a vision of where they want to go, be able to change their strategy if called for, increase their revenue base, build a strong organization, have viable succession plans, and top management must have powerful strategic partnerships.

Unfortunately, I know not supporting friends and allies who poorly manage the nonprofits is hard. We are very sensitive to the fact that within those poorly managed nonprofits, staff members have families, many of them serving the community for twenty to thirty years, just not well. It will be difficult to do, but we must withdraw our support when necessary and provide support where it will matter most.

The other reality is that major corporations are now being very particular to whom they are funding. Unlike in the sixties, they are developing tougher criteria for giving, and their bottom line is impact and achievement of specific goals. Their foundations are also insisting nonprofits get out of their silos and partner with other nonprofits to maximize scarce resources.

9. Conduct research.

We have to conduct more in depth research. I know I am biased since I have been a consultant for more than forty years, but we as blacks do not do enough in-depth research. And I do not mean research in just business economics but research in areas that affect people, the most important being:

- education
- politics

- health
- environmental
- business/investments

In-depth research will tell us where we have been, where we are now, and where we should be in the future if we want to survive in these difficult times. Historically, we have relied on journals, newspapers, TV broadcasts, teachers, and professors. In the majority of these cases, the research was done by a nonminority; rarely was an author of the research black.

In the forties and fifties, black newspapers such as the *Chicago Defender, Pittsburgh Courier,* and the *Michigan Chronicle* were widely read and gave invaluable resources for sharing data, insights, and issues affecting blacks. Unfortunately, these great newspapers either died or weakened over the years. Almost standing alone to fill the critical gaps were our black publications, *Ebony, Jet, Essence,* and *Black Enterprise.*

Over the years, I was shocked how few students, friends both rich and poor, and even professionals outside of their industries had even a basic understanding of the laws, innovations, people, and global events that were affecting their lives. In the past, we could forgive not devoting long hours spent in the library conducting research but not now. With the internet and handheld devices, there are few facts that the average citizen cannot discover within minutes.

Over the years, African American studies and African America history concentration has been established in HBCUs and non-HBCUs across the nation. When I conducted an analysis of these programs at our top schools, I noticed that few had courses on African American economic development or business. How can we have studies on blacks in America without analyzing the impact that the US free enterprise system had on blacks, good or bad? Our educators must educate us on the ways to both create and distribute wealth.

As a wise old philosopher once stated, "The truth will set you free." We as blacks have to gather the facts to determine our own truth and destiny.

10. We have to stop the crabs-in-the-barrel mentality.

I made this statement once when I was at a public forum with mixed groups of people at Harvard Business School. The blacks in the back of the room gasped. I heard one embarrassed student whisper, "No he did not go there." I said to myself, almost every day black friends or associates make the same statement, but we are not supposed to say this in public. I reminded them we should not be afraid. We are not airing our dirty laundry because we know we act that way. If we were honest, within our culture, this mentality was developed by whites hundreds of years ago on the continent of Africa, pitting one African tribe against another. In slavery, they pitted light-skinned blacks from the house against the dark-skinned blacks working in the fields.

In modern corporate America, I encourage black professionals to protect their own elite blacks in the C-suite. Our failure to support one another has always bothered me in working in and for major corporations, especially when I see how other groups support and sponsor one another. I witnessed Jews support other Jews, Asian Americans support other Asian Americans, and Mormons promote other Mormons. Why should blacks be afraid to do the same for other blacks?

Over my fifty-year career, I have been very fortunate to have many black mentors, coaches, and sponsors. Because of favors they gave me, I have gone out of my way to assist other blacks. But this is not to say I have not had other blacks trying to take me to the bottom of the barrel. I will never forget a meeting with a very powerful elected official where we, a black business, were advocating for a larger slice of the procurement pie. The official listened for about an hour and then made a statement I will never forget. He said, "When I award the contract to other ethnic groups, I receive praise. But when I give a contract to a black business, before I can even get to my office to sit down, I get five calls asking, 'Why didn't you give that contract to me?'" It was a good lesson, and it was clear to me this powerful elected official was very aware of the reality that within our community, the crabs-in-the-barrel mentality was ever present. Rather than compete with one another, blacks have to work together, invest in one another, and, equally important, praise one another. If we do not, we will continue to suffer.

CHAPTER 18

OPEN LETTER TO YOUNGER GENERATIONS

As I reflect on my professional journey of the past fifty years, I will admit much progress has been made. Yet today, as I am forced to observe through social media, nightly newscasts reports, and newspaper articles, I can't help but feel like we are regressing. This greatly depresses and saddens me for the following reasons:

- I feel powerful people are trying to take us back to the America that caused my grandfather to flee Mississippi.
- The very institutions that made this nation great are being challenged.
- There has never been a time when strong partnerships among historical global partners were needed to confront Russia and other nations threatening our democratic process.
- Although the new laws might assist certain industries' economic victories because of tax policies, ultimately, for the majority of the US, politicians will lose.
- The poorest citizens will sink lower economically because of the huge wealth disparity.

The four hundred richest Americans now have more wealth

than the bottom 61 percent of the US population. The twenty individuals at the top of the pile control more wealth than the bottom half of the population. The richest households own more assets than the entire African American community, and a mere 182 individuals on the Forbes List have more assets than the entire US Hispanic population.

A recent study by Princeton Economist Angus Deaton and Anne Case found that the mortality rate among white middle-aged Americans with limited education is increasing, while those of every other group and the citizens of every other advancing country continue to drop. The increase in rates of death among this group is attributable to what the *New York Times* describes as "an epidemic of suicide and afflictions stemming from alcoholic liver disease and overdoses of heroin and prescription opioids." One theory, offered by Sam Pizzigati, is the population suffers from thwarted aspirations having been raised with expectancy of upward mobility that never came to fruition. Unfortunately, skillful politicians are able to convince many Americans that they were denied upward mobility by minorities, Jews, and immigrants.

Maybe I am naïve, but I strongly believe that if we involved all people in a meaningful way in the US free enterprise system, not only would world citizens benefit, but the nation would be stronger. I see the US free enterprise system as a vehicle to improve race relations and provide hope for those in need, be they white, black, or brown. It was for this reason I dedicated my life to minority business development and diversity and inclusion; maybe I am too stubborn to forsake my dream.

I believe that although our principles and institutions might be threatened, America will survive. I believe this for many reasons, the most important being my faith and trust in the goodwill of people, irrespective of race, religion, or gender, as well as my faith in the younger generation. I spend a significant amount of time with young people between the ages of seventeen and forty-seven. They might be different from my generation and the generation after mine, but they believe in the same philosophy that has been this nation's great dream. For me, the key to success would be to combine the brilliance and drive of the millennial and younger generations with the wisdom of the older generations.

If we work together, we can defend our nation against serious strife from internal and external global threats. We will not be able to win this fight by merely having half a million people marching, well-written op-ed pieces in the *New York Times*, or investing inordinate amounts of time in under-resourced nonprofits. That might be the noble thing to do and at times very heart warming, but alone they will not win the battle. The forces we are confronting are too powerful, too well financed, and too well organized. To turn the tide, we must have both a near- and long-term strategy that accepts capital accumulation is critical, as I have stated throughout this book, if we want to fight the battle against those who desire to wield their clout often. I strongly believe in the US free enterprise system. I accept there are good and bad capitalists. The key questions one has to ask are how capital is being utilized, for whom, and for what greater good.

In the near term, there will be those political and business leaders who will do their best to confront the negative forces. But to effect greater change and safeguard our historic institutions and organizations, our mission has to create a workplace where everyone has a sense of purpose. To quote from Mark Zuckerberg's Harvard 2017 Commencement Address: "To keep our society moving forward, we have a generational challenge—to not only create new jobs but create a renewed sense of purpose. But it's not enough to have purpose yourself. You have to create a sense of purpose for others." Zuckerberg goes on to outline the challenge when he states, "Our generation will have to deal with tens of millions of jobs replaced by automation like self-driving cars and trucks. But we have the potential to do so much more together."

My generation opened the doors, and the next generation opened opportunities for millions. The millennials and younger generations have to lead a global transformation. The advice I offer during this pivotal time is as follows:

1. Vote for and support politicians who believe in what you believe in.
2. Embrace the US free enterprise system and make it better.
3. Train yourselves and others to be invaluable assets in the new global, technological economy.
4. Be bold and think big.
5. Invest in one activity in business and another in personal life.
6. Have the passion to be a change agent.
7. Accept the wisdom of those who have had meaningful journeys.
8. Join hands with people all over the world and appreciate cultural differences.
9. Delay instant gratification and celebrate every milestone along your journey.
10. Accept that there will be those who oppose you. Fight them fairly with collaboration, well-thought-out plans, and positive acts.

I have faith in the younger generation. In my heart, I know you will be the leaders I pray you will be.

CHAPTER 19

THE MOTIVATION TO STAY INVOLVED

When I started my journey, America was on a mission for societal greatness. With a Kennedy in the White House, affirmative action laws were being passed at all levels of government, and for the first time, corporate America was opening its doors to people of color. Things were positive, and it was a hopeful time. I knew my journey was going to be exciting, worldly, and financially rewarding.

Over a fifty-year period, I saw a man walk on the moon, Jackie Robinson become the first black baseball player, and people of color and women become CEOs of Fortune 500 companies. I saw entertainers like Jay-Z, Beyoncé, Chance the Rapper, P. Diddy, Jessica Alba, and John Legend become business moguls and change the rules of the game. I saw a black man elected to the White House as our first minority president. I was proud of my country, my people, and my generation.

With fifty years of societal progress behind me, I was ready to retire and thank my generation for a job well done. I was going to relax at home, watching endless streams of basketball games, good movies, Sunday-morning news programs, and spend many hours with good friends, loved ones, and my daughter, Camille. Sadly, my plans cannot be realized, as today my life and my dreams are once again in turmoil. I am forced to reexamine the past fifty years of professional service and positive change I thought I had helped to cement for a better world. I am asking myself daily, what is happening to the America I knew? Once again, the stinging words of hatemongers have gained power. Established laws and policies that people fought and died for are being eviscerated. American citizens of color are again being shot and told to leave the country, while still others are being told they cannot enter.

This is not the America Jack Kennedy, Martin Luther King Jr., and others envisioned and gave their lives for. This is not the America I have spent my entire personal and professional life representing and that I worked so hard to make better. For the last two years, I have been in shock, avoiding the Sunday-morning talk shows I once loved to watch, alternatively losing myself in comedy films and basketball games. But while I have not given up hope, I am forced to accept my planned retirement must be put on the back burner. I am normally a very positive person, but I have been in a deep funk. I found myself singing "Let's Get It On," my favorite Marvin Gaye song. My journey has to continue; my generation's work is being undone. As a result of what I feel is a total degradation in the progress we gained, I've made the following commitments to myself:

1. Keep a positive mental attitude and believe things will get better.
2. Keep love in my heart for the people close to me, my community, and even for the people who hate me for the color of my skin.
3. Educate the younger generation on our nation's history, both good and bad, to prepare them to be better leaders in the future.
4. Foster business through growth and strategic partnerships with people of goodwill, irrespective of color, religion, or gender.

5. Continue to write books and articles and give speeches to educate, motivate, and inspire others.

6. Ask my friends and allies to also write books or share their experiences with the larger community.

7. Reach out to leaders in both parties, especially persons of color, to do the right thing for the community they represent and for America.

8. Invest even more time in my lifelong passion of minority business enterprise development, with a goal of creating billion-dollar businesses in cities across the nation.

9. Share the business case for diversity in major corporations across the country.

10. Continue to reach out to students and young professionals to motivate and inspire them to be outstanding leaders in the next generation.

The old leaders have either died or moved on, with a few still hanging on, desperately trying to remain relevant in a changing landscape better suited for a newer guard. They played their roles and carried out their mission. But as I have said many times before, business leaders and entrepreneurs call the shots in the US free enterprise system. Why should minorities operate differently? Our new leaders must come from the business community.

When I was a young professional in the sixties, people made you feel guilty if you earned a lot of money. I urge young professionals in business schools across the nation to earn as much money as you can, because wealth allows you to sit at the table of power. The question for all of us is, what do you do with the power once you are at the table? Example: Mark Zuckerberg, Bill and Melinda Gates, Warren Buffett, Robert F. Smith, President Barack Obama, Mayor Bloomberg, and Jay Pritzker.

In my more than forty years in the field of minority business, no one is a better model of the success of MBED than John

Rogers, founder of Ariel Capital. John was the only son of Jewel Lafontant, the first female graduate of the University of Chicago Law School and an ex–inspector general and general counsel, and former assistant United States attorney in Chicago. His father, John Rogers Sr., was a distinguished public servant and ex-Tuskegee airman, with more than one hundred combat missions of service during WWII, and eventually a Cook County judge for more than twenty years. One of John Rogers's great-grandfathers owned the Stratford Hotel in Greenwood, Tulsa, Oklahoma, which was at one time considered the Black Wall Street. The hotel was destroyed in the Tulsa race riot of 1921.

After graduation from the University Chicago Lab School, John Rogers attended Princeton University, where he was voted the most valuable player on the team's basketball team. His father encouraged him at an early age to invest in stocks and bonds. In July 1983, after a couple of years at William Blair, he decided to start his own investment company with $10,000. Along with his mother and a few others, I was fortunate enough to be one of the early investors, and today Ariel Capital has grown to more than eighty employees with more than $13 billion under management. Many of his employees were recruited from the top universities in the country, with Princeton University being his number one choice and where he served on the board. In 2008, Rogers became the first African American winner of the Woodrow Wilson Award from Princeton for his service to the university.

Not only has John been an outstanding entrepreneur and loyal Princeton alumni, he has also been a mentor and inspiration to thousands of young black professionals, encouraging them to enter the fields of investment banking and entrepreneurship. I cannot mention John without also sharing similar accolades with his now cochairman of Ariel Capital, Mellody Hobson Lucas. John met Mellody on the campus of Princeton when she was a student. He offered her a job as an intern in 1991. Mellody, a dedicated and quick learner, quickly rose to become the firm's senior president and director of marketing. In 2000, she became the president of Ariel Capital, and in 2019, she assumed co-CEO responsibilities.

Like John Rogers, Mellody Hobson Lucas has been a strong advocate for giving back to the community and minority business enterprise. Her TED Talks on both subjects are a collector's item and repeatedly shown across the country. In addition to being a sought-after public speaker, she is an active board member, serving JPMorgan Chase, Starbucks, and Estee Lauder. She also serves as the chairman of After School Matters, a nonprofit that provides Chicago teens with high-quality, out-of-school programs. She is a board member of the Chicago Public Education Fund, George Lucas Education Foundation, Lucas Museum of Narrative Art, and the Sundance Institute, where she has been appointed emeritus trustee. In 2015, Mellody was named to *Time* magazine's annual list of the one hundred most influential people in the world.

John and Mellody are outstanding models illustrating that, if given the opportunity, blacks can perform at the highest levels, be strong advocates and philanthropists for the communities they came from, and be steady contributors to the American free enterprise system.

For those who dream of becoming entrepreneurs, I recommend that they first learn critical skills and gain valuable experience before starting their own business. I share the following advice:

- Accept and appreciate the opportunities being offered to you in four growth industries: health, energy, construction, and IT.
- Build the biggest and strongest businesses you can create.
- Surround yourself with people smarter than you.
- Form strategic domestic and global partnerships.

- Be civic leaders, giving your time and resources to those in need.
- Employ our youth and give hope for a better life.
- Sell and diversify your business, as it is financially wise to do so.

As all businesses prosper, our nation will continue to prosper. This is a fact. For all who are in America, whether recent immigrants who bring intelligent and innovative insights, or the ancestors of those who came over often against their will in our not-so-distant slave past, or just the millions of average US citizens, we are all tied together economically. The greater harmony we have as a nation, the stronger our great nation will be. The opposite will also be the case.

We have come a long way in our short history. To move forward, it is our responsibility to keep the ideas of influential civil rights champions who came before us in the forefront of our minds. It is our duty as citizens of a unified nation to be cognizant of and believers in these notions of allowing love to overpower hate as a means to future success. It is in all our best interests to create economic growth and foster development in the inner cities.

I will never retire. My back may be weak, but my heart and spirit remain strong. To all Americans, I say let's make the world a better place to live. Let us join together to be global leaders, utilizing intergenerational wisdom and skill sets, and move our society to achieve higher, more ambitious goals.

APPENDIX A

JAMES H. LOWRY & ASSOCIATES ALUMNI

Arnita Goodman: BA/MBA, Harvard University

Arthur Glenn: BS, Western Michigan; MA, University of Michigan; MBA, Emory University

Barbara Gomez-Day: BA, California State University

Barron Harvey: BS/MBA/PhD, University of Nebraska

Bill Lowry III: BA, Emery College

Brenda Welburn: BA, Howard University

Cameron Pilcher: BA, Lake Forest University

Caren Yancey: BA, Tufts University; MA, Atlanta University

Carlton L. Guthrie: BA cum laude / MBA, Harvard University

Carolyn Welmon: BA, Clark University

Charles E. Stevenson: BA, Loyola University; MBA, Harvard University

Charles Stevenson: BA, Loyola University; CPA, MBA, Harvard University

Cheryl B. Leggon: BA, Barnard College; MA/PhD, University of Chicago

Cheryl Hamilton: BS, Northwestern University

Chris Hollins: BA, Grinnell College; MBA, Wharton School of Business

Clarke Lowry: University of Southern California

Darrell Boyd: BA, University of North Carolina Chapel Hill

David Morrison: BA, St. Louis University; MA, Catholic University of America; MBA, University of Chicago

David Rone: BA, Tufts University; JD, Northwestern University

Dennis J Brownlee: BA, Princeton University

Diana Smith Sykes: BA, Roosevelt University

Donald H. Ogilvie: BA/MBA, Yale University

Dr. Claudia Barriga: PhD, University of Wisconsin

Ed Howard: MBA, American University

Edgar Frank Bridges: BS/MS, University of Wisconsin (Milwaukee); PhD, Florida State University

Emerson Hall: BA, John Hopkins University

Evan Lowry: BA, DePaul University

F. Marvin Hankah: BA/MA/PhD, University of Wisconsin (Milwaukee)

Fargo Thompson: BA, University of Pittsburgh; MBA, Wharton School of Finance (University of Pittsburgh)

Frank Montgomery: BA, University of Iowa

Frank Pokorny: BA, Columbia University; MBA, Michigan State University

George Boykin: BS, New York University; MBA, University of Chicago

Gloria Jackson, M.D: BS, Xavier University; MD, University of Illinois

Godfrey A. Gordon: BA/MA, Howard University; PhD, University of Maryland

Haley Licata: BA, Washington University St Louis

Herschel Tolson: BS, Xavier College

Iris Harvey: MA/MBA, University of Southern California, Los Angeles

James Ekblad: BS, University of Illinois; CPA, University of Illinois

James Ragland: BA, Texas A&M University

James Simmons: BA, Grinnell College; MA, University of Chicago

Jane M. Thompson: BA, Cornell College; JD, University of Virginia

Janice Hinkle: BA/MBA, Harvard University

Janice Sullivan: BA, Prince George's Community College

Jayne Thompson: JD, Northwestern University

Jeffrey Davidson: BS/MBA, University of Connecticut

Jerome Simmons: BA, Grinnell College; MBA, University of Chicago

Jon Pearson: BS/MPA, University of Pittsburgh

Josie Gough: BA/MEd/JD, Loyola University Chicago

Judy Matthews: BA, Eastern Illinois University; MBA, University of Notre Dame

Karen Jackson: BA, College of Holy Cross

Karl Lewin: BS, Southeastern University; MBA, Fordham University

Kathy Berry: BA, Southern Illinois University

Ken Tatum: BA, Tuffs University; MBA, Harvard University

Kevin Booth: BA, Howard University

Kia C. Coleman: BA, Wesleyan University, MBA, University of Chicago Booth School of Business

Kim Pilcher: BA, Drake University

Kirti N. Patel: BBA, Sardar Patel University of AAIA; MBA, South Gujarat University, India

Langdon Neal Jr.: BA, Trinity College

Lydia Mallett: BA/MA/PhD, Michigan State University

Maggie Butler: BS/MS, Governor's State University

Marilyn Booker: BA, Spelman College; JD, Illinois Institute of Technology

Marilyn Cherry: BA, Spelman College; JD, Illinois Institute of Technology.

Melody Irvin: BA, Howard; MBA, Wharton

Michael A. Kilpatrick: BS, Hulman Institute of Technology; MS, Purdue University

Michael Bonner: BA, Howard University

Michael F. Meyer: BS/MBA, University of Chicago

Michael Holzman: BA, Northwestern University; MA, University of Chicago; JD, Loyola University

Michael R. McKillip: BA, St. Mary's College; MA, University of Chicago

Michael V. Bonner: BA/MA, Howard University

Michele Lomax: BA, University of Washington; JD, University of Chicago Law School

Nancy Sprow: BA, Rutgers University

Olivet Ames: BA, Smith College

Pauline Prater: BA, DePaul University

Peter C.B. Bynoe: BA cum laude, MBA, and JD Harvard University

Reginald C. Burton: BS, Roosevelt University; MBA, University of Chicago

Richard C. Holland: BS, Cornell University; MS, Massachusetts Institute of Technology; MBA, Columbia University

Richard Crawford: BA, University of Illinois

Richard I. McCline: BS, University of Illinois; MBA, Northwestern University

Robert Holland Jr.: BS, Union College; MBA, Bernard Baruch Graduate School in NYC

Rolf K. Blank: BA, Luther College; MA, University of Wisconsin; PhD, Florida State University

Samuel Cooper: BA, University of Pennsylvania; JD, Harvard University

Sharon A. Morgan: BS, Northeastern Illinois University

Sharon Collins: BA, Whittier College; MA, University of Southern California. Los Angeles; PhD, Northwestern University

Steve Abington: BA, Louisiana State University

Thea E. Lunn: School of the Art Institute of Chicago

Tobi Klein-Marcus: BA, Grinnell College; MA, London School of Economics; PhD, University of Bristol Kosty

Vicki Weiss: BA, Georgetown University

Victor Chears: BA, Yale University; EdD, Fielding Graduate University

William A. Lowry: BA, Lake Forest College; JD, Loyola University

William J. Holleran: BA, Union College; MA, American University

William E. Lowry, Jr.: BA, Kenyon College; MS, Loyola University

INDEX

H

Hale, Alan 61
Hancock, Herbie 37, 104
Harlem Globetrotters 11
Harmon, Sidney 139
Harris, Carla 209, 240
Harris-Dugger, Liz 135
Harris, Ira and Nicki 114
Harris, Nettie Camille Anthony
       vii, 100, 101, 102, 103,
       152, 153
Hartigan, Neil 114
Harvard African American
       Alumni Board 110
Harvard University Program for
       Management Development
       106, 107, 108, 111, 115
Harvey, Barron 142, 239,
       240, 276
Hashemipour family xi
Hatcher, Richard 56
Henson, Dan 136, 144
Herman, Alexis 247
Herzog, Katie 210
Hightower, Dennis 112
Hobson, Charles 75, 81
Hobson Lucas, Mellody xi,
       273, 274
Holland, Richard 161, 162, 164,
       167, 240
Holland, Robert 88, 89, 90, 99,
       111, 116, 160, 161, 166, 192
Hollins, Chris 120, 276
Hooks, Reverend Ben xv
Howard, Edward 147, 276
Howroyd, Janice Bryant 239, 254
Hunter-Gault, Charlayne 28, 38

Huntley, Walter 171
Hunt, Vivian 193
Hutchins, Dwight 193

I

Inside Bedford-Stuyvesant 75, 81
Irons, Edward 141

J

Jack and Jill of America 23, 27,
       35, 100, 155
Jackson, Don 181
Jackson III, Curtis James (50
       Cent) 259
Jackson, Maynard 57, 97, 166,
       171, 172, 185
Jackson, Phillip xii
Jackson, Reverend Jesse xv, 27,
       159, 185
Jacobs, Don 237, 238
Jacobs, Eli 73
Jacobson, Walter 184
Jacobs, Pat 145
James H. Lowry & Associates x,
       13, 87, 116, 138, 144, 148,
       178, 276
Jarrett, Valerie 13
Jasinowski, Jerry 134, 139, 158
Jay-Z (Carter, Shawn Corey)
       259, 270
Jensen, Ray 167, 169
Jet magazine xv, 14, 15, 16, 263
Jobs, Steve 243, 246
Johnson, Jerry 193, 254
Johnson, John 13, 14, 79, 253
Johnson, Lyndon 57, 63, 71
Johnson Publishing 13, 221

Lowry, William A. x, 182, 278
Lowry, William E., Jr. 3, 4, 5, 7,
    9, 10, 11, 12, 17, 19, 20, 29,
    112, 114, 117, 208, 212, 215
Loyd, Bernard 193
Lucas, C. Payne 71, 91

M

Mack, John 207, 208
Management Leadership for
    Tomorrow (MLT) 257
Manetta, Beatriz 239
Mankiewicz, Frank 66
Martinez, Arthur 237, 238
Matassoni, William x
Mathews, Judy 145
Mawjis, Piloo and Maroon 49, 51
Mayisela, Ethan 49
MBN USA Magazine 162, 261
McArthur, John 110
McDonald's Corporation 17, 170,
    174, 213, 214, 215
McGhee, Camilla xi
McGuire, Raymond J. 156, 257
McKinsey & Company 84, 85,
    86, 87, 88, 89, 90, 91, 92,
    93, 96, 99, 100, 101, 102,
    103, 105, 106, 107, 108, 109,
    110, 111, 112, 113, 115, 116,
    117, 118, 120, 121, 122, 134,
    138, 143, 145, 158, 159, 160,
    162, 163, 165, 171, 172, 181,
    191, 192, 193, 194, 201, 207,
    208, 213, 220, 222, 223,
    224, 225, 226, 227, 230,
    237, 241, 242, 265
McLeary, Tom 239
McNeely, Don 162

Medinah Country Club 186, 214
mentoring 195
Meyer, Michael 142
Michael Reese Hospital
    Board 236
Michel, Harriet xi, 163, 169,
    237, 238
Miller Brewing Company 228
Miller, Tony xi, 193
Miner, Judd 119
Minority Business Development
    Agency 82, 139, 140,
    141, 145
Minority Business Enterprise
    Development 118, 139, 141,
    171, 172, 173, 176, 177, 181,
    185, 187, 249, 250, 272
Minority Business Enterprise
    Development in the
    1980s 144
Minority Business Report,
    The 181
Mitchell, Adrian 233
Mitchell, Parren 136, 150, 169,
    187, 256
Mitchell, Robbin 233
Moe, Kari 175
Monroe, Sylvester 156
Monsanto 204
Montgomery, James 175
Morgan, Randall 242, 245
Morgan Stanley 117, 203, 206,
    207, 208, 209, 210, 211,
    212, 213, 225
Morris, Peter 142
Moseley Braun, Carol xi,
    188, 205
Motley, Marion 11

Mr. Contract 180, 183, 185, 186, 187, 193
Mullin, Leo 134, 135

N

O

P